WARS IN THE WOODS

Wars in the Woods

The Rise of Ecological Forestry
in America

SAMUEL P. HAYS

University of Pittsburgh Press

Published by the University of Pittsburgh Press, Pittsburgh, Pa., 15260

Library of Congress Cataloging-in-Publication Data

Hays, Samuel P.
  Wars in the woods : the rise of ecological forestry in America /
Samuel P. Hays. — 1st ed.
     p.   cm.
  Includes bibliographical references and index.
  ISBN 0-8229-4328-X (cloth : alk. paper) — ISBN 0-8229-5940-2
(pbk. : alk. paper)
    1. Forest reserves—United States. 2. Forest policy—United
States. 3. Forest management—United States. 4. Forests and for-
estry—Political aspects—United States. 5. Forest ecology—United
States. I. Title.
  SD565.H39 2007
  634.9'20973—dc22   2006025172

For Polly

CONTENTS

PREFACE

This book reflects both a personal and a scholarly journey. First of all, it takes me back to my first forestry experience in the 1940s as a twenty-two-year-old, when I worked for the Oregon and California Revested Lands Administration (O&C) west of the Oregon Cascades. The daily tasks consisted of routine forestry activities—tending a nursery and planting trees, fighting forest fires, building an access road to salvage a burn—and a multitude of collateral jobs such as blacksmith, auto mechanic, and cook. In the process I became interested in the O&C, and soon I was learning about its history and program. In one respect the O&C was a pioneering forest agency for its time. When in 1937 Congress spelled out in a separate law the policies to guide O&C management, it was one of the first such detailed statutory directives for any of our federal public forests. I became a convert to sustained-yield wood production, and I now reread a lengthy paper I wrote about the agency's history and future prospects with a mixed degree of nostalgia and recognition of just how much it expressed a view of forestry that in recent years has come under fire.

After writing my first book on the history of conservation during the Theodore Roosevelt administration, and taking a vacation from conservation writing, in about 1970 I became interested in environmental affairs and began to look into this as a subject for investigation. I found myself taking up where I had left off, with an instinctive interest in forestry as a part of the larger environmental scene. To delve more deeply into the issues I became both a participant and observer and soon found out that much had changed in the past twenty-five years, as "environment" had been added to "conservation." I served for a number of years as chair of the conservation committee of the Pennsylvania chapter of the Sierra Club, where I learned much more about the mysterious ways of environmental politics than I contributed. Soon I was writing papers about the management of the Allegheny National Forest, drawing up forestry proposals for the newly developing eastern state club chapters, serving on a state advisory committee to formulate recommendations for a state wild and scenic river system, and participating in a variety of forums pertaining to state forest management.

This personal experience dovetailed nicely with a more conventional scholarly approach to historical investigation. Seeking to combine both I tried to make my observation of day-to-day events form the pieces of longer-range historical understanding. I searched for documents to chart the environmental scene I was observing, especially in forestry, and to help make sense out of my personal experience in forestry affairs in Pennsylvania. What was the substance of the debates going on, and what were the issues in controversies over the objectives of forest management? Through attempts to understand the varied points of view, I identified the issues themselves as public affairs of considerable importance.

Now, some thirty years later, in this book I attempt to put together both personal experience and historical research into a coherent story that makes sense of it all. It seems obvious that the forestry world has been beset with considerable tumult over these years, that new forces are at work and old forces are rallying in defense of past forest institutions. New actors seeking to shape the forest scene now abound; new issues have arisen to define the arena of "forest politics." As I watched all this happen and participated in it, my continuing question as a historian was "What does this mean for the long run?" My answer in the following pages may smooth the path of understanding for others interested in forest affairs and perhaps aid them in their own attempts to make sense out of new and often confusing events.

I developed special interests in several aspects of the forestry scene. My conventional interest in the national policy debates expanded to include an interest in the people who were engaging forest agencies directly and advocating new on-the-ground practices. As a social historian who sought to examine governmental affairs in the context of the relationship between society and politics, I raised questions about the "social roots" of interest in forest reform. I chose to focus on state forest affairs, rather than taking an exclusive interest in the national forests. By examining the state forest spectrum, in contrast with the more uniform perspective of national policy, I could get closer to the roots of forest affairs. I had to find some way of placing that broad and varied state forestry spectrum into the larger picture.

The role of administrative choices—some might call it administrative politics—was another subject to which I was increasingly attracted, both on the federal and state levels. Usually carried on quietly and removed from media visibility, administration was a forum for forestry decision making of equal, if not greater, importance than that of public debate and controversy. I developed my own sound bite for this—"politics begins after a law is passed"—and began to sort out the various ways in which choices made by administrative agencies were an integral part of forest management. The issues—issues such as judgments about science and the balance of costs and benefits, the composition of advisory committees, and the participants invited into the circle of decision makers—became more elaborate and often more sharply defined as the scene shifted from legislation to administration. One simply could not understand how forest affairs evolved without a firm grasp of the politics of administration.

I continued to give attention to the reactions of forestry institutions to the "winds of change," or to their various degrees of acceptance or rejection when confronted with new demands and ideas. My thinking was shaped by the theme of "innovation and response," a context for thinking about American history which I developed in my first book, The Response to Industrialism. This was a way of distinguishing between those institutions and values that were associated with the new forces of industrialization and modernization in the nineteenth century, and those defending earlier and competing institutions and values. Could these responses to new ideas in forestry be arranged in a similar continuum of different degrees of acceptance and rejection of new proposals in forest management? Among the many state and federal forest administrations, professional organizations, and scientific institutions, I found a wide range of responses, and in several of the following chapters I use this theme of variation as a strategy to describe the impact of ecological forestry.

To explore these questions involved a much more extensive and penetrating analysis of the forest scene than was possible through the dramatic events emphasized not only in the media but by specialists as well. Controversy over the Pacific Northwest Plan formulated by the Clinton administration led most observers to focus on the spotted owl. But this attention seemed to obscure much in the debate. Ecological forestry emerged in many areas of the country, not just the Pacific Northwest; it involved many more issues than the declining population of a "signature" species; many of the issues were not dealt with by the mainstream media; and there was a distinct neglect of the larger ecological culture that was sprouting up in different regions of the United States and amid many sectors of society. I became convinced that much could be learned, for example, by charting the involvement of citizens and scientists in forest planning throughout the country, most of it well beyond the Pacific Northwest.[1]

To follow through with these lines of inquiry about forest affairs, however, presented a major problem of evidence. The usual array of prominent newspapers and official documents, the customary sources in research libraries, were less than adequate. To follow citizen activities I subscribed to the newsletters and magazines of environmental organizations. In order to ferret out issues at the state level I acquired material from the state environmental organizations and state administrative agencies and subscribed to selected state and regional newspapers. New types of newsletters on administrative politics arose in a number of environmental fields—the first was *Environmental Reporter*—but these were quite costly and I could finance only a few; I was frustrated by the fact that libraries did not acquire them. Specialized organizations in fields such as public lands, endangered species, forest litigation, and ecological science began to cover the issues in which I was interested.

Printed sources increased in number and availability as environmental issues became more extensive and more complex, but the possibilities for research expanded by several degrees of magnitude with the Internet. In the mid-1990s, when I began to use the Internet, my acquisition strategies changed sharply. Several Internet sites gathered and reported articles from newspapers and made them available online. I could access articles in state and regional newspapers that provided much richer coverage of site-specific forestry issues than was available in the national newspapers. Speeches, proceedings of conferences, scientific reports, legal briefs and judicial opinions, newsletters and reports of commodity forest organizations, plans proposed by citizen reform groups, and comments on administrative proposals were now available. The notes in this book make clear the vast increase in documentary sources that the Internet made available.

As I tracked the steady impact of environmental and then ecological objectives on forest management, I came to the conclusion that this was not a mere question of policy objectives, in which one could weigh one set of policies against another, but was rooted much more deeply in the cultural attitudes of the participants, which shaped strongly felt perspectives. Nor was it a matter of tracking a social movement with its strategies of organization and advocacy, whereby one could readily argue, as the commodity advocates did, that the issues were generated by the need for organizational enhancement, rather than being "real" issues. The differences lay deeper, rooted in the participants' values as to the meaning of forests. They could be understood only through the unique personal process of direct engagement with forested areas, direct aesthetic experiences, and scientific observation. Contesting parties were displaying preferences that could hardly be swayed by more superficial arguments, when their values were at stake.

The significance of values in the contest between ecological forestry and commodity forestry appeared even in the 1970s, shortly after the National Forest Management Act was passed in 1976. The first survey of public values to catch my attention was sponsored in 1977 by the American Forest Institute, an industry think tank; in this survey Americans expressed the view that the predominant meaning of the nation's forests was as wilderness and habitat for wildlife, and that wood production was of far less importance.[2] A variety of similar surveys at regional and state levels repeated the finding. In Pennsylvania, for example, among a list of services provided by the state's forests, clean air, clean water, and wildlife habitat stood at the top, and wood production was at the bottom.[3] In its own surveys of opinion the U.S. Forest Service identified the same pattern and frequently described it as differences in values.[4] I sought to bring together these values and perspectives under the phrases "ecological forestry" and "commodity forestry."

I especially sought to pin down specific on-the-ground management activities associated with an ecological forestry perspective. I paid particular attention to the specific proposals that both citizen groups and ecological scientists were bringing to the debates, especially during their participation in the development of forest plans. While it was difficult to define a term like "ecological forestry" or any of the new terms that were arising, such as "new forestry," "ecosystem management," "sustainable forestry," or "good forestry," it was not difficult to describe the management specifics.[5] These, discussed in chapter 2, included such objectives as biodiversity management, the protection and enhancement of diverse flora and fauna; using habitats rather than "stands" as units of management; maintaining a structural diversity of tree species and age; promotion of native forests and old growth; organizing forest management around watersheds; protecting forests from disturbances such as roads, harvest methods, motorized recreation, and mineral extraction; and soil erosion and depletion of soil nutritional capacity.

Ecological attitudes about forests, moreover, were not isolated in their meaning and origin, but seemed to be one expression of the growth of a wide-ranging ecological culture with a generalized but comprehensive focus on nature and natural processes, a perspective that influenced many aspects of life in the late twentieth century. It infused education at all levels, inspiring an outpouring of books for children, and influenced religion, intellectual pursuits in the study of the natural world, scientific discoveries in a wide range of biological fields, recreation and leisure activities, the choice of desirable occupations among young people, even law, economics, and the media. A new sense of wonder and inquiry and of enjoyment and knowledge of nature brought a new sense of meaning to many human activities. All this comprised not a momentary intellectual fad but a perspective and direction of values that, like most values, were often both deeply held and beyond rational explanation.

A wide range of forest plants and animals, far beyond the customary range of trees with marketable wood fiber or of animals hunted as game, now became the focus of both popular and scientific interest. The age of a forest now was not just the time span needed to grow a harvestable tree but a much greater span of three hundred or five hundred years or longer. And the forest of ecological interest was no longer just the early, middle, or later successional forest, thought of as stages leading to the harvest of "mature" trees, but the "old" or "ancient" forest with its own distinctive flora and fauna. All around me was abundant evidence that both scientists and citizens were changing what a forest meant to them and to the larger society.

In my conversations with commodity foresters on options in forest management I found much the same depth of commitment to values as among citizen advocates, although their values were quite different ones. They vigorously defended wood production on the nation's forests as both legitimate and necessary. To them the forest was composed of plants that could be a source of wood, measured in terms of board feet and cubic feet, categorized in terms of ages of sapling, pole, and mature timber, all steps on the way to wood harvest. It seemed that, in their mind's eye, the few biological forest elements called "commercial trees" obscured a more comprehensive vision of the vastly larger complex of ecological elements.

During the decades after 1970 I observed a growing gulf between commodity foresters and both the citizen groups and scientists with an ecological perspective. The two groups spoke different languages, used different terminology, engaged in different research, were associated in their training with different sections of colleges and universities, and had formed their own separate organizations. Even though commodity foresters complained vehemently about the political and legal actions of ecological forest advocates, in most of their activities they hardly recognized their existence and seemed indifferent when I tried to describe to them the nationwide engagement of citizens and scientists in the vast array of forest species, habitats, and ecological processes, about which they seemed to know little. And when ecological scientists joined to urge forest reform in an ecological direction, commodity foresters were prone to dismiss them as unreliable scientists in contrast with tried and true silviculturists, who were the reliable "forest scientists."

Thus, in the 1970s I began to form the view that the emerging conflict in American forestry could be described as a divergence in perspective between ecology and silviculture, customarily defined as the practice of cultivating forest trees. The issues seemed to become increasingly detailed and esoteric, and their resolution shifted sharply to the level of administrative decision making, in which the politics of science and economics shaped policy. Moreover, even then there were rumblings about the way in which forest issues were being adopted into political party agendas. By the beginning of the twenty-first century, issues were shaped heavily by party strategies. I was struck by how little of this, or of the wider environmental scene, was known to the general public—the issues were so vast and complex that they were beyond the grasp even of many who described themselves as "foresters"—and how limited was the media's interest in or understanding of these issues. Under the George W. Bush administration, the wood products industry, the forestry profession, and the Republican Party have used executive power and authority with considerable imagination in an attempt to hamstring ecological forestry advances. In the end, I make no prediction as to who will win this "war in the woods" but only state that the war itself is alive and healthy. I hope that this book will provide a historical context for those who wish to understand the ongoing controversies more effectively.

WARS IN THE WOODS

CHAPTER 1

New and Old Forestry

A Confrontation in the Making

Late-twentieth-century controversies over forest management—the "wars in the woods"—emerged in clear form in the 1970s, but they had significant roots in previous decades. They developed out of two divergent tendencies: an ecological approach to forest management based in a prior environmental perspective, expanding the focus on outdoor recreation in a natural setting into emphasis on forests as complex ecological entities; and more traditional commodity forestry, emphasizing wood production, whose proponents resisted the acceptance of ecological objectives and gradually sharpened their own strategies to defend a more limited commodity production role for American forests.

From Environment to Ecology: The Beginnings

Ecological forestry grew out of citizen activity that was more aesthetic than ecological in its perspective. The central thrust of that beginning was popular interest in outdoor recreation, highlighted by a post-1920 outburst of interest in outdoor recreation that continued unabated after World War II. This broad-based citizen activity led to national legislation—the Wilderness Act of 1964 and the National Trails and National Wild and Scenic Rivers acts of 1968—and counterparts among the states as well. These had little ecological content; instead, they emphasized the beauty of natural forests, high mountains, lakes, rivers, and the outdoors generally. But they did provide new opportunities for citizen initiatives to advocate that more and particular areas be established and legally protected—"set aside" as the phrase went—for enjoyment of their natural beauty. One can therefore root much of the subsequent citizen participation in environmental and ecological affairs in these outdoor recreation programs and the aesthetic impulse that lay behind them. The evolution of ecological forestry involved the growth of citizen participation and the addition of ecological objectives to the earlier emphasis on aesthetic objectives in the natural world of the "outdoors."[1]

The expansion of citizen involvement in the national wilderness program established in the 1964 legislation soon took that program well beyond what Congress had anticipated and involved a much larger public. That law had designated a number of areas as official units of the National Wilderness System, but it had also provided for "wilderness study" areas, that is, areas that the U.S. Forest Service and other land management agencies should examine and propose for addition to the system by Congress. In its investigations the agency frequently sought the suggestions of citizen groups. However, wilderness proposals soon went beyond those formally identified in the law as wilderness study areas when citizen groups brought a wider range of "wilderness candidates" to the table. Often these were proposed not through the Forest Service but directly to Congress in the manner of traditional constituency proposals to members of the House and Senate. They led to a considerable expansion of what was called "de facto" in contrast to "de jure" wilderness, that is, areas that citizens argued in fact had wilderness qualities equal to the areas recognized in the 1964 law.[2]

These citizen-inspired wilderness areas within the national forests extended the focus of the wilderness system from the earlier emphasis on alpine areas, known dismissively as "rock and ice" wilderness, to more heavily forested areas below tree line. The U.S. Forest Service vigorously resisted this transition in order to preserve forest lands for wood production, but citizens continued to press to expand the venue for wilderness action. A symbolic episode of sorts in the incorporation of fully forested areas into the wilderness system occurred when an uncut forested watershed, the French Pete Creek in Oregon, was added after a twenty-year battle pressed by citizen advocates. Little by little, ecological realities of forested lands became an integral part of the recreation movement. This was reflected in changes in outdoor guidebooks, which earlier had been written for mountain climbers. Previously the aim of climbers hiking through forests was to get to the beginnings of the vertical climb as quickly as possible; the trails through the forest to reach that point were often sketched only briefly. The revised guidebooks, however, greatly expanded description of the forested trails, including the flora and fauna that the climber might encounter. Thus, in several ways one could trace gradual changes in the wilderness movement that enhanced the potential interest of the outdoor adventurer in forest biology, as well as geology.

The growing citizen involvement in forested wilderness areas was especially striking in the East, where the de facto wilderness movement was almost wholly within the context of forested rather than alpine "rock and ice" areas.[3] The potential for the inclusion of eastern areas in the wilderness system attracted eastern members of the Sierra Club who, having experienced western areas, turned to their own backyards. Most of the new eastern chapters of the club, formed state by state in the early 1970s, grew out of wilderness proposals in their nearby national forests. Club chapters sponsored outings to scout potential wilderness areas, prepared slide shows to convey the attractiveness of the areas to a larger audience, drew up proposals with maps and detailed descriptions of biological as well as geological characteristics, and enlisted their representatives in the Congress to introduce bills to include the areas in the wilderness system. These proposals were consolidated in omnibus bills and served to establish in a 1974 law the first eastern components of the wilderness system.

The Wilderness Act of 1964 grew out of citizen activity in the form of the Wilderness Society. Initially this was a relatively small group of advocates, located primarily in the East. But action subsequent to the act of 1964 greatly expanded the number of people involved in promoting wilderness protection, enlisting advocates throughout the nation. A "movement" started by a few gradually became a nationwide effort on the part of many. Confined at the start to an advocacy group in the nation's capital—even as late as 1977 the Wilderness Society had only one western state chapter, in Montana—by the 1980s wilderness activity had brought together a number of national organizations, but, more important, it had generated regional, state, and local action throughout the country. As interest in the ecological characteristics of the national forests emerged in the 1970s, many in those organizations added ecological and watershed objectives to their interests, creating an ecological forestry perspective in addition to the environmental forestry of the outdoor recreation movement.[4]

The Clear-Cutting Issue

Wilderness activity served gradually to bring the nation's forests closer to the American people. Events pertaining to the forest at large, not just areas of wilderness potential, augmented the process by which forested areas became more visible to the public, and enhanced public interest in how they were managed. A number of events between the mid-1960s and the mid-1970s were important steps in this direction.

The first of these that grew out of the Multiple-Use Act of 1960 was initiated by the wood products industry when it sought to amend that act to give it more emphasis on wood production. The 1960 act had identified the "multiple uses" under which the national forests should be managed: wood, water, grazing, recreation, and wildlife, with the stipulation that wilderness would not be "inconsistent" with these objectives. However the act did not set priorities among these uses, and the industry argued that it should, and that wood production should rank high among them. In the late 1960s the industry took a bold step in this direction by proposing legislation, the Timber Supply Act of 1969, giving wood production a much greater role in much of the national forests. The environmental coalition that had successfully fought for the wilderness, trails, and rivers acts of 1964 and 1968 applied its influence now to this proposal and defeated it.[5]

Almost immediately, however, the issue of clear-cutting and how forests should be harvested came to dominate the national forest debate. Clear-cutting not only engaged the nation's capitol in debate over the national policy, but affected the many Americans who had explored the out-of-doors since World War II. As the Forest Service adopted clear-cutting in the 1960s as the preferred method of harvesting trees, those who hiked and camped in the woods could see the results for themselves. They considered the remains of a clear-cut to be utterly repugnant and reacted not just with their minds but with their emotions. Pictures of the results of clear-cutting reached an even larger audience and expanded further the public that would feel involved in the ensuing debate.

Reaction against clear-cutting arose initially in the Bitterroot Forest of western Montana and the Monongahela Forest of West Virginia. In both areas, citizens called upon their legislators, Senator Lee Metcalf in the first case and Senator Jennings Randolph in the second. In Montana, Professor Arnold Bolle, dean of the Forestry School at the University of Montana, authored a report highly critical of the Bitterroot clear-cut.[6] In West Virginia it was a citizen fisherman's group, the Izaak Walton League, which took up the cause and with the help of an attorney with the Sierra Club, Jim Moorman, devised a legal argument that clear-cutting was contrary to the 1897 act, the initial management statute under which the Forest Service operated. That act, Moorman argued, directed that only mature trees be sold and that they be marked individually for sale.

Clear-cutting soon became the subject of hearings in Congress, sparked by Senator Gale Magee of Wyoming, after which a legislative proposal was developed to restrict its practice.[7] The Nixon administration, customarily ambivalent about environmental matters, drew up an executive order to restrict clear-cutting in the national forests but as the issue heated up, withdrew it.[8] The issue, however, remained dramatically alive when the federal courts accepted the claims of the environmental plaintiffs and declared the practice contrary to the 1897 act. To the wood products industry it was obvious that the law needed changing to legitimize clear-cutting, but doing so opened the door to a much more extended debate over management of the national forests, in which a number of critics of national forest management had an opportunity to make themselves heard. The resulting National Forest Management Act of 1976 became a focal point in the clash between the new and the old that set the stage for the steady evolution of ecological forestry and perfected and hardened the vigorous reaction of commodity forestry advocates.

The management issues set off by the controversies over clear-cutting were argued and decided at the upper levels of government in Washington, D.C. But as the issues evolved they came to involve the wider public more fully. The initial human reaction to clear-cutting was aesthetic; the devastation evident in the tangle of discarded pieces of trees and brush seen when one came upon a clear-cut during a hike was a sharp contrast to the beauty of the full canopy forest. But it did not take long for the hiker with an inquiring mind to explore what else was involved. The destruction was more than aesthetic. Clear-cutting, many came to believe, had a profound effect on forest plants and animals, destroying a complex range of habitats from the canopy to the ground level and implicitly raising questions as to just how long the effects of the cut would last and if recovery would ever take place. Wilderness of rock and ice did not raise such questions. But the fully forested wilderness established a new visual image of wilderness to be protected, and called attention to the seemingly dim prospects of recovery from massive timber harvesting. Clear-cutting had the potential of moving the interested citizen in a new direction, toward a more complex and more comprehensive ecological view of what had been destroyed and what should be restored.

Both the expansion of wilderness affairs from de jure to de facto objectives and the clear-cutting issue had immediate effects on the public context of national forest management. But they also had more slowly evolving consequences by focusing public interest on just how the forested areas of the country should be managed. The ecological perspective that gradually influenced management objectives was not implicit in either de facto wilderness or the reaction against clear-cutting but had significant roots in the fertile circumstances established by those developments. That perspective also had roots in the elaboration of two new contexts for public debate that came onto the scene in the same years, the environmental impact statement (EIS) required by the National Environmental Policy Act of 1969 (NEPA) and the Endangered Species Act of 1973 (ESA). The steady evolution of an ecological perspective on forests brought together citizens' direct experience of forests and the opportunities that both NEPA and ESA provided for citizens and scientists to participate more fully in national forest management.

Legislative Innovations with Ecological Potential

Both NEPA and the ESA had a potential to influence national forest management that was only dimly recognized when they were enacted, and neither act had an immediate impact on the development of an ecological approach to forest management. However, as the debate over forest management sharpened and the provisions of both pieces of legislation were used more frequently, their influence came to be so extensive that commodity forest advocates looked on them, and rightly so from their perspective, as crucial. They worked mightily to cut them back sharply or even to repeal them.

The National Environmental Policy Act had some wide-ranging policy provisions, as its title indicated, but both the Council for Environmental Quality (CEQ), which was established to administer it, and the courts let that part of NEPA remain unused.[9] They declined to interpret the act as mandating agencies to make policy decisions in a favorable environmental direction. However, in Section 102 the act also contained a procedural requirement that the environmental consequences of federally approved actions be carefully analyzed before those actions could take place. The provision for environmental impact analysis did not require the agency to take action one way or another, but by simply requiring that careful and thorough study precede action it potentially could bring a wider range of factors into consideration for forest management than had traditionally been the case. Hence it provided an opening for ecological concerns to become a part of decision making.

Environmental impact analyses, so the requirements ran, had to be comprehensive, interdisciplinary, and searching. They could not be simple and one-dimensional, and the courts frequently made decisions that agencies must live up to that requirement. The EIS process also required that alternative courses of action with different consequences be fully examined and that the agency make a reasoned choice among them. All this meant that a broader view was now called for as to what a forest comprised and what had to be taken into account in comprehensive forest management. It was now legitimate, indeed required, to consider the more central aspects of ecological forestry, such as a much wider range of species than those capable of producing wood fiber, as well as more complex and longer-term ecological processes.

Gradually, over the years, ecological forestry advocates, both citizen groups and scientists, found in the EIS an opportunity to bring the latest in ecological forest science to bear on forest plans. The citizen groups followed the relevant scientific literature closely and spread widely those scientific studies with ecological implications. They consulted with scientists as to the latest knowledge about the ecological consequences for forest conditions of human actions such as logging, road building, or recreational vehicle use. At times they served to bring scientists together to make joint statements about the ecological wisdom of proposed courses of action. As a result of these efforts, the agency often financed impact studies by individual scientists or consultants and at times hired their own specialists, particularly in the regional offices, in order to ensure that their environmental analyses would pass legal muster. In such ways the Forest Service was forced to bring a broader ecological perspective into the agency, although it did so piecemeal and often with great reluctance.[10]

The nation's endangered species program, which evolved through a series of enactments but reached a relatively comprehensive form in the Endangered Species Act of 1973, also required the agency to manage more broadly and provided opportunities for citizen groups and scientists to pressure it to do so. The act was administered by the U.S. Fish and Wildlife Service (FWS), and its provisions were imposed upon all federal land and water management agencies. The agencies were required to call upon the FWS to investigate, through a "biological opinion," whether or not a species on agency lands might be endangered or threatened. Moreover, members of the public could petition the agency to list species as endangered, as provided for in the act. The agency, in turn, called upon biological specialists in the species in question to determine the relevant population levels, whether or not they were declining, and if so, if they had reached levels that could not sustain the species.[11]

It took some time for the program called for by the ESA to be developed, for an active constituency on the part of citizen groups and biological specialists to form, and for the agency to bring together a group of scientists, both in-house and externally, to implement it. But as it did so it revealed the way in which the program served as an instrument to link the public, the scientists, and the agency in a common endeavor.[12] Accomplishments under the act always lagged behind its potential. But over the years, both the ESA and NEPA provided important mechanisms whereby ecological forestry took shape. The National Forest Management Act of 1976 established even more comprehensive opportunities for the expression of this new approach to forest management. Ecological forestry evolved not just through the new procedures available to its advocates; it also took shape through intensive give-and-take with commodity forest advocates in the Forest Service, the forest profession, and the forest industry. A variety of commodity forest organizations were unprepared to bring emerging ecological ideas into the orbit of their thinking and accepted them only with reluctance and often vigorous resistance.

The Response of the Old to the New

The proposals advanced by advocates of ecological forestry presented a significant challenge to established forestry institutions, represented by the U.S. Forest Service, the forestry profession, and the wood products industry. Since the late nineteenth century those institutions had provided the main impetus in shaping forest management. Over the years of the twentieth century, these institutions and their leaders had shaped the scientific and managerial practices in wood production forestry to the extent that the word "forestry" in both technical and popular language implicitly meant "wood production." The forestry leaders and institutions now were so firmly committed to wood production that, when confronted by the press of new objectives in environmental and ecological forestry, they had difficulty in accepting them. Often they considered these new ideas as threats to their primary interest in wood production rather than as opportunities to broaden their vision as to what forests constituted and how they were to be managed. Hence, when the drive toward ecological forestry began to emerge in the 1970s, the leaders of traditional forest institutions were not prepared to exercise constructive leadership in the growing pursuit of environmental and ecological objectives.

This reluctance reflected deep-seated professional values and commitments from which a silvicultural perspective had emerged over the years. That perspective was one-dimensional, focused sharply on that small piece of the forest, species of trees that were marketable as lumber and also for pulp for paper products. This viewpoint was rooted in commitment to a sharply specialized branch of "forest botany" that greatly narrowed perspective in training, profession, and management. Many of the earlier foresters had training in traditional botany, which introduced them to a wide range of plants and plant evolution. But in the process of becoming field foresters and forest managers, that perspective was narrowed to increasingly detailed knowledge about those relatively few plants that contained marketable wood fiber. Hence a more limited field of botanical knowledge called "dendrology" came to replace a broader botany. By 1950 the most widely used dendrology text book, authored by Harlow and Harrar, advised the reader that "It is felt that students of forestry should first know well the commercial species of North America."[13]

The Evolution of Wood Production Practices in the Forest Service

The Forest Management Act of 1897 stipulated two major objectives in management of the forest reserves: wood production and watershed protection. The agency soon became preoccupied primarily with the first. The 1897 law provided little guidance about wood production, save to authorize a policy to maintain a "continuous supply of timber" and to stipulate that only mature timber be cut. The agency took this authorization as a broad mandate. Elaboration of that authority in practice came to be the agency's central preoccupation over the years of the twentieth century.

Pressures arising from the market shaped the agency in a number of ways. One was the need to sell wood to return agency income, a need in which the agency inevitably conformed to the requirements of the market. Hence sales contracts were shaped so as to be attractive to timber buyers. The agency developed the practice of organizing these contracts around lumber mills and soon thought of its responsibility as one of providing a continuous supply of timber for specific mills that sustained community economies. Often this desire to foster a local wood products economy resulted in the agency shaping the details of contracts, their length and terms, so as to be more acceptable to timber buyers.[14] In this way the requirement for a "continuous supply of timber" became a major statutory instrument for fostering an industry and establishing a community economic base resting on resource extraction. All this was intended to bring about a major change from instability in the industry and communities that resulted from the "cut and run" practices of earlier years.

Equally significant and evolving early in the agency's history was the penchant to eliminate older trees and to replace them with the fully "regulated forest," which would be subject to continued careful control from planting to harvest.[15] Sound forest management, in the eyes of the foresters, could advance only by removing the old to make way for the new. Those who valued old forests for their aesthetic and later for their ecological characteristics and who spoke of "old growth" or "ancient forests" stood outside the pale of scientific forestry.[16]

A third major tendency in production forestry practice involved the way in which the market undercut one of the most widely accepted features of good silviculture, that of removing smaller trees through thinning—to "thin out judiciously and advance the crop," as the phrase went. This practice was continually stymied by the unwillingness of buyers to purchase thinned products. In almost all sources of wood supply from the smaller forest woodlot to the larger holdings, market pressures led to a preference for cutting the larger trees and leaving the smaller ones, a practice that came to be known as "high-grading." These market pressures played an important role in undermining selection silviculture, which, while it emphasized cutting the larger and more merchantable trees, also embraced thinning as a strategy for producing future marketable trees.[17]

Agency Response to Objectives Other Than Wood Production

The firmly established wood production objectives of the Forest Service made it difficult for the agency to integrate other objectives into its program.

The first challenge to the agency's objectives came early in its history amid the popular view that the nations' public forests served both as parks with desirable aesthetic qualities and as sources of wood products. This view was expressed most frequently by one of the most extensive and vigorous advocates of the forest reserves, the General Federation of Women's Clubs.[18] Their support led eventually to the formal designation of reserves as national forests where wood production would occur, but also to the designation of areas—local, state, and national—as parks where it would not. This dual role of forests was expressed widely by a Coloradan, Enos Mills, who had close connections with the Federation of Women's Clubs and who was hired by Gifford Pinchot, the head of the newly designated Forest Service, to "spread the gospel" of the national forests. Mills spoke throughout the nation, and his main constituency was the network of state chapters of the Federation of Women's Clubs. His speeches reflect the two roles of forests—as parks and for production—which he, like many members of the public, did not see as incompatible.[19]

Gifford Pinchot, however, the nation's most forceful advocate of national forests, could not bring himself to include both sets of forest management objectives as legitimate functions of the new agency. He opposed park proposals that stipulated a no-cutting policy and sought to incorporate parks into the national forests with explicit approval that they provide for wood

harvest.[20] By the time of the celebrated Governor's Conservation Conference
in 1908, Pinchot's distinction between forests and parks had become sharpened to the point of almost irreconcilable alternatives. Pinchot refused to
give either Mills or the Federation of Women's Clubs an integral role in the
conference proceedings or in the proposals arising from it.[21] Silviculturists
and park proponents went their separate ways. The main objective of the
park proponents thereafter was to establish a national park administration
separate from the Forest Service, and despite Pinchot's vigorous opposition,
they won when Congress in 1916 established the National Park Service.[22]

These events established a rivalry between the two agencies. The most
significant result was their competition for land, resulting in a loss of U.S.
Forest Service jurisdiction over forest land when a series of new national
parks were carved out of national forests.[23] However, the rivalry had even
more extensive significance for the future. For while the National Park Service provided over the years a forum for concern over a wide range of forest species and ecological processes, the Forest Service (not always without
hesitation) maintained a rigid rejection of a wider view of its own ecological
resources and resisted their inclusion in its management program.[24] As it
confronted ecological forestry in the 1970s and after, these earlier commitments to wood production constituted an agency burden that greatly limited the ability of the old to respond constructively to the new.

The watershed program of the Forest Service, also derived from the
1897 Forest Management Act, carried a similar burden. That provision grew
out of the desire on the part of western towns and cities on the one hand,
and irrigators on the other, to protect the watersheds from which their
water supplies were drawn.[25] These water users were primarily concerned
about watershed erosion and silting in their reservoirs, and the tendencies
of both logging and grazing to cause erosion. However, in administering
the 1897 act, the Forest Service shifted the focus of its watershed program
from the role of forests in protecting watersheds and water supplies to their
role in facilitating the loss of water through transpiration. To prevent that
loss trees on the watershed should be cut, rather than be retained to protect
against erosion.

Thus a program that might well have called for restriction on logging in
order to protect watersheds was turned into a justification for timber harvest
to enhance water supplies. These developments constituted the early stages
of an issue that evolved with considerable force in later years as ecological
forestry placed great emphasis on the protection of aquatic species—salmon
was the most dramatic case—through restricting timber harvests in order to
maintain watershed protection functions. In the face of these new demands

on forest management the Forest Service had little experience or management skills on which to rely, not even a system for inventorying or measuring the health of watersheds.[26] A traditional management orientation focused on commodity forestry now proved to be a roadblock in the agency's ability to take up a major element in the ecological forestry program, one that, ironically, constituted an action to recapture a statutory mandate in the 1897 act.

Recreation

In the 1920s the national forests entered into a new social milieu as a result of their increasing accessibility by automobile. The national forests in the East, acquired under the 1911 Weeks Act, were especially subject to increased use from a more mobile public. The Forest Service was now called upon to accommodate driving for pleasure as a form of recreation, which came to be the most extensive noncommodity use of national forests, and a growing public interest in hiking, camping, and wildlife.

Driving for pleasure came to impact the forests in the early stages of the automobile era, when in the 1920s the effect of timber cutting, and especially clear-cutting, on the visual quality of forest roads became a subject of internal debate in the Forest Service. Should clear-cutting to the edge of the road be permitted or prohibited? Advocates of clear-cutting argued that while the public might object, this objection could be overcome by a careful explanation that the practice was silviculturally sound. But advocates of prohibition expressed considerable doubt that such an explanation could overcome public objections on aesthetic grounds. To prohibit clear-cutting down to the road edge would reduce the amount of forest available for harvest, and this amounted to a considerable acreage if it were applied to all car-traveled roads throughout the national forest system. The agency chose to keep the area along roads—the "visual corridor"—free of clear-cutting.[27]

Closely associated with driving for pleasure was the growing popularity of car camping in the national forests. Beginning in the 1920s, car camping grew steadily in the 1930s, amid the development of an extensive recreational infrastructure in the nation's parks and forests created by the Civilian Conservation Corps. Car camping often led to scattered campsites and the spread of forest fires; the agency met these problems with a series of planned campgrounds and the requirement that camping be confined to those areas and be prohibited elsewhere.

Both visual corridors and specified campgrounds established a pattern of land classification or zoning on the national forests that separated "special uses," where timber harvest would be restricted or prohibited, from the "general forest" where harvest would prevail as the dominant use. This reflected the agency's approach to noncommodity uses in which they were separated from the general forest, with the implication that they were secondary uses and generally incompatible with the main forest's more important use for wood production.

In the 1960s these approaches were extended to the national wild and scenic rivers and national trails system that were then evolving. Each was planned with scenic visual corridors. These seemed naturally to be required for aesthetic enjoyment of both river recreation and hiking, and therefore the policy was extended to the new recreational uses. In the earlier years when the wood products industry was relatively uninterested in the national forests, there had been little objection from that quarter to visual corridors. Now in the 1960s, with a much more lively interest in the national forests, the industry was quick to complain that the forest acreage required by this zoning practice would greatly restrict wood production. But the practice had long been established, and in the new circumstances it prevailed.

Wildlife

Greater public accessibility to the national forests opened them to a steady increase in hunting and fishing and brought wildlife as a resource more directly into the realm of forest management. Over the years this presented national forest managers with problems that were even more difficult to deal with than was the case with recreation. For while recreation could be isolated from wood production through zoning, wildlife with its varied and complex habitat requirements was a more integral part of the forest. The earlier focus of wildlife protection was on nesting and the reproduction of the young and was simple enough for the agency to deal with, but as information derived from radio telemetry greatly expanded knowledge about the geographical range and complexity of wildlife habitats, the integration of wildlife with wood production became ever more difficult. Moreover, wildlife was subject to the jurisdiction of the states, not federal authority, and national forest supervisors had to work within the context of decisions made by state game commissions.[28]

During the 1930s wildlife as a public management issue became increasingly important. Hunting on public lands grew steadily. The National Wildlife Federation was established.[29] The Wildlife Society was founded as a professional organization.[30] Thus, on both public and scientific fronts, wildlife commanded a new presence. A report by a special committee of the Society of American Foresters on wildlife emphasized the difficulties of integrating wildlife into traditional forest management.[31] The Forest Service responded to these new circumstances by increasing its resources for wild-life management in the 1930s. But different priorities during World War II brought this to an end, and after the war that commitment was restored only slowly.[32]

During these early postwar years, prior to the emergence of environ-mental and ecological objectives in forest management, the roles of wildlife and silvicultural management were dovetailed in the "early successional" forest, that is the young forest in its first decade or so of regeneration after harvest. These new forests provided considerable food for browsing ani-mals, such as deer and ruffed grouse. This satisfied the interests of both deer and grouse hunters, on the one hand, and some wood production interests, on the other. In the Great Lakes states, the accommodation of both interests was especially firm, since the replacement of the older pine forest with as-pen, raw material for the pulp and paper industry, gave rise to a short-lived forest in which the early successional stage would be repeated frequently every fifty years or so. Hence both the pulp industry and the game hunters forged a firm partnership to object to creating older, late successional forest acreage.[33] In Pennsylvania the relationship was more tenuous, since here the wood production goal emphasized hardwoods, and successful regeneration of the best hardwoods was jeopardized, since the seedlings were prime deer food.[34]

These varied adjustments of wildlife to silviculture came at a time when wildlife interests were primarily matters of game hunting. The emergence of ecological forestry, however, brought a new twist to the role of wildlife, emphasizing nongame animals and human appreciation rather than hunt-ing.[35] Among wildlife professionals, as those, for example, in the Wildlife Society, the new nongame wildlife interests were more readily accommo-dated.[36] The changes were also reflected in the revised North American Game Policy, which appeared with a new title, the North American Wildlife Policy.[37] Amid the new interest in a wider range of nongame wildlife, the accommodations in earlier years between silviculturalists and hunters were not so easily repeated, and those accommodations actually became a major roadblock in the adjustment of the old to the new.

The Challenge to Agency Autonomy

The varied demands for use of the national forests, which seemed to in-crease steadily over the years, led to proposals to incorporate some uses into the agency's management mandates. Thus, the Multiple-Use Act of 1960 formally identified five acceptable uses of the forests—grazing, recreation, wildlife, watershed protection, and wood production—and declared that wilderness, though not included in the list, was "not inconsistent" with those uses. Three of these uses, grazing, recreation, and wildlife, were not included in the Forest Management Act of 1897. Decisions as to which uses should be allowed or favored on specific forest lands were still in the hands of the Forest Service, and this continually prompted proposals on the part of interested sectors of the public for legislation to preempt the agency's authority to enhance the role of one or another use.

Proposals challenging the agency's autonomy were not without precedent. In the past, failure to respond more positively to external demands had led to significant losses of the agency's freedom to make its own decisions. Because of its rejection of national park objectives, the Forest Service failed to prevent the establishment of a separate national park agency and faced the transfer of a significant number of its lands to the National Park Service; because of its resistance to permanent wilderness designations on national forest lands it lost the authority to establish such areas to Congress in the Wilderness Act of 1964 and the Eastern Wilderness Act of 1974; in the endangered species program the agency, as with all of the federal land management agencies, was faced with decisions by another agency, the U.S. Fish and Wildlife Service, about important species and habitat designations on its own lands.

The issue of agency autonomy and the continual possibility of statutory restraints on that autonomy, therefore, lurked behind the emerging controversies of the 1970s. Environmental and ecological advocates hoped that the application of the National Environmental Policy Act of 1969 would impose restraints on the Forest Service on behalf of their objectives. But when the administrators of NEPA and the courts seemed to abandon the substantive requirements of that law and confine it to acceptable procedures—how the agency should make decisions and not what the substance of those decisions should be—the would-be reformers turned increasingly to new legislation that would include such substantive requirements.

By the middle of the decade, therefore, commodity forest advocates were primed to seek new legislation to legitimize clear-cutting, and environmental and ecological advocates were prepared to join in with their own proposals for statutory reform that would specify more precisely their environmental and ecological goals. The result was a legislative struggle leading to the National Forest Management Act of 1976 (NFMA), an enactment that was as promising for sharpening a new and more formalized setting for the conflict between commodity and ecological forestry as it was for solving the immediate problems of defenders of commodity forestry.

The Forest Management Act of 1976

The immediate impetus for congressional action leading to the National Forest Management Act of 1976 was the Monongahela decision, in which the court decided that clear-cutting was contrary to the Forest Management Act of 1897, under which the U.S. Forest Service had long administered the national forests.[38] The decision created a crisis for both the wood products industry and the Forest Service, which had been committed to clear-cutting as the preferred method of harvest for over a decade. The drive for changes in the law to permit the practice was spearheaded by the industries that harvested and processed wood, but, taking a lesson from the failures in the drive for the Timber Supply Act of 1969, the industry now sought to organize the entire wood products industry, from the woods to the finished product and including lumber mills, commercial outlets, and labor, in a massive drive under the rallying cry that the future of the entire industry was at stake.[39]

Almost immediately, however, legislative proposals took a somewhat different turn. The initial bill was introduced by Senator Hubert Humphrey, who had long argued that a new climate in forest affairs took it well beyond wood production alone, and who had been searching for an approach that would broaden the context of forest management.[40] Humphrey's proposal would establish a wide-ranging planning process in which the agency and each national forest would periodically establish plans to guide their activities over the following decade or so. The proposal was brought forward under the rationale that planning conducted within the context of "scientific" natural resource information would become the prevailing method of making national forest decisions and would replace the evolving context of political controversy and litigation. A way had now been found under which future national forest decisions would move forward smoothly and outside the realm of politics.[41]

Competing with the Humphrey proposal was another proposal arising out of the environmental community and focusing on the emerging substantive environmental and ecological issues in national forest management. It was sponsored by Senator Jennings Randolph of West Virginia, who had established close relationships with environmental groups during the controversy over clear-cutting in the Monongahela National Forest.[42] These groups were wary of circumstances in which the Forest Service would have sole administrative authority to make national forest decisions and desired to include in the new law specific substantive provisions in the form of policy requirements. Some of these groups had wanted to use NEPA to establish substantive goals for forest management and were disappointed that the courts and the Nixon administration had turned that law into an overwhelmingly procedural device. They now came to the debate over the new forest act hoping to work substantive provisions into it.

A number of these specifics pertained to silvicultural standards, such as the use of clear-cutting and selection cutting, or that land be classified into levels of productive capacity and timber harvest be restricted to lands of sufficient potential for regrowth, or that harvest not be permitted unless regeneration could take place within a limited time after harvest.[43] But others dealt with environmental and ecological objectives, such as maintaining the diversity of plant and animal communities and protecting riparian areas. The agency resisted these objectives and the standards that they implied on the grounds that these were "technical" matters that had best be left to "the professionals," but the citizen environmental organizations argued that they were far more than mere technical matters and the agency would not reform itself unless required to do so through substantive requirements enacted through legislation.

The initial significance of the 1976 NFMA was to fulfill the main goal in the industry drive by legitimizing clear-cutting, though under some restriction. Moreover, the law established the planning process that Senator Humphrey had promoted. Commodity forestry advocates were particularly relieved that much of the prescriptive element of the Randolph bill that would have reduced the autonomy and influence of the agency was considerably softened. This self-confidence on the part of commodity forestry advocates played a major role in prompting the industry to become involved with the Reagan administration with a firm belief that it could count on continued influence in national forest policy and to encourage the forest industry as well as the Forest Service to belittle and ignore the persistent but unspectacular growth of ecological forestry.[44]

The long-term significance of the act, however, was to extend the Forest Service planning program that had already begun to develop in the agency into a comprehensive and forest-wide process. Each forest now was required to develop a fifteen-year plan and to propose alternative courses of action and justify which one it chose to approve. Opportunities for citizen input into the plans would be required, and appeals to modify the plan for any national forest could be taken through the agency administrative appeal system. The process by which these plans were developed and their application in on-the-ground management from this time forward constituted the focal point of debate over national forest policies. And ecological forest management proposals became a critical aspect of this debate.

Initially the planning program established by the 1976 act aroused considerable enthusiasm on the part of those who envisaged a sharp reduction of controversies over national forest management. The program, so it was predicted, would replace a highly politicized national forest scene with a smoothly running decision-making system under the direction of a professional and value-free administrative agency. In later years, since public debate did not lessen, but in fact increased, and since litigation as a part of that debate continued, these planning advocates looked upon the act as a failure. However, use of the act's planning program by citizen and scientific groups shaped it into a major forum for the environmental and ecological objectives emerging in the wider society to work themselves out in the context of specific forests. In this view, one can well look upon the 1976 act not as a failure of planning but as a successful mechanism for the gradual, even glacial advance in expression of environmental and ecological forest objectives.

That the act would play this role became apparent soon after it was approved in 1976. Initially it took the form of a handbook for citizen forest reformers as to how they could use the act's procedural and substantive provisions to advance their objectives.[45] Published originally in 1980 after the agency developed the initial regulations under which the act would be carried out, and then reissued in 1983 after the revised regulations themselves had been approved in 1982, the handbook was a joint venture of the Wilderness Society, the Sierra Club, the National Audubon Society, the Natural Resources Defense Council, and the National Wildlife Federation. The handbook served as a how-to guide to citizen reformers in their efforts to participate in the planning process. More important, it served to identify a midpoint in the emergence of ecological forestry, a stage in which earlier impulses in that direction were consolidated and from which, through the forest planning process, they were integrated to shape a more fully developed nationwide ecological forestry initiative.

In using the planning program now required by the 1976 act, ecological forestry advocates applied not just the substantive provisions of the act, but also the requirements of NEPA that environmental analysis be multidisciplinary as well as comprehensive and "searching," and also the requirements of the ESA of 1973. Hence a variety of procedural and substantive requirements under which national forest management now took place were brought together, often to reinforce each other, as citizens and ecological scientists sought to bring an ecological perspective to bear on decisions made by the Forest Service.

The focus on planning in each national forest soon led to a process by which forest reform groups with an environmental and ecological perspective organized their efforts around individual national forests. They stepped up their work to investigate and discover in greater detail the circumstances of individual forests, to identify objectives and problems in site-specific terms, and to create citizen-sponsored plans to compete directly with the plans formulated by agency personnel. In each major region of the country, more local groups formed regional organizations that increased their resources and capabilities in developing regional multi-forest strategies and mobilizing wider public support.[46] Several national organizations, mainly those that had joined in developing the citizens' handbook, and in particular the Wilderness Society, developed "citizen support facilities" in order to assist groups with technical advice and resources.[47]

During the 1980s, these organizations steadily increased their presence in national forest affairs, and through their continual engagement with the Forest Service they identified and sharpened a complex of issues that specified the elements involved in an ecological approach to forest management. By the end of the twentieth century, this complex of policies had come to constitute a body of knowledge and objectives that could rightly be described as ecological forestry. Organized forest reform activities and the policies that they shaped are the subject of the next chapter.[48]

CHAPTER 2

Shaping an Ecological
Forestry Program

The debates over forest policy in the last third of the twentieth century identified the elements of ecological forestry so that by the beginning of the
twenty-first century they constituted a coherent and well-established set of
specific objectives. These were shaped by influences from both citizen reform organizations and ecological scientists. The reform organizations were
much involved in critiquing forest plans and tended to formulate their views
in terms of forest characteristics such as flora and fauna; the areas that might
be managed as old forests; and specific threats such as wood harvest practices, pollution, or motorized vehicles. Hence their activities led to issues
that had considerable meaning on the ground.[1]

Ecological scientists identified similar issues but usually in more conventional scientific language. They spoke in terms of disturbance and recovery as general concepts; or fragmentation with its implications for habitat;
or acid rain as a general biochemical disturbance. The views of scientists
were formulated in different venues than those of forest reformers, in different publications and rarely in formal cooperation. Yet the two were continually aware of each other, and reformers enlisted the help of ecologists in
drawing up their management proposals. As a result, in the realm of public
debate over forest policies, a loose but reinforcing connection evolved between the two streams of ecological thinking about forests. Often scientists
played the lead role in shaping the ideas in ecological forestry, while the

citizen organizations took the lead in applying those ideas to the specifics of forest management.

Citizen Actions for Ecological Forestry

In the years after the National Forest Management Act of 1976, a considerable number of citizen forest reform organizations were formed throughout the nation. They represented a distinctively new agenda and a new type of organization on the environmental scene.[2] Most of them originated in efforts by those who lived near national forests to become involved in forest-wide plans and projects, an involvement that the new law facilitated. By the mid-1980s local groups were coming together into regional organizations. These took on a wider regional perspective and combined the resources of smaller groups with assistance from national organizations and more recently organized service centers specializing in such matters as roads and endangered species, as well as law. They often obtained the support of foundations that preferred to support regional objectives rather than the more limited goals of local groups.

These groups sought to advance specific objectives of ecological forestry as applied to forest lands in their own areas, and they pressed forward in negotiations with federal and state forest agencies. They formulated plans, often in competition with the plans of the national forests; put forth critiques and proposals with reference to specific projects; supported inventory and monitoring programs; and often sponsored active work by citizens on projects such as field studies, road identification, wildlife monitoring, and a variety of forest restoration activities. While their efforts at resisting major disturbances such as clear-cutting, road construction, motorized off-road vehicles, mining, and cattle grazing attracted most attention from the media, their positive objectives in support of biodiversity and watershed health constituted the driving inspiration for their activities.

While the state and regional organizations were focused on particular sites, they displayed striking similarities in their goals, and they shared ideas as to appropriate forest practices. Their ecological objectives arose not from some central source but from widely shared personal experiences with forest conditions and forest managers. Citizens' engagement in forest affairs gave rise to a strong desire for scientific understanding of ecology, which led in turn to a continual search for the latest in ecological science that they might then apply to the forests around them.

Most of the various local, state, and regional ecological forest organizations seem to have evolved from the decentralized wilderness movement of the 1980s. That movement shifted the focus of wilderness activity from the national to the state scene, as advocates worked with their congressional delegates and elicited congressional support for legislative proposals involving forests in their districts. Organizations within the states worked to acquire more detailed information about legislative proposals, and this gave rise to voluntary fieldwork by citizens that enhanced their knowledge of the biology and geology of the state's wildlands and increased their interest in ecological forestry.[3]

These varied citizen activities attracted a number of skilled professionals. Some who were adept at aerial analysis of forest areas were assisted by volunteer pilots to produce aerial photographs of forest vegetation. Some with botanical and zoological skills and knowledge of candidate areas explored the presence of distinctive flora and fauna. As wilderness advocates prepared photographic records in order to attract wider interest in the protection of wilderness areas, the areas came to be prized for their biodiversity as well as their remoteness; plants and animals soon were added to spectacular mountain scenery as assets that were now at stake. Advocates of wilderness reserves now added the protection of biodiversity to their objectives. And they thought in a manner similar to professional ecologists in emphasizing disturbances in natural systems from human activities such as timber harvest, mining, road building, or motorized recreation. Thus, their perspective became shaped by the infusion of ecological values into the values of wilderness experience.

These were subtle but powerful changes in values that can be traced to a wide variety of activities in which more and more people came to experience, investigate, and enjoy the natural world. Some of this was the result of exposure to natural history education, as in an elementary school environmental education program; some was the result of field trips emphasizing natural history sponsored by citizen organizations such as the Audubon Society, the Nature Conservancy, the Sierra Club, or by the innumerable land conservancies known popularly as "land trusts." Many adults satisfied their desire to understand the natural world by visiting areas owned and managed by land trusts. These activities grew as people interested in the out-of-doors aged and replaced more strenuous activities with activities of personal observation and photography that could be enjoyed with less physical effort. Magazines, books, television programs, and photographs by hobbyists conveyed the intricacies and beauty of the natural world through photography. Often the term "wilderness" was replaced with "wild," which emphasized biodiversity as well as the experience of dramatic scenery and gave rise to the terms "wilding" and "rewilding" to describe efforts to protect and re-store the biodiversity of wildlands.

The decentralization of wilderness and ecological forestry activities soon took on an additional regional form of organization.[4] Within regions such as northern New England, the Southern Appalachians, the central Rockies, or the Pacific Northwest, organizations were formed to deal with varied environmental circumstances. State branches of national organizations such as the National Audubon Society or the Sierra Club joined the regional or-ganizations in coalitions that enabled issues to be dealt with on a wider basis. Often these coalitions arose with a broader regional focus defined in geographical terms, such as a forested region, a watershed, or an ecosystem. Some of these regional forest alliances were the Northern Forest Alliance, the Southern Appalachian Forest Coalition, the Southwest Forest Alliance, or the Sierra Nevada Forest Protection Alliance. Such groups mobilized re-sources for regional ecological description and analysis or the formulation of regional resource management plans.

Several organizations that specialized in distinctive ecological prob-lems were formed, publicized their own special skills, and assisted regional organizations. These included the Wildlands Center for Preventing Roads, located in Missoula, Montana. Its publication The Road RIPorter provided sci-entific information about the adverse ecological impact of roads.[5] The Cen-ter for Biological Diversity located at Phoenix, Arizona, undertook many initiatives under the Endangered Species Act to list species at risk and pro-vide critical habitat for them. The Old Growth Campaign gave assistance to those protecting old forests and developed a program of enlisting "grove guardians." The Wilderness Society issued a monthly letter with informa-tion about the course of wilderness activity. The Forest Service Employees for Environmental Ethics provided a daily news service about national for-est affairs. The environmental law centers throughout the country devoted some of their time to forest issues and served as sources of legal talent to conduct environmental cases. The most extensive was Earthjustice, an out-growth of the former Sierra Club Legal Defense Fund, with headquarters in Oakland, California, and regional offices in Juneau, Oakland, Denver, Talla-hassee, Honolulu, Bozeman, Seattle, and Washington, D.C. Several regional environmental law organizations provided legal talent for cases within their own areas such as Western Resource Advocates (formerly Land and Water Fund of the Rockies) of Denver, Colorado, the Western Environmental Law Center in Eugene, Oregon, and the Southern Environmental Law Center in Atlanta.[6]

Far less noticed, but providing ecological interest and skills of value in regional and locally organized activity, were the many organizations specializing in a given species, such as bats, loons, wolves, raptors, elk, frogs, salamanders, invertebrates, and wild flowers.[7] These organizations tended to bring together both citizens and scientists to enhance knowledge about a given type of flora or fauna and often provided informal links among individuals working on both knowledge and action, rather than giving rise to formal organizational connections. Networks of many and varied sorts, facilitated by the vast number of Web sites that they generated on the Internet, marked the development of ecological activities. These organizations gave significant new meanings to old terms. While "wildlife" formerly had referred primarily to game animals, the new and rather awkward term "non-game wildlife" expanded this meaning to include invertebrates and plants. Even more significant was the way in which the term "conservation" now extended beyond its earlier focus on the management of trees with commercial wood fiber potential to the management of a host of individual species in programs such as bat conservation, bighorn sheep conservation, and raptor conservation. Specialized groups advanced programs to "save" these species from the population declines generated by human disturbances.

Planning and implementation served as the primary focal points of these organizations, which spent considerable time scrutinizing and evaluating the forest plans mandated by the 1976 National Forest Management Act.[8] They frequently advanced beyond that to develop their own plans, which they used to convey their objectives to their constituencies and the public and to confront the agencies with a perspective beyond specific forest plans and projects. Over the years a number of such plans emerged to constitute a major body of ideas and actions that indicate the nationwide significance of ecological forestry. These organizations followed closely the management of the forests in their areas in terms of ecological forest objectives such as inventory and monitoring of species, and combating significant forest disturbances such as harvest practices, motorized recreational vehicles, road building, or mining. In both planning and implementation, the agendas of local, state, and regional ecological forest organizations were strikingly similar.

In these strategies federal statutes were widely used, especially the National Environmental Policy Act (NEPA) and the Endangered Species Act (ESA). While most legislative requirements for administrative agencies were discretionary, as reflected in the use of the term "may," a few were mandatory with the wording "shall" or "must." Hence NEPA and the ESA with their mandatory provisions provided special leverage to citizen forest organizations in their negotiations with the agencies. While ESA worked directly in requiring agencies to act in a particular way on endangered species issues, NEPA tended to have a more diffuse and long-term effect in requiring only that the agency fully understand and explain its proposals in a "searching and interdisciplinary" way. This dealt more with knowledge, such as inventory and monitoring, rather than implementation, which involved management choices. Hence the historical question of whether or not "full disclosure" requirements brought about change in the agency's ecological thinking was quite different from whether or not they led to immediate changes in action.

Both NEPA and the ESA sustained and advanced the distinctive role of science in the agendas of ecological forest organizations. On the one hand, NEPA provided the organizations ample opportunity to bring to bear on agency activities the latest scientific information about both ecological forest resources and their conditions, and the effects of major disturbances on those resources. In this manner, science had significant potential influence on actions of environmental agencies, but this potential was not always realized. The ESA, on the other hand, was more bothersome to the Forest Service, because its requirements arose from the views of scientists outside the agency as to what species were threatened and endangered and what were the habitat requirements for recovery. The problem became even more critical for the Forest Service as the scope of biodiversity management expanded from rare and endangered to sensitive species, with the mandate falling upon the national forests to maintain the viability of all such species. This mandate gave rise to policies and hence measures to provide external scientific review of such decisions.

Tension over the role of science in forest ecological affairs arose when scientists within the Forest Service were called upon to render scientific judgment about ecological conditions to their management superiors and were then overruled. The resulting personnel problems were highlighted in several sensational incidents and led to a contest between the professional judgments of agency scientists and the policies that forest management sought to implement. These conflicts led to the organization of the Forest Service Employees for Environmental Ethics (FSEEE), which over the years developed a number of ecological programs including a distinctive environmental education package with a much stronger ecological perspective than the most widely used curricula, Project Learning Tree and Project Wild. FSEEE also instituted a new quarterly, Forest Magazine, the first such semipopular magazine with an environmental and ecological perspective in forest mangement.[9]

Regional Variations in Shaping Ecological Forestry

The ecological forestry agenda that began to take shape in the last third of the twentieth century arose from direct engagement of citizens with forest agencies throughout the country. The forest plans required by the 1976 National Forest Management Act were the vehicle for this interaction. The specific elements of an ecological perspective were shaped one by one as citizens formulated critiques of the plans initiated by the individual forest administrations, drew up their own alternative plans, appealed specific elements of the plan to the regional foresters, took appeals further to the Washington office of the Forest Service, and, in a few cases, went to the courts. Since conditions varied widely among the individual national forests, so did these specifics, in so many individual cases that it would be more than tedious to catalog them. Often, however, those engaged with an individual forest found themselves coming together with others into regional groupings, groupings often fostered by the agency's own promotion of multiforest planning. Looking at regional planning provides fewer cases to examine in detail in order to emphasize the process as both nationwide in extent and varying in specific content from one geographical area to another.

The Northeast

Forest reform activity by citizens in the far Northeast (northern New England and New York) evolved within the context of the region's dominant late-twentieth-century forest crisis: the decision by large industrial timberland owners to sell their holdings in anticipation that traditional forest uses—wood production, hunting and fishing, and forest recreation—would give way to permanent development. As owner after owner sought to sell their forest lands and made clear that the value of the lands for development was far greater to them then their value for wood production, a host of proposals arose, ranging from land purchases and conservation easements to protect forest land from development, to competing "forest certification" programs, to state regulation of cutting practices and restrictions on "liquidation forestry," to a proposal for a national park, each with its own advocates. All this produced a welter of contrasting voices throughout the region, amid which proposals for ecological forestry obtained only a limited audience.[10]

The most comprehensive group to express some elements of an ecological forestry program was the Northern Forest Alliance. It brought together some forty-four citizen organizations from throughout the region with a set of issues that sought to balance both ecological and wood production objectives. Its mission statement read: "To work together to protect and enhance the ecological and economic sustainability of natural and human communities in the Northern Forest." The alliance described an ecologically viable forest as "a more structurally complex forest with more mature trees; more stands of mixed species, size, and age, and the full diversity of naturally occurring plants, animals, and natural communities." The alliance's wood production goals, maintained alongside its ecological objectives, emphasized that "Northern-Forest based businesses can benefit by focusing on growing and processing high quality saw logs. Paper-making will remain part of the region's economic mix, but will not dominate forest management to the extent it has in the past." The alliance thus sought to carve out an extensive niche for ecological forestry alongside "value-added" wood production objectives. It looked to willing buyer/willing seller arrangements to acquire land rights to provide "permanent protection" for "forests of high ecological value" and at the same time to create "a safety net of forest practice regulations to protect public values."[11]

Several documents produced by the alliance helped to define its position on forest issues more sharply. One described a program for the management of the Nulhegan and Victory Basin wildlands of the northern forest, which emphasized the multiple ecological values of roadless areas.[12] This was a comprehensive statement of the adverse impacts of roads on biodiversity and watershed integrity, complete with extensive scientific and technical documentation. At the same time the alliance sponsored an extensive and critical analysis of conservation easements, advising precautions in drawing up such easements and emphasizing the need to make clear the positive uses that the easements authorized as well as the uses that were to be prohibited.

This "middle ground" of opinion about forest ecology in New England was identified by the absence of two significant groups from the list of participating organizations, the Society for the Protection of New Hampshire Forests and the Sierra Club. The New Hampshire society was one of the nation's oldest state forest organizations; it had been active in the political movement to add eastern lands to the national forest system in the early twentieth century and had long acquired and managed its own forest lands for both wood production and aesthetic objectives.[13] In recent years it had become a major force for obtaining state funds for state forest land acquisition in New Hampshire. But such actions had been carried out within a context of traditional sustained-yield timber management, without considering ecological objectives or the establishment of national parks. The most vigorous statement of its position came in a document published in

2001, "New Hampshire's Vanishing Forests: Conversion, Fragmentation and Parcellization of Forests in the Granite State." But in sharp contrast with the way in which ecological objectives identified the fragmentation of forested areas as a threat to native biodiversity, the society's publication identified fragmentation as a roadblock in the management of the state's forests for wood production. Differences in the positions of the Northern Forest Alliance and the Society for the Protection of New Hampshire Forests explain the absence of the society from the list of groups that made up the alliance.

The Sierra Club and its allies championed an alternative to the Northern Forest Alliance that brought together two related policy ideas that the alliance rejected. One was a proposal for a three-million-acre national park in north central Maine around the existing Baxter State Park, and the other was opposition to green certification (see chapter 3) as an effective alternative to regulation of state forest practices. The national park idea was brought into the forest policy fray by a group called RESTORE: The North Woods that was founded in 1992 under the inspiration of Michael Kellet, then regional director of the Wilderness Society in Boston, and led in Maine by its state director, Jym St. Pierre. The proposal appeared to be popular among Maine voters, as was indicated by several public opinion polls. The first, conducted by Abacus Associates of Hatfield, Massachusetts, and sponsored by the Sierra Club, concluded that 63 percent of Mainers supported the national park proposal, 22 percent opposed, and 15 percent were undecided. RESTORE identified its objectives as "ecological restoration," that is, to "restore the ecosystem as closely as possible to its pre-human 'wildness.'"[14]

In tandem with the proposal to establish a Maine Woods National Park the state chapter of the Sierra Club expressed skepticism about the certification movement. Certification was popular among many members of the Northern Forest Alliance, but the Maine Sierra Club was wary of the ability of the certification movement to serve as a major initiative for advancing biodiversity or "native forest" objectives. The alternatives were the Sustainable Forestry Initiative (SFI) of the American Forest and Paper Association, and the Forest Stewardship Council (FSC) (both described later). The Sierra Club choose not to deal with this issue in general terms but, instead, to evaluate in depth one of the more publicized cases of certification in Maine, that of the holdings of J. D. Irving Company's Allagash woodland. It commissioned a report by a well-known Maine forest analyst, Mitch Lansky. In his evaluation Lansky argued that in using quantitative scores for certification eligibility and monitoring the results in later evaluations, the certifiers compromised the purported standards; the high marks given to woodland management were based more on promises than on performance. The report documented many forestry practices that did not meet FSC standards, and served as the basis for the Sierra Club's conclusion that green certification of the Irving Allagash woodlands was unacceptable.[15]

The Northern Forest Alliance gave considerable support to the FSC "green certification" program, which served to distinguish it from Sierra Club views on both a national park and on certification. Maine citizens, moreover, seemed to consider the park proposal as a preferable alternative to the popular conservation easements; the opinion survey concluded that "54 percent of respondents favor the government's gradually buying land for a national park where no logging would be allowed, compared to 25 percent who favored buying development rights from timber companies and allowing them to continue to log the land."

The Southeast

The evolving public attitudes toward forests in the Southeast were captured in 2002 by a U.S. Forest Service survey in preparation for the development of forest plans in the agency's southeastern region.[16] In the survey, 5,222 interviews were completed with residents in the seven states, in which thirteen national forests were located. Three general topics were measured involving values in national forest management, management objectives, and general environmental attitudes. The respondents gave strong support to natural values of forests and weak support to extractive activities. The authors summarized the results: "At the top, they [the forests] are viewed as important for their importance in passing along natural forests for future generations, followed by protecting sources of clean water, providing protection for wildlife and habitat, providing places that are natural in appearance, emphasis on forest health, and protection of rare or endangered species." The authors continued: "The values most often emphasized in the management of national forests, i.e., outdoor recreation and timber, are in the second or lower ½ of the list of values." In summary they stated, "The people [who live here] clearly put ecosystems and naturalness above utilitarian objectives in the management of these national forests."[17]

Citizens made two environmental/ecological initiatives in the Southern Appalachian region. One emphasized the impact of chip mills, which had become a major development in the newly extensive southern private forest industry.[18] This turn of affairs in the wood products industry had major impacts on both water quality and future wood supplies. The other initiative grew out of activities in the national forests of the Southern Appalachians and was more ecologically comprehensive in the scope of its interests, with special attention to biodiversity, wildlife, and habitats. These two initiatives worked from two different origins and in two different directions; yet they tended to come together in a regional ecological approach to forest affairs and a shared critique of wood production.

Chip mills had become a major part of the southern forest industry whose primary objective was to produce pulp for paper. The industry now preferred a raw product that could be supplied with smaller trees of younger age, and this gave rise to plantation production, short rotations (the life of a tree between planting and harvest), clear-cutting, and even-aged management (managing all trees within a given area to be of the same age). The mills themselves were the most visible part of the enterprise, places where logs were turned into chips, which were then shipped to pulping mills located elsewhere, both in the United States and abroad. The chip mills created an enormous demand on southern forests, becoming a major factor in the conversion of hardwoods to pine plantations and generating denuded forests very much like the cutover lands of the North a century earlier.

Citizen organizations arose to highlight the resulting effects on wildlife and watersheds and to demand that the environmental impact of the industry be examined before it proceeded further. An investigation and report known as the Southern Forest Resource Assessment (SFRA) was completed in late 2001.[19] The most important future problem, so the SFRA argued, was the decline of southern forested land as the result of its conversion to urban development, much like what was taking place in New England. The report incorporated neither the ideas of ecological forestry nor its specific proposals or concepts such as biodiversity inventory and monitoring, habitat analysis, old growth, forests of multiple age, clear-cutting, and even-age management.

About the same time that the Southern Forest Resource Assessment was released, the Southern Appalachian Forest Coalition, composed of twenty citizen groups located in six southern states, produced a quite different assessment of southeastern forests called "A Conservation Vision for the Southern Appalachian Region."[20] The member groups of the Forest Coalition had all promoted citizen engagement with the national forests since the 1976 National Forest Management Act, each with its own history and its own issues. They had come together in 1994 with similar perspectives about forest affairs and now attempted to link their programs and resources into a region-wide approach to the management of the Southern Appalachians.

The two reports represented in rather striking fashion the two sets of visions about forest management that were at odds in the South as well as in the nation at large. One envisioned a future organized largely around the benefits of wood production, and the other stressed the environmental and ecological role of southern forests in the region's future. There was perhaps no region of the country in which these two perspectives now stood in such stark contrast, each expressed in its own "futures" document.

Over the years since its organization, the citizen's coalition had conducted an extensive survey and mapping program for the public lands in the Southern Appalachians, "identifying conservation and heritage resources, setting conservation priorities, and placing local conservation prospects within a landscape perspective." These had used geographical information systems (GIS) resources to identify areas for both potential public acquisition and management, within the framework of a proposed network of conservation areas throughout the region. The GIS maps identified regional wilderness and roadless areas, protected wildlands, unprotected wildlands, old-growth forests, hot spots of biodiversity, aquatic diversity area watersheds, high-priority areas for public acquisition, conservation easements, and cultural/heritage areas. Special emphasis was placed on biological diversity in the Southern Appalachians, especially as a unique area of over three thousand species of flowering plants.

The public report of the Southern Appalachian Forest Coalition, titled "Return the Great Forest: A Conservation Vision for the Southern Appalachian Region," was endorsed by almost two hundred organizations throughout the region, including Republicans for Environmental Protection, and by President Jimmy Carter with the supporting statement, "I am very impressed by this bold vision of how to restore and preserve the Southern Appalachian Forest." The launch of the report at a press conference in Greenville, South Carolina, on July 26, 2002, was timed to coincide with the revision of the U.S. Forest Service plan, which was to begin in late August. It showcased eleven South Carolina organizations that had pledged their support for the program's issues. Ten individuals and foundations had provided funds for the coalition's proposal.[21]

Not directly connected with the coalition but providing specialized support for the unique role of the national forests in the advancement of biodiversity was a Southern Appalachian project of Defenders of Wildlife that outlined in considerable detail the crucial issues of the diversity provision of the 1976 act and, in response, the subsequent development of the provision for species "viability" drawn up under that act. A report, "Southern Lessons: Saving Species Through the National Forest Management Act," prepared by David John Zaber and sponsored by Defenders of Wildlife, elaborated on the crucial role of the Forest Service in saving the nation's biodiversity resources.[22] The general statement was supported by seven case studies in which Forest Service action under the requirements of the law had saved species throughout the Southern Appalachians.

The Midwest

Citizen actions for forest reform in the Midwest focused heavily on national forest management. Activity emerged in the 1990s in the form of a regional organization known as Heartwood.[23] Heartwood grew out of a series of citizen actions on national forests in the Ohio Valley that came together in the winter of 1990 and 1991 to form a regional organization, the Heartwood Forest Council, and soon to expand its reach to the larger Midwest and form a series of regional activities. By the early twenty-first century, fifty-five local and state groups had become member organizations of Heartwood.

In its earlier years, Heartwood's constituents had come to believe that its environmental and ecological objectives could be fostered only by reducing and perhaps eliminating logging on the various national forests that it represented. That objective served to unify groups of people that were widely dispersed. Most of the national forests in the region were separate from each other, were relatively small, and, in the absence of significant national parks, were the largest forested areas in the experience of mid-westerners. This wide dispersion led Heartwood's role in promoting local and state organizations and educating them about procedural opportunities open to citizen reformers under the 1976 National Forest Management Act and its subsequent regulations.

The extension of Heartwood's constituency broadened its program to include policies for the entire Central Appalachian region and beyond. This was known as the Appalachian Restoration Campaign and was described as a project "dedicated to the restoration and protection of the Central Appalachians" with the more specific aim of developing "an interconnected system of reserves in which human activity is compatible with ecological recovery and health." It believed that "humanity's rate and intensity of land" use had now surpassed "natural disturbances" that "increasingly threatened . . . the integrity of the Appalachians." And it especially noted that parks and reserves in the region were isolated and failed "to represent and interconnect the region . . . denying its natural large-scale functions." Its specific program was aimed at providing support to Heartwood member groups "in the form of maps, research, data, and other information."[24]

One of the main projects of the Appalachian Restoration Campaign was to provide GIS maps on a variety of subjects such as the distribution of threatened and endangered species listed by both federal and state agencies, the ecological units of the eastern United States, roadless areas in eastern national forests in general, specific national forests such as the Daniel Boone National Forest in Kentucky, or specific issues such as the proximity of timber sales to endangered species.

Two citizens' organizations associated with Heartwood, one in Indiana and the other in Pennsylvania, reflected the varying situations and successes of ecological forest action in the region. In Indiana the Hoosier National Forest became the target of citizen action in the early 1980s. In 1996 seven groups formed the Indiana Forest Alliance to coordinate forest reform activities on both the Hoosier National Forest and the state forests as well. One of the early, successful reform objectives of the alliance was the exclusion of motorized recreation vehicles from the forest, and beginning in 1998 no timber was harvested on the Hoosier, largely because of potential threats to the Indiana bat, a federally protected endangered species. In 2001, under the leadership of the alliance, thirteen groups joined to produce "A Conservationist's Alternative Plan for Management of the Hoosier National Forest," which defined a central role for wildlife and watershed objectives. In 2002 the alliance brought a court suit to require environmental assessments of timber harvests on state forests as required under the Indiana code, which at this writing is still pending.[25]

In Pennsylvania, the Allegheny Defense Project (ADP) went through a different development. While the Hoosier National Forest in Indiana contributed only about 4 percent of the state's timber supply, the Allegheny National Forest (ANF) held an important part of the Allegheny Plateau's prized hardwood timber, especially black cherry, and hence any reform effort faced a highly influential hardwood timber industry and a forest management deeply committed to wood production. Public interest in ecological objectives on the ANF was both limited and sporadic, and the few attempts to advance them met only limited success.[26]

The Southern Mountain West

The mountain West spawned a number of alliances of citizen forest groups with an interest in ecological forestry. These varied not only with geographical area but with broader ecological or ecosystem conditions.[27]

SOUTHWEST FOREST ALLIANCE

The Southwest Forest Alliance, with headquarters in Flagstaff, Arizona, was founded in 1994 and by 2003 was composed of sixty-seven separate groups located in Arizona and New Mexico.[28]

One of the alliance's primary objectives, under the slogan "Old Growth

Forever," was to protect and restore old-growth forests in Arizona and New Mexico. It lamented the undesirable but continued logging of rare old-growth trees in the Southwest, and emphasized that "the Kaibab Plateau [on the North Rim of the Grand Canyon] is home to the greatest remaining density and distribution of old-growth pines. Numerous sensitive wildlife species, including the Mexican spotted owl, the Kaibab squirrel and the northern goshawk and the Apache trout depend upon this unique area." Over the last one hundred years, the alliance argued, "forest management practices including logging, grazing, and fire suppression have greatly decreased forest viability throughout the Southwest. Forests have become heavily fragmented, average tree diameter has decreased, and fuel loads become increasingly more dangerous every fire season." One of the alliance's major publications was *Disappearing Legacy, Destruction of the Ponderosa Pine Ecosystem.*[29]

During the early years of the Southwest Forest Alliance, the role of fire and the response to it became a major issue in the region. As one approach to fire the alliance stressed the need to protect the large trees "which are the most fire resistant and represent the next generation of old growth." Also as a fire prevention strategy, it emphasized the need to reduce the risk for communities located in and around the national forests. In this strategy the alliance cited surveys of voters across Arizona expressing a major opinion that preventing forest wildfires "could be better accomplished by removing small trees and brush than by logging large trees" and "that efforts to thin forests of brush and small trees should be concentrated near forest communities rather than in the wooded back country."

SKY ISLAND ALLIANCE

The Sky Island Alliance was formed in 1992 in response to a proposal by the Forest Service to turn the Coronado National Forest in southeast Arizona into a national recreation area.[30] The group presented an alternative plan or design to the Forest Service at a conference in 1994, and at the same conference biologist Tony Povilitis offered another reserve system for the Sky Islands that would include as well the Gila and Apache National Forests to the north. In December 1995 the alliance and the Wildlands Project hosted a three-day workshop to begin a conservation area design for a Mogollon Highlands/Greater Gila/Sky Islands region. This then led to the formation of a Sky Islands Wildlands Network Conservation Plan, released in the fall of 2000, to which over two hundred individuals and a dozen groups contributed.[31]

The Sky Islands Conservation Network comprises about 17.3 million acres and extends from the Mogollon Rim in east-central Arizona and west-central New Mexico south to the northern Sierra Madre Occidental in Chihuahua and Sonora, Mexico. At the center of the region, covering about 9.9 million acres, are the Sky Islands. This term, coined in 1967 by Weldon Heald, identified mountain ranges that are isolated from each other by intervening valleys of grasslands or desert. The valleys of this basin and range country act as barriers to the movement of woodland and forest species. The region is a center of biological diversity for several groups of species, whose diversity stems from the region's location, elevation, and history. It is oriented north and south between the Rocky Mountains and the Sierra Madre Occidental of Mexico and is a meeting point of temperate North American species and warm subtropical species.

The Sky Islands network is a complex of cores, linkages, and compatible use zones in an ecologically defined area. The alliance has used the relatively new term "rewilding" to describe a scientific approach to protecting and restoring native ecosystems and large wilderness, with selected focal species to represent larger groups of species important to maintaining ecologically healthy conditions. The process of rewilding the Sky Islands involves intensive resource mapping, the reintroduction of extirpated species, ecological restoration, and issuing guidelines for management and standards for compatible economic use.

A distinctive aspect of the alliance program is the large number of volunteers that it attracts.[32] Over a three-year period it reported that over two hundred volunteers had spent over 5,000 hours mapping a half million acres of national forest lands and nearly 1,000 miles of legal and illegal dirt roads threatening the wildness of the Sky Islands. Volunteers monitor wildlife populations, close and revegetate illegal roads and collect varied information important to guide conservation. Specific projects include the closure and ecological restoration of the Slavin Gulch Road in the Dragoon Mountains as a demonstration project; an inventory of leopard frogs and identification of threats to them and possible sites for reintroduction; and a project in cooperation with the Natural Resources Department at the Arizona Department of Transportation to install remote sensing cameras to detect and photograph the movements of animals under highways.

SOUTHERN ROCKIES FOREST NETWORK

The Southern Rockies, the mountain chain located primarily in Colorado but extending into Wyoming on the north, played a distinctive role in ecological forestry both in citizen organization and science. The Southern Rockies Forest Network (SRFN) was composed of twenty-six constituent groups, many of which had been tracking national forest activities since

before the 1976 National Forest Management Act.[33] It evolved in the context
of an extensive group of regional professionals in the natural and social sciences on which it could draw for diverse scientific information., a context
that was well represented by *Rocky Mountain Futures*, Jill Barron's collection of
essays by thirty-four specialists in regional institutions.

A biodiversity conservation program was one of the network's major
activities. A description of this program read: "The wild inhabitants of the
Southern Rockies—including lynx, cutthroat trout, goshawk—are struggling for survival in the face of rapid human population, rampant urban
sprawl, and unchecked resource extraction. Using science and citizen advocacy, SRFN member groups aim to secure lasting protection for the plants
and animals, and habitats that make the Southern Rockies unique."

Another of the network's programs was the Southern Rockies Ecosystem Project to promote the region's health and integrity. The project identified its objective in this manner: "a healthy ecosystem falls within the range
of conditions that existed before Euro American settlement, including pre-
settlement components (e.g., native species), structures (old-growth forest
characteristics, landscape patterns), and dynamics (e.g., natural processes
such as fire). Native species of the Southern Rockies have adapted to these
pre-settlement habitats and natural processes over long time periods. As
ecosystems deviate from these natural conditions, native species may not
be able to persist and ecosystems may not function properly." This project
was followed by the *Southern Rockies Wildlands Network Vision* published in 2003,
which outlined the direction of the network's program.[34]

Actions to implement ecological forestry in the Southern Rockies took
several turns. One was to develop, in cooperation with the Colorado Environmental Coalition, mapped reserve plans for three national forests and an
attempt to persuade those forest administrations to analyze the reserve plans
as official planning alternatives, to use the reserve plans both as a scientific
reference for monitoring Forest Service compliance with environmental laws
and as rallying points for citizen input to the Forest Service, and to establish
a legal and scientific basis for possible later appeals of Forest Service plans.
This focus on three forests became the initial step in working toward an
ecosystem protection plan for the entire Southern Rockies, and a Southern
Rockies Ecosystem Protection Act. The project organizers extended mapping and citizen involvement, especially its Forest Watch network, beyond
the three original forests to the entire state of Colorado, thereby developing
its constituency more broadly and establishing more local support in these
regions.

The Northern Mountain States

GREATER YELLOWSTONE COALITION

The Greater Yellowstone Coalition was formed in 1983 in order to focus attention on the region of Yellowstone National Park and its surrounding areas.[35] Around the park were seven national forests that together with the Grand Teton National Park comprised the Greater Yellowstone Region. In the earliest days of the coalition the region was identified primarily by the range of movement of the large animals: grizzlies, elk, and bison. These large mammals could not be managed simply by focusing on their activities within the park; the scope of attention had to be extended to the entire region. Around this regional approach, the coalition found a wide range of support; by the early twenty-first century it included 11,700 individual members; 80 local, state, and national conservation and outdoor organizations; and over 230 businesses within the region.

In later years the concept of "ecosystem management" came to be popular in national forest affairs. This concept seems to have been established with some degree of concreteness by this focus on the Yellowstone ecosystem. In the 1980s and early 1990s there were serious efforts to develop more effective formal relationships between the National Park Service and the U.S. Forest Service to work out the ecological interconnections within the region in terms of concrete management activities. However, these initiatives within the agencies foundered amid the opposition of those whose interests lay in the national forests. They feared that ecological influences arising from the park would spill over to the surrounding forests. Opposition from the Wyoming delegation in Congress, bolstered by regional logging interests, led to an abrupt end to the proposal, with forced transfers from their positions of agency officials who had promoted it.[36]

The Greater Yellowstone Coalition, however, continued to work in a less dramatic and yet still comprehensive fashion, within the general context of the "greater Yellowstone ecosystem," arguing forcefully that the entire region had to be thought of as a broad ecological system, and then establishing that context as the framework within which individual programs and projects were given relevance. In doing so they tackled a wide range of environmental and ecological conditions in both park and forest management. The coalition stated that "a healthy, wild ecosystem can prosper only if it is kept whole. Rivers, migrating wildlife, even boiling water shifting below ground do not stop for lines drawn on a map." The expanding wildlife focus of the coalition was especially noticeable, for while much of its initial impetus grew out of its interest in the large mammals, somewhat in the spirit of the nineteenth-century role of Yellowstone as a game refuge, in late-twentieth-century fashion it incorporated broad biodiversity concerns as well.

From its earliest days the coalition gave special attention to the economy of the Greater Yellowstone area with an emphasis on both the economic changes within the region itself and the rapid development that was taking place on its periphery. It assembled economic information that emphasized the sharp decline in the traditional forest, range, and mining economies, and the growth of white-collar and professional activities and retirement communities that were becoming far more important in terms of jobs, investment, and income. The coalition took this information to the communities around the park to advocate local initiatives to foster the new as the old declined.

Early in its history, the Yellowstone Coalition established close relationships with scientists interested in the region, and soon it was holding annual conferences to highlight their scientific work. While this drew on scientists from diverse institutions throughout the nation, the coalition soon gathered together a smaller group of western scientists to serve as a Science Council, chaired by Dr. David Challinor, forest ecologist from the Smithsonian Institution. The council included specialists in ecology, wildlife biology, fisheries, soils, botany, economics, and political science. The last two were especially noticeable, as they drew into the science council both Thomas Power, economist at the University of Montana, whose studies about economic changes in the West were widely known, and John Freemuth, political scientist at Boise State University and a specialist in the analysis of the public lands.

ALLIANCE FOR THE WILD ROCKIES

The Alliance for the Wild Rockies encompasses the northern Rockies from Idaho through Montana and Wyoming in its area of interest and is much like the Greater Yellowstone Coalition in its ecological setting and its program.[37] In fact, it includes the Greater Yellowstone ecosystem as one of the five ecosystems of the "Wild Rockies." The others are the Glacier/Northern Continental Divide ecosystem; the Greater Salmon-Selway ecosystem in central and southern Idaho; the Greater Cabinet/Yaak/Selkirk ecosystem to the north, and the Greater Hells Canyon/Wallowa ecosystem to the west. The alliance draws these five regions together under the general name "Wild Rockies bioregion."

While the alliance advocates the expansion of the region's designated wilderness areas, it does so with the caution: "Large areas have been protected under the 1964 Wilderness Act, but the resulting wilderness areas, chosen mostly for scenic and recreational attributes, have failed to protect biological diversity." This transition in objectives from wilderness preservation to biological diversity, as I have observed before, was one of the major changes that took place between the 1960s and the 1980s and beyond in public efforts to modify the previous pattern established in the national forest multiple-use program. But, as with the Greater Yellowstone Coalition, the predominant feature of biodiversity emphasized by the alliance was the role of the large mammals such as wolves, elk, and grizzly bears, and the habitat that they required. It was no wonder that among the alliance's board of advisors were three of the major figures in the attempt to protect and restore the grizzly bear in the northern Rockies: the scientist Dr. John Craighead; Dr. Charles Jonkel, an internationally recognized bear biologist; and Lance Olson, founder of the Great Bear Foundation.

The alliance's special interest in large mammals and their habitat shaped major elements of their program. One was the issue of roads and their role in fragmenting forests and grizzly bear habitat. The Wildlands Center for Preventing Roads, the national center to advocate road closures, grew out of concern for this problem in western Montana, and continued its work from headquarters at Missoula, Montana. At the same time a number of constituent groups of the alliance fostered citizen inventories of roads, many of them not on the records of the national forests, often supplementing that information with GIS mapping, and these groups worked with the Forest Service to close roads permanently. With the help of personnel enlisted in the Roads Scholar Project, more than 5,000 miles of roads were inventoried in 1994 and 1995, of which 6 percent had not previously been mapped or accounted for by the agency. At the same time the Wildlands Center documented the effectiveness of road closure devices.

The public lands on which the alliance concentrated, although within the same general region and therefore ecologically related, were often separated through their distinctive histories, having been administered through the years by different agencies for different purposes. In conventional ecological forest strategy this placed a special focus on the need to connect areas through biological corridors so that fragmented landscapes could take on larger habitat significance. Of the five large ecosystems within its concern, the alliance explained: "The areas most threatened by fragmentation in the Wild Rockies are also the most important to the health of wildlife and plant populations: the biological corridors connecting the region's five core ecosystems. Individually, none of these ecosystems are large enough to support self-sustaining populations of wildlife; they are dependent on each other for new and varied genetic stock. Wildlands between ecosystems serve as biological bridges, permitting migration and genetic interchange of both plants and wildlife."[38]

A wide range of proposals that the alliance generated were brought together in the Northern Rockies Ecosystem Protection Act, which helped to focus the attention of diverse groups on the region as a single "bioregion." It involved a wide range of land use projects: over 18 million acres of wilderness; two national park and preserve studies, one in the Hells Canyon area and the other in the Flathead National Park and Preserve Study Area adjacent to Glacier National Park; 1,810 miles of wild, scenic, and recreational rivers; almost 2.5 million acres of the wilderness proposed as "biological connecting corridors"; a pilot system of almost one million areas as a "National Wildland Recovery System" to restore native vegetation and species diversity, reduce erosion, and close and revegetate needed roads; and a Blackfeet Wilderness adjacent to Glacier National Park to recognize and protect Native American uses and treaty rights.

The Pacific States

CALIFORNIA

In the late 1990s a number of state organizations interested in California's wildlands came together in the Sierra Nevada Forest Protection Campaign to focus directly on the national forests of the Sierra Nevada.[39] The campaign soon participated in a federal program to develop a region-wide management plan for the national forests in the Sierra Nevada. A series of events, reports, and controversies led to a study—the Sierra Nevada Ecosystem Project (SNEP)—completed with $7 million funding from the federal Congress—which produced "the most detailed ecosystem analysis ever." It documented significant human impacts to the mountain range, to aquatic and riparian systems, old growth, and species, all that had arisen from a variety of sources, particularly logging and fire suppression. In response to this study the Forest Service made two failed attempts to design a management plan for the Sierra Nevada, which proposed to double the logging in the range and offered few specific protection measures for the spotted owl or other at-risk species. The proposal, in the form of an environmental impact statement, for the most part ignored the SNEP information and was withdrawn by the Clinton administration.

In response to these developments, the Sierra Nevada Forest Protection Campaign was formed to inject ecological forestry objectives into the next round of plans and studies for the Sierra Nevada. Several further reports about the entire process ensued, including a critique of past planning efforts conducted by a federal advisory committee of scientists. Under the active leadership of a new regional forester, Bradley Powell, another planning effort began that involved a wider range of specialists from other federal and state agencies as well as academics, in which the citizen Protection Campaign participated. The plan, called the Sierra Nevada Framework, incorporated ecological forestry objectives far more extensively than had any previous national forest regional plan. Powell signed the resulting "Record of Decision of the Sierra Nevada Framework" on January 12, 2001.

The goals involved in this process and stated in the program of the Protection Campaign covered the entire range of the ecological forest objectives that were taking shape throughout the country: protection of diverse plants, wildlife, and habitats; watershed protection; preservation of old-growth forests; and reduction of massive threats to forest ecology from humans in the form of logging, dams, and motorized recreation. The campaign's program gave special emphasis to two related themes that were developing around ecological forestry campaigns. One was a strategy to restore fire to the ecosystem and as part of that strategy to reduce fire threats to the interface between forests and surrounding human communities by thinning young trees there, while retaining older growth, which was more fire resistant. The other was to enhance the economies of forest communities by emphasizing the growing importance of recreation and living in an attractive forest environment as the region's future economic promise, in contrast to the continually declining and now very small role of extractive industries such as logging and grazing in the Sierra Nevada.

OREGON NATURAL RESOURCES COUNCIL

The citizen group in Oregon with a specialized focus on public forest lands is the Oregon Natural Resources Council (ONRC).[40] The council was formed in the 1970s to establish a new stage of the Oregon wilderness movement. Heretofore Oregon wilderness proposals sponsored by those who had participated in the first wave of wilderness action had been confined to the Cascade Mountains in western Oregon. Proposals by citizen groups elsewhere in the Oregon Coast Range in western Oregon or the mountains of northeastern Oregon were resisted on the grounds that they were not true wilderness. Since earlier advocates such as the Sierra Club would not take these up, those interested in an expanded set of wilderness areas formed the Oregon Natural Resources Council to advocate new de facto wilderness proposals and over the years succeeded in adding wilderness areas throughout the state. Through its proposals, which became part of the Endangered

American Wilderness Act and the Oregon Wilderness Act, more than 1.2 million acres were added to Oregon wilderness.

Still later, as old growth, wildlife, and biodiversity issues infused the wilderness movement with new objectives, the council expanded its range of activities to include them. The ONRC was the first group to appeal a Forest Service timber sale based on concern for the spotted owl, and by this time the Sierra Club, through its Legal Defense Fund, took up the issue, which led to a virtual halt of logging in spotted owl habitat managed by the federal government. By the end of the twentieth century this new direction had led to the creation of the Oregon Wild Campaign to protect the state's public forest roadless areas 1,000 acres and larger, to stress habitat for salmon as well as rare and endangered plant species, and to emphasize forests as a source of clean drinking water.

A major feature of the Oregon Wild Campaign was the construction of maps to provide visual images to demonstrate the "critical link between wild forests and the ecosystem services they provide, including clean drinking water, fish and wildlife habitat and other values." Together they constituted an atlas of the state's wild areas, and with the use of geographic information systems identified approximately five million acres of Oregon forests suitable for wilderness designation. ONRC Web sites contained maps of the wilderness proposals and specialized maps of watersheds supplying municipal drinking water, old-growth forests, salmon and elk habitat, roaded areas, and clear-cuts on lands managed by the Forest Service and the Bureau of Land Management. This wild forest program enlisted the support of seventeen core conservation groups and endorsements from over 280 organizations and businesses and fifty-eight elected officials. This support included an urgent statement from four of the state's five members of the U.S. House of Representatives to "protect the values of roadless areas . . . from all activities that will harm their wild character."

WASHINGTON STATE

Forest ownership and administration in Washington State was probably the most complex in the nation, with very large holdings in national forests, in state forests, and owned by private industry. Forest governance, therefore, is carried out in three ways: under U.S. Forest Service and federal statutes; by the state Department of Natural Resources, which manages lands under state legal authority; and by the public regulation of forest practices on private land. The three different sets of management arrangements provide an opportunity to compare the ways in which different state and federal forest conditions gave rise to quite different mixes of objectives, which incorporate ecological strategies to varying degrees.

The citizen organization with the largest clientele and the most extensive program was the Northwest Ecosystem Alliance, which was known to the public through the activities and personality of its leader, Mitch Friedman.[41] One of the alliance's most successful ventures involved an approach to state trust lands, which under the state's constitution assigned predominant importance to economic returns to the state's educational system, with only minimal concern for ecological values. While some attempted to revise this traditional interpretation, the alliance focused on the Loomis Forest in northeast Washington with the proposal to purchase 25,000 acres of it from the state land commission and transfer its title to the Department of Natural Resources to be managed under a broader mandate with strong ecological objectives. With a vigorous fund-raising campaign assisted by several very large contributions from wealthy individuals in Washington, the strategy worked, and $16.5 million was raised from more than 5,000 citizens, making possible the purchase of the Loomis tract.

The ecologically inspired purchase of the Loomis Forest tract met roadblocks when it came to permanent management, however. The Loomis Forest was part of the state land trust system, in which lands were managed under mandates to maximize economic returns on behalf of the state educational system. On their purchase, the Loomis lands were transferred to other sections of the Department of Natural Resources to be managed as a forest conservation area. However, as the details for this management evolved, they moved in a direction of multiple uses, much like the national forests, and the alliance found itself struggling to inject ecological objectives into the management program. Thus, the broad ecological goals of the Loomis purchase, including elimination of future wood harvest and road building, were threatened amid the intricate political maneuvering within the Department of Natural Resources.

The alliance took up a variety of other projects pertaining more to the national forests in Washington: it reviewed many national forest timber sales, in some of which wood harvest schedules were modified; it engaged in a number of court cases, as citizen organizations had done many times before; and it took the lead in protecting the lynx, listed as "threatened" by the U.S. Fish and Wildlife Service in 2000. It formed the Cascades Conservation Partnership, a three-year campaign to purchase and protect over 75,000 acres of privately owned forests that would link the northern and southern Cascades. Among its contributions to phasing out roads in the national forests was a successful lawsuit on the Okanogan National Forest, which required the forest to keep inventories and control of old logging roads, many of them "ghost roads," as required by the National Forest Management Act of 1976, and to carry out the requirement that temporary roads not intended to be part of the permanent road system should be closed and revegetated within ten years.

SOUTHEAST ALASKA CONSERVATION COUNCIL

Alaska has its own distinctive setting for applying ecological forest objectives.[42] The Tongass National Forest, the largest of the U.S. national forests, has been the focus of over thirty years of controversy over its management objectives, and the Southeast Alaska Conservation Council has focused its energies on the forest in seeking to advance wildland objectives, including the protection of land, wildlife and habitat, and water quality from the adverse impact of wood production.

The starting point for these events was the advent of industrial-scale logging in the 1950s, marked by the 1947 Tongass Timber Act, in which Congress created a timber-first management regime. After passage of the act the Forest Service granted the Ketchikan Pulp Company and the Alaska Pulp Corporation fifty-year contracts to purchase Tongass timber in exchange for their agreement to build and operate pulp mills in Ketchikan and Sitka.[43] These contracts were the culmination of the longtime Forest Service objective dating back to the early twentieth century to organize timber management around the mills that would process the lumber, in effect tying sustained-yield wood production to the market rather than to scientific silviculture. The fifty-year contracts were the only ones of that length among all the national forests and they guaranteed that wood production, with its attendant clear-cut harvesting and road building, dominated the objectives of the Tongass National Forest. This management strategy was enhanced by the 1971 Alaska Native Claims Settlement Act, which created thirteen native corporations and allowed them to select more than 500,000 acres of the Tongass National Forest, which were then almost all clear-cut within twenty years, with virtually no protection for salmon streams and wildlife habitat.

By the late 1960s, several aspects of this arrangement had come sharply into focus. One was the fact that intensive logging was not uniform throughout the Tongass—in fact two-thirds of the forest is noncommercial, either nonforest or scrub, and about half of the commercial forest land is composed of low-volume stands. Only 4 percent of the entire forest is composed of high-volume old growth involving stands greater than 30,000 board feet per acre. By 1970 this high-volume portion of the Tongass was prized equally by the timber industry and by ecological forest advocates as valuable fish and wildlife habitat.

Amid these developments, the Southeast Alaska Conservation Council (SEACC), a coalition of eighteen Southeast Alaska conservation groups, "has been dedicated to ensuring protection for the unique environment of South-east Alaska. The values found in old-growth forests—wildlife, water quality, fisheries, recreation opportunities and solitude—are essential for perpetu-ating the Southeast Alaskan way of life." In pursuing these objectives, the council has continually stressed that the Forest Service plan envisaged in the fifty-year contracts was detrimental to the region's economy, and that "a healthy economy must protect the health of the ecosystem upon which it depends. . . . [It] minimizes the export of raw materials and maximizes the manufacture of finished goods, . . . manufactures and exports finished goods made from local materials, . . . keeps more money floating through it than it sends out of the community, . . . [and] contains a diversity of enter-prises and revenue-producing activities."

Throughout the 1970s, misgivings about the harm that wood produc-tion had wrought to the forest, water, and wildlife habitat resources of Southeast Alaska began to take shape. In the Alaska National Interest Lands Conservation Act of 1980, 5.4 million acres were protected from develop-ment (of which 3.6 million acres consisted of rock, ice, muskeg wetlands, and noncommercial forest). These included lands in the Admiralty Island and the Misty Fjords National Monuments, but at the same time the act set a legislative timber target of 4.5 billion board feet per decade and established a permanent timber appropriation of at least $40 million per year to sup-port the timber industry. In the 1990 Tongass Timber Reform Act, a more ecological direction was enhanced when the high timber targets of the 1980 act were revoked and the automatic $40 million annual appropriation was repealed, one million acres of watersheds were protected, and modifications were made in the long-term pulp contracts. Later the 1997 Tongass Land Management Plan revised the logging schedules to limit harvest at 267 mil-lion board feet per year and required improved salmon and wildlife habitat protection. Yet by establishing such a high cut level, the SEACC argued, the Forest Service continued to demand that hunting, sport and commercial fish-ing, subsistence, tourism, and recreation take a backseat to timber interests.

An Ecological Forestry Perspective

By the early twenty-first century, the landscape of citizen organizations seeking to influence national forest affairs differed markedly from that some twenty-five years earlier. The conservation groups that had been instrumental in pressing the Randolph bill in the debates leading up to the National Forest Management Act of 1976 had reflected the past controversies over the legislation of the 1960s. But while some of these, such as the Sierra Club and the Wilderness Society, continued to play a role in the new complex of ecological forestry advocates, most local and regional ecological forestry groups were of relatively recent origin and drew from newly energized constituencies. They had come into existence around the new context of national forest affairs shaped by the 1976 act and its provisions for planning and citizen participation, procedural requirements of the National Environmental Policy Act, and the substantive provisions of the Endangered Species Act and the 1976 act. By the end of the century, the regional organizations that had emerged since the 1976 act had accumulated several decades of experience in negotiating with the Forest Service and had given rise to a varied set of alternative forest plans and programs.

The most striking consequence of these activities was that they forged a set of ideas that, despite their varied regional origins and settings, expressed a remarkably unified perspective that was infused with ecological objectives and ecological science. While ecology as an approach to the natural world had been expressed in varied ways by diverse advocates in previous years, ecological ideas had not yet been put together to focus on forest management. Only in a few cases did the term "ecological forestry" appear. Now, after several decades of practical give-and-take between ecological forestry advocates and commodity forestry advocates, in which the process of engagement was continually shaping new ideas and new on-the-ground management practices, a clearly defined perspective emerged to bring all this together in a common set of ideas to which the term "ecological forestry" gives focused expression.

Biodiversity

Among forest reform organizations the protection and enhancement of diverse forest flora and fauna was uppermost in concern.[44] This was popularly known as the biodiversity issue. To the public the most visible aspect of biodiversity was in the realm of threatened and endangered species, especially the implementation of the Endangered Species Act of 1973. But the issue went much further to include the "viability" of a wide range of forest species, a program developed under the authority of the 1976 National Forest Management Act. Driving this approach was the rapid discovery in the last third of the century of the vast array of species in the national forests.

Forest reformers emphasized species inventory, management, and monitoring, with special emphasis on "sensitive" species, that is, those that were declining in population, so as to take action before that decline reached a "threatened" or "endangered" condition.[45] There was special attention to the fact that forest managers had limited knowledge about forest species other than those valuable for wood fiber, and that there was considerable discrepancy between the availability of management resources for the small number of woody, commercial species and the much larger number of forest flora and fauna that received only minor management concern. Moreover, reformers felt that forest managers were more than indifferent to the adverse impact of forest practices such as roads, harvesting, and silvicultural methods on diverse species, and the agency showed limited interest in and ability to track those effects through monitoring. Frequently the entire issue came to be organized around particular species that had come to earn a high degree of visibility, such as salamanders, frogs, butterflies, neotropical migratory songbirds, snails or mussels, lichens, fungi, mosses, or various species of wildflowers. Species-specific information gave the reform movement considerable ammunition to challenge forest policy.[46]

Habitat

In close connection with biodiversity issues were issues of habitat. The traditional category of forest classification on the part of wood production foresters was the stand, a group of trees of relatively similar species or condition, which then became the unit of analysis. Those interested in a wider range of forest species, however, argued that this was inappropriate in identifying forest areas relevant to most species and that a habitat classification was more in order.[47] The classic case was the wetland as a habitat for both plants and animals. Equally important to reformers was the old forest as an area of unique plants and animals, a habitat that in the course of forest history had been all but completely destroyed as wood production marched across the nation in the nineteenth and early twentieth centuries. Then there were riparian habitats, with flora and fauna unique to them, deep forest and fragmented forest habitats, canopy, midstory, understory, and ground habitats, ridge and cove habitats, habitats covering the movements of wide ranging vertebrates, and more confined habitats of animals of more limited range and immobile plants. To give this problem specific attention, forest reformers took up the relatively new strategy of gap analysis, in which areas of richer clusters of flora and fauna were identified as distinct from those areas containing species of less common occurrence, with the objective of concentrating land acquisition and protection resources on these habitat "gaps."[48]

Structural Diversity

A major aim of ecological forestry is to develop and maintain a structural diversity of species composition and age. The multi-aged forest is preferred to the single-aged forest and a multispecies forest to the more engineered monoculture of industrial forestry, because it provides a more diverse species habitat.[49] While contemporary management sought both to foster and maintain forests of an even age, ecological forestry looked to a forest of diverse ages as the benchmark for successful forest practices. And in regions where there is a major drive toward species conversion, such as hardwood forests to pine in the Southeast, there is an attempt to restrain these tendencies and move forest conversion toward a more mixed-species and mixed-age structure. Or, to take another example, in the Great Lakes there is much opposition to maintaining large areas of early successional aspen forest for deer and grouse, and similar opposition to an extensive policy of replacing sixty-to-eighty-year-old hardwoods with younger forests to provide deer browse.

Native Forests and Old Growth

The benchmarks toward which ecological forestry seeks to turn forest management are focused on the native forest that existed prior to massive manipulation of forests by European settlers in terms of structure, habitat, and resident species.[50] Species that have become extirpated or are in a state of continuous decline should be restored or reversed; silvicultural management should move toward reestablishing significant acreage of tree species that existed before the cutover eras of the nineteenth and twentieth centuries; the benchmark of biodiversity should be the species in the forest habitats before commercial cutting. Forest reformers argued that a significant acreage should be devoted to restoring earlier species and habitat, especially in the face of the continued drive by industrial forestry to foster even-age, short-lived monocultures for intensive wood production.

The retention and recovery of old growth was a widely supported version of the interest in native forests. This issue was especially prominent in the Pacific Northwest, the major regional location of forests that were several hundred years old and known as "ancient forests." They were prized for their diverse and distinctive ecological characteristics and were often the focal point of ecological forestry action. Here the emphasis was on the retention and protection of the remaining old growth. In the East, where most older forests had been cut down and managers had never experienced an old-growth forest, those remaining were small in size and usually only small tracts remaining from previous logging. Here the old-growth movement by the late twentieth century was only in its infancy and devoted much time to cataloging and publicizing known old-growth areas while at the same time discovering new ones, especially in the Southern Appalachians. Here the intact forests were rarely more than one hundred years old, and there was considerable attention to restoration as well as protection. Eastern old-growth conferences were held in the 1990s to bring together citizen reformers and ecological scientists, who shared an interest in the ecological value of older forests.[51]

Watersheds

Ecological forestry also gave rise to an interest in the organization of forest management around whole watersheds and gave close attention to the relationship between forest cover, species habitat, soil erosion, and management of watersheds from the upper headwaters to the main streams below.[52] In this issue, reformers sought to focus sharply on the riparian buffer area, especially its width and vegetation management within it; on the need to protect headwater and intermittent as well as perennial streams; and on in-stream biochemical water quality as well as erosion and sedimentation. Reformers went beyond both riparian areas and in-stream water quality to emphasize entire watersheds, their degradation and need for restoration. Management of whole watersheds required monitoring far beyond the monitoring of main streams that most water quality programs performed, and often included a strategy for classifying watersheds based on quality as a strategy for selective protection and restoration. The so-called best management practices for protecting streams from sedimentation, policies common in many states, were the target of many forest reform strategies because most were simply advisory rather than mandatory and were weakly implemented.

Protection and Restoration

Forest reformers developed a dual action program of protection and restoration.[53] On the one hand, they sought to reduce forest uses that presented a threat to the existence and health of ecological resources such as clear-cutting, mineral extraction, and motorized vehicle recreation. On the other, they sought to restore what they felt were more desirable forest conditions, which those practices had degraded. Both protection and restoration objectives were shaped by the idea that human activities were responsible for the degradation of forest resources and that restoration required a shift in management strategies from more to less intensive human impact. Forest protection had long emphasized action against fire and disease, while forest restoration had emphasized the regeneration of trees. But while those twin objectives had been organized around wood production, forest reformers, with a much broader range of resources in their mind's eye, now attempted to organize them around the forest as an ecological system in which wood production would play a more subordinate role.

By the early years of the twenty-first century, the focus on forest restoration had provided an umbrella under which forest reform organizations across the country came together to present a common agenda for the nation's forests.[54] This appeared in the form of a restoration agenda that had been hammered out through a series of meetings of national forest reform leaders. While this effort was a logical step in the evolution of their agenda, it was furthered considerably by the growing emphasis on the dramatic wildfires of the early twenty-first century, whereby the commodity forest community sought to funnel many forest issues into one issue—fire—and the Forest Service itself moved in a similar direction. Fire ecology provided an opportunity to debate the issue of forest health, and post-fire restoration provided an equal opportunity to define the characteristics of a healthy forest. In pursuing the debate, the forest restoration agenda drawn up by the forest reform community served as a major document that brought together many aspects of evolving ecological forest issues into a statement about forest reform objectives.

Ecological Forest Science

The contributions to ecological forestry from ecological scientists were shaped far less by continual give-and-take with forest managers, as was the case with forest reformers, and more by research and attempts to assess and integrate the resulting knowledge.[55] The initial starting point for scientists was much like that of the reformers; they were equally intrigued with the vast range of species in the nation's forests, the way in which they were interrelated, and their evolution over time.[56] The term "biodiversity" held similar meaning for both.[57] Among both groups, for example, there was a perennial call that more resources should be devoted to inventorying species as a starting point in ecological forestry. But while the reformers attempted to apply this interest to management practices, the scientists devoted their time and efforts to activities more detached from land management. The massive focus of research in the International Biodiversity Observation Year, which linked ecologists around the world in a similar set of species investigations, typified these activities.

This preoccupation with biodiversity was supplemented by a broad interest in disturbance and recovery in ecological processes.[58] Forest reformers tended to emphasize specific forest disturbances such as harvest practices, mineral extraction, road building, the use of pesticides and herbicides, motorized recreation vehicles, or excessive deer population.[59] But while ecological scientists worked on such problems of human impact in their research, they were more interested in a systematic analysis of disturbances, both natural and human, among many forest sites, and a wide range of other ecological systems as well, in order to shape generalizations that cut across space and time. For example, they reported research on the way in which urbanization both reduced biological diversity and increased the presence of invasive species, a subject that rarely entered the strategies of groups preoccupied with management of forested areas.[60] They were especially interested in recovery processes, and this led them into historical analysis of the long-term effects of disturbances such as fire and windstorms in earlier periods of time, or the persistence of the effects of agricultural plowing on soils in later regenerated forests.[61]

Ecological scientists were generally skeptical about the widespread practice of even-aged management because of its tendency to foster a monoculture rather than a variety of species and to promote a single-aged rather than a multi-aged forest. Such attempts to simplify forest habitats were detrimental to the maintenance of the varied forest conditions that were more congenial to biodiversity. Tendencies fostered by even-aged management were held partly responsible for the decline in species diversity. Views of both ecological scientists and forest reformers on this issue were quite similar, as the reformers continually sought to challenge Forest Service policies that converted mixed forests to forests in which the trees were of the same age and species. Closely connected with this set of ideas was the common interest in native forests as a benchmark for the desired forest, that the mix and age of regenerating species should approach as much as possible the characteristics of forests at the time of European settlement.[62]

In the late twentieth century ecologists began to emphasize the role of forest fragmentation as a major disturbance, the way in which farmsteads, roads, and utility lines had broken up large, intact forest areas into smaller ones, fracturing a larger habitat into smaller pieces.[63] They noted the close relationship between unfragmented habitats and fragmented ones and the different species that were found in each. The study of fragmentation emphasized forest ecological changes over long periods of time, a process that reformers found difficult to work into forest plans of short duration, and hence reformers did not share the scientists' interest in fragmentation as fully as they did their emphasis on disturbance and recovery.[64]

However, a similar, even joint, interest was expressed by both in old forests. Ecologists had long mourned the end of earlier forests and often advocated that the remaining old growth be protected from further inroads. Scientific interest in old forests was expressed especially in the research conducted in the last third of the twentieth century at the Andrews Forest Experiment Station of the U.S. Forest Service in Oregon.[65] In the midst of remaining sizeable tracts of old forest lands in the Pacific Northwest, the species composition and ecological processes of forests of three hundred years of age and more were the subject of intensive investigations. Forests in the East contained far less old forest acreage, but the old-growth protection movement in the East was well supported because old forests were considered to be an ecological asset by scientists who also favored the protection of forests of lesser age, for example, eighty to one hundred years, so that they could become future old growth.[66]

Ecologists tended to agree with citizen reformers that the development and maintenance of a forest of mixed ages and species, usually thought of as characteristic of "native" forests, should be a goal of forest management.[67] Hence they were skeptical of both clear-cutting and even-aged management, which led to a reduction rather that enhancement of diversity of habitat and therefore of species. One approach to this fostered by some ecological scientists emphasized not the abandonment of clear-cutting but the retention of a larger number of trees during harvest in order to establish more effective bridges between the older and the regenerating forest. From a practical point of view this permitted some clear-cutting, in which trees left after the cut might well constitute at least a quarter of the potentially harvestable trees.[68]

Ecological forestry involved quite a different group of scientists, hydrologists, in watershed issues. Hydrologists were far more inclined than were ecologists to think of watersheds as a focal point for observation and analysis. Hence citizen forest reform organizations found themselves working in tandem with hydrologists rather than ecologists on those issues. These two different facets of ecological forestry came together especially in the Pacific Northwest Forest Plan where the role of salmon in the forested watersheds of that area led to a single set of management objectives. Much as was the case with the biological species of forests, an emphasis on watersheds involved inventories and monitoring as the beginning point of management. The Pacific Northwest Forest Plan gave rise to an extensive program for watershed-wide inventory and monitoring of habitat conditions for salmon.

At the same time the effect of forested watersheds on coldwater fisheries had long played a role in forest issues throughout the nation, and in the environmental era the focus on aquatic conditions expanded to include the chemical composition of streams as well as temperature and sedimentation. In both cases, however, modern hydrological science expanded the scope of watersheds to include both the cumulative effects of many and diverse watershed events and the integration of intermittent and perennial main streams.[69]

While one set of ecologists, represented by the Ecological Society of America, remained content with scientific investigations for their own sake, another, the Society of Conservation Biology, was eager to put science to work shaping policy, and still another, the Natural Areas Association, was preoccupied with ecological management of natural areas. These took quite different directions, and the several groups seemed to bypass each other with their separate organizations, meetings, and publications, but together they helped to develop and advocate major ideas in ecological forestry, which were quite similar in overall meaning and perspective and linked them intellectually with the forest reformers. Together they established the broad cultural climate of modern ecological forestry.

The relatively common ecological outlook of both forest reformers and ecological scientists can be observed through the common technical terminology they used in contrast with the terminology of commodity production forestry.[70] Traditional forestry had its own distinctive set of concepts and words, such as the stand; board feet or cubic feet; saplings, poles, and sawlogs as stages in the age of trees; economic maturity and biological maturity, all of which revolved around accounting for and managing trees containing commercial wood fiber. Ecological forestry introduced new terms associated with species and habitats such as keystone species, management indicator species, microhabitats, understory species, soil mycorrhizae, colonization, and retention. Few of these terms, used by ecological forest writers, entered the literature of traditional forest affairs such as the publications of the Society of American Foresters or the reports of the American Association of State Foresters. And when each group came to report forest research that it felt to be significant, a similar gap prevailed. One could find out little about ecological forestry or its advocates in the pages of the wood-production-oriented journals.

The citizen movement for ecological reform and biological scientists with new ecological interests tended to work in tandem. To the public the reformers were the more visible of the two, but in terms of the timing of historical development it appears that often the scientists led the way and the reformers followed the course they charted. The issue of the spotted owl in the Pacific Northwest forests is an instructive case. As the Forest Service and the Bureau of Land Management took up that issue under the mandate of the Endangered Species Act, it called upon a diverse group of ecological scientists to help develop a policy. The scientists shifted the context from the owl itself to the owl's habitat on the conventional ecological ground that one could not maintain a satisfactory owl population without a satisfactory owl habitat. Once this shift in perspective occurred, the scientists brought into it a wide range of plant and animal species that were distinctive to old forests and depended upon them as habitat.

The close connection between ecological science and ecological action could be observed in the ecological science that appeared in the forest plans and in litigation undertaken by ecological forest reform organizations. On occasion it also appeared in the letters signed by ecological scientists in support of forest reform policies, especially during the second Bush administration, when the role of ecology in forest affairs was under attack. The role of ecologists in forming the Pacific Northwest Forest Plan was particularly significant because of the prominence that they gave to the vital but publicly less discussed "lesser" species, plants and especially invertebrates. The documents involved in drawing up that plan detail not only categories of species such as mosses, lichens, fungi, vascular plants, mollusks, amphibians, and mammals, but also describe their vital role in the viable functioning of the region's ancient forests. While the media could accept the role of the more dramatic species, such as the spotted owl and wild salmon, they were far less enthusiastic about the vital ecological role of these less visible species. They rarely discussed them, and when they did they usually were disparaging. As future events would reveal, the scientists were far less able to defend biodiversity when programs to identify and inventory these lesser species came under attack.[71]

The growing claim of ecological forest advocates to greater influence in forest affairs did not go unchallenged by those who had long dominated forestry with a commodity emphasis. As with many types of historical developments, however, both changes and resistance to them were more gradual than sudden. Thus, the beginnings and expansion of influence of ecological forestry generated a spectrum of responses. Some with intense "production forestry" traditions resisted with a high degree of "commodity absolutism"; others were far more receptive to change; and the most intriguing cases are in the middle, in which some forest institutions sought to express an association with ecological objectives while retaining traditional commodity practices. Chapter 3 explores this variety of reactions to the growth of ecological forestry.

 CHAPTER 3

The National Response
to Ecological Forestry

My objective in this book is not only to describe ecological forestry as a reflection of changes in social values and biological science but also to identify
its impact on traditional forest institutions. In what ways was it incorporated
into customary thinking and activities in private and public forest affairs,
and in what ways was it not? In this chapter I examine relative degrees
of acceptance and rejection of ecological ideas, policies, and programs. On
one end of the continuum of reactions are those forest leaders and institutions that reflected a dominant focus on wood production; I explore their
strong and public opposition to ecological forestry first. I then proceed to
those cases that combined ostensible public acceptance of ecological objectives with resistance to change in practice, often giving rise to a confused
mixture of reactions. And finally I take up those activities that incorporated
some ecological forest policies in a more positive but still tentative and in-
complete fashion.

The View from the Fringe

Forest policy, like so many aspects of public affairs in the United States, did
not escape those who viewed the world from the fringes of the political
spectrum. Here there was a tendency to think of forest issues as a clash of
political ideologies cast in terms of the intrusion of alien forces into Ameri-

can life. The most common factor among these opponents of ecological forestry was a radical commitment to the combined ideas of private enterprise and private property with minimal responsibilities to the wider society. Ecological forestry was not a matter of debate over legitimate alternatives in public land management but of a threat to traditional American values and a call for action to ward off insidious and subversive influences. The target of attack for these "fringe" advocates was not so much the issues themselves, with which they dealt primarily in terms of ideological opposites, but of the people who spoke in favor of ecological forestry. They focused their attacks on the messenger rather than the message.

One of the more prolific and cited speakers to challenge the role of ecological forestry was Michael Coffman, a professional forester who taught at Michigan Technological University and until 1992 was a manager for Champion International, a major forest and paper products company in the United States.[1] His contribution to the complex of anti-ecological thinking was to argue that biodiversity as a general idea and the Endangered Species Act in particular were the product of external global influences and a pantheistic environmental scheme. Coffman elaborated this theme in his book *Saviors of the Earth? The Politics and Religion of Environmentalism*. In what he described on his Web site as "a miracle from God," he states that he played a key role in stopping the ratification of the Convention on Biological Diversity in the U.S. Senate "an hour before the Senate was scheduled to vote on its ratification." In 1999 Dr. Coffman began to publish "Discerning the Times Digest," a monthly newsletter "designed to help busy Christians understand world events as related to the Bible and their Christian lives." His Web site also contains an article that focuses on his central message, "International Domination of U.S. Environmental Law and Private Property."

Robert G. Lee, a professional forester with sociological interests and a member of the faculty of the School of Natural Resources at the University of Washington in Seattle, was an equally popular critic of ecological forestry from the fringe. He was especially well known for his book, *Broken Trust, Broken Land: Freeing Ourselves from the War over the Environment*.[2] His critique was broad-based, less focused directly on ecological forestry and more on its broader economic implications, arguing especially from the viewpoint of private enterprise and private property with the persistent theme that concern for environmental protection was a violation of human rights. Fundamental freedoms in America, so his argument went, were being undermined by a movement using moral persuasion to "save the earth," with the result that the nation was moving closer to a totalitarian society. Lee's views were quite similar to other generalized anti-environmental arguments that tended to ignore the practicalities of environmental affairs in favor of sweeping ideological statements, but his background and institutional involvement in forestry affairs made him especially well regarded by the most traditional and conventional supporters of commodity forestry.

Patrick Moore, author of *Greenspirit* and a Web site by the same name, was one of the most sought-after speakers opposing ecological forestry and the environmental movement. He was prized especially because he could be billed as one of the early organizers of the well-known environmental group Greenpeace; he had been active in its earlier phase when it conducted sensational raids on nuclear sites, but he no longer associated himself with the environmental community. In his later years Moore had become active in wood production affairs in British Columbia and had become a forceful exponent of the social benefits of forests managed for wood production. He expressed little recognition of the ecological components of forests; "trees are the answer" was the theme on which he became a crusader. At the same time he aroused an enthusiastic audience with his attacks on the "environmental movement" as "anti-human," "anti-science and technology," "anti-trade," "anti-business," and "just plain anti-civilization."[3]

The most forceful and perhaps the most widely cited of the fringe commentators on ecological forestry came from a different quarter. Alston Chase was a philosopher whose point of attack was against the notion that one could restore an earlier "pre-settlement" natural forest, which he deemed a subversive idea that both underlay the entire environmental movement and served as a serious threat to American civilization. Chase's initial foray was his 1986 book, *Playing God in Yellowstone*, in which he castigated efforts to restore earlier ecological conditions in the park and from which he launched a brief journalistic career as a regular columnist in a number of western papers. He elaborated his ideas further in a 1995 book, *In a Dark Wood: The Fight over Forests and the Rising Tyranny of Ecology*, in which his target was ecological thinking as a whole.[4] He tended to formulate the ecological versus commodity forestry disputes in broad theoretical and moral terms with a special focus on "biocentrism" as a corroding influence in human society.

One of the most vigorous critics of ecological forestry, and especially those segments of the community such as college and university forestry schools, forest management, and sectors of the forest profession, was Harry V. Wiant Jr., a twenty-four-year member of the faculty at West Virginia University and in 2002 named as the first holder of the Joseph E. Ibberson Chair in forest resources management in the School of Forest Resources at Penn

State University. Wiant became involved in the conflicting sectors of the
Society of American Foresters (SAF) and responded to the pleas of the traditionalists to run for president of the organization, because "many of our
members were giving up in the struggle for meaningful forest management
and were buying into politically correct but scientifically dubious management philosophies." He won the SAF vice presidential election in 1996
(which automatically elevated him to the presidency the following year)
with 52 percent of the vote, amid a campaign that he described as an attempt "to move SAF to the right." To elaborate his views he wrote a paper,
"Stand Up for Forestry," which he presented frequently to audiences of foresters.[5] In it he dismissed ecological forestry as "eco-nonsense which threat-
ens our economic prosperity and basic freedoms." And he argued that every
forester should be required to read Alston Chase's In a Dark Wood, Robert G.
Lee's Broken Trust, Broken Land, and Michael Coffman's Saviors of the Earth.

These observers tended to cast their arguments in broad theoretical
terms with limited reference to the human interest—scientific or popular—
in ecology and the practicalities of the effort to incorporate nature into a
society which continually turned natural into developed lands. They shifted
the controversy from the concrete circumstances of land management,
which formed the context of most of the issues discussed in this book, into
a clash of theories quite divorced from human circumstances.

The Reaction from the Forest Establishment

The most determined and uncompromising practical resistance to ecological forestry came from the forestry establishment, for whom wood production was the primary objective of forest management and who either
sought to eliminate ecological forestry from their radar screen or to attack it
frontally as stupid or dangerous. The most prominent of these and the most
resistant to change was the private wood products industry, which took a
jaundiced view of the first stirrings of "environmental forestry" in the 1960s
before it evolved into "ecological forestry." The industry opposed the drive
to establish a national wilderness system and equally opposed the legislation
to establish a system of national trails and national wild and scenic rivers.[6]
All of these the industry looked upon as an undesirable removal of land
from the "timber base" on which annual allowable cuts were calculated. It
was especially concerned with the increasing insistence on the part of wilderness advocates that the long-standing wilderness candidate areas above
tree line be augmented by areas of lower elevation that were more heavily
timbered.[7]

The American Forest and Paper Association

The forest industry was represented in public affairs by the American Forest and Paper Association (AF&PA), which was formed in 1993 as a merger of two previous organizations, the National Forest Products Association and the American Paper Institute.[8] It quickly became the leading advocate of national forest policies on behalf of wood production and the leading industry critic of environmental and ecological forest policies.

The forest industry was unhappy with the Multiple-Use Act of 1960 because it did not establish priorities among the uses that it designated; the industry-sponsored Timber Supply Act of 1969 was intended to rectify this by making wood production the dominant use of many portions of the national forests.[9] The environmental forest movement had developed sufficient strength arising from the wilderness and wild and scenic rivers campaigns to forestall this proposal, and it failed. Not until the heady days of the second Bush administration did the industry return to this objective and urge that the uses identified in the 1960 act should be prioritized, with the implication that wood production should be identified as the dominant use in significant areas of the national forests.[10]

Shortly after the defeat of the Timber Supply Act, the timber industry was faced by the successful environmental lawsuit in which the court agreed that clear-cutting was contrary to the 1897 Forest Management Act. Faced with this potentially massive change in national forest harvest practice, the industry mobilized to a greater extent than ever before, energizing not only the wood products companies, but the entire industry down to the retail lumber level and labor as well, from workers in the woods to mills and furniture manufacturing. The resulting National Forest Management Act authorized clear-cutting; this, along with the failure of the environmental community to establish statutory standards for forest management in that law, contributed to the widespread view that the act was a victory for the forest industry.[11]

In the early years after the 1976 act, the wood products industry maintained considerable influence in national forest affairs. By the 1980s it had gained strong support from the Republican Party, and it played a decisive role in the new administration of Ronald Reagan. Reagan selected John Crowell as assistant secretary of the Department of Agriculture with jurisdiction over the U.S. Forest Service; Crowell was a general counsel of the Louisiana-Pacific Timber Company, the largest purchaser of timber from the national forests. Crowell proceeded to tighten control over national forest affairs from the Washington office and directed forest supervisors to increase considerably the timber harvest levels. The massive increase in cutting that resulted generated a backlash of protest from forest supervisors throughout the West on the grounds that it would greatly harm the legal mandates to protect watersheds and wildlife. This resistance from the supervisors contributed to steady reductions in timber harvest.[12]

In an equally quiet but persistent fashion, the citizen reform movement was able to use the machinery of the 1976 act, the environmental review process mandated by the National Environmental Policy Act, and the Endangered Species Act to bring to national forest affairs a perspective far broader in scope than the emphasis on wood production that the forest products industry had brought to the Reagan administration. Over the eight years of the Clinton administration, these efforts produced some shift toward a more ecologically oriented forest policy. Even these limited changes, however, gave rise to a sharp backlash from the industry, and once again after the election of 2000 they established close relationships with a Republican administration, that of George W. Bush.[13] This led to a massive change in the administration of the national forests under the direction of a new undersecretary of agriculture, Mark Rey, who for many years had been chief lobbyist for the American Forest and Paper Association. This time, however, the strategy was not to mandate allowable cut levels from Washington, but instead to attack the procedures which the citizen groups had used to obtain their foothold—the EIS and administrative appeals—and to give forest supervisors freedom to make their own assessments about the relevant ecological science free from external scientific review.

The most visible periodical that spoke for the forest industry in public affairs was *Evergreen Magazine*, an offshoot of the Canada-based Evergreen Foundation. Jim Peterson, spokesman for the foundation, was active on the speaking circuit, with his favorite topic being the threat to the forest industry from evolving environmental and ecological policies. While he continually presented arguments against the objectives of forest reform groups in forest policy, his more vigorous attacks were reserved for environmental groups. A pithy quote from his speeches was his statement that "the only thing being protected in the public forests today is the political influence of environmental groups whose decades-old objective has been to retain power for themselves while disfranchising other stakeholders."[14]

The National Council for Air and Stream Improvement

While the American Forest and Paper Association was the most visible and publicly vocal of the industry's organizations, a quieter and even more influential advocate for the industry was the National Council for Air and Stream

Improvement (NCASI).[15] This was the forest industry's research arm, which funded research to obtain the science that would support the industry's policies. Scientific knowledge about ecological forestry was a relatively new and evolving field, and its implications for wood production were also evolving steadily. The industry sought to be in the forefront of new discoveries so that, as one NCASI researcher put it, the organization could "position industry and management agencies with the data needed to lead rather than react to these issues as they emerge." By funding selected research projects closely related to emerging regulatory issues, NCASI was able to use its own version of scientific knowledge to defend the industry's wood production objectives:

NCASI was established in 1943 to deal with the two main regulatory issues which the industry faced at that time—air pollution and water pollution from pulp and paper plants. As its Web site states, "NCASI was originally established to assist the pulp and paper industry in addressing wastewater treatment issues." On the onset of the environmental era, this traditional preoccupation with industrial wastewater expanded to include the newer issue of the impact of timber harvest operations on stream water quality. Still later, as the effect of wood production and harvest activities on the larger forest ecosystem became increasingly prominent, the work of NCASI broadened even further to new frontiers of forest biology and ecology. Soon NCASI represented itself as "an environmental resource for the forest products industry since 1943," so that there was a considerable gap between its traditional title and the subject matter of its research. NCASI's activities were shaped not so much by a clearly defined body of knowledge but by the impact of regulation, actual or potential, on wood production activities. Its research interests, so it stated, arose because "there are numerous 'hot' issues that have the potential to, or are currently, reducing management opportunities."

NCASI's most extensive work dealt with watershed issues, with special emphasis on attempting to refute the claim that logging practices in the woods made an important contribution to water pollution. The issue was nonpoint sources of water pollution. The approach of the wood products industry and NCASI to this problem was to prefer action at the state rather than the federal level, and voluntary action rather than regulation. They affirmed rather frequently that since most states had some sort of program in place to promote "best management practices" to control erosion from timber harvesting, the problem was well in hand. However, there was evidence that the state programs varied enormously in their content, their compliance, and their results. Hence both the industry and NCASI were under some constraint to work toward more uniform approaches at the federal level, for example, a system of monitoring, on which basis more convincing judgments could be made about the impact of forest practices on water quality.

Of potentially greater consequence, however, was the fact that the new emphasis on ecological forestry expanded NCASI's activities beyond the earlier emphasis on air and water pollution to a wide range of ecologically identified issues with which the industry was now confronted. The research problems that NCASI now began to take up involved the wider realm of forest biology and ecology and especially problems of endangered species. The list of the organization's research projects now included studies of amphibians, forest raptors, gopher tortoises, salamanders, Allegheny wood rats, bats, forest birds, the Canada lynx, and the red-cockaded woodpecker. The objective of this research was to expand knowledge about the presence of distinctive species in various settings of wood production management, such as early, middle, or late successional forests, or in forests of various geographical extents. Many habitat variations had remained unexamined as endangered species issues evolved, and new knowledge about selected forest settings might well enable the wood product industry to lessen regulatory constraints on desired management activities.

Issues of forest ecology were now potential subjects for research. Some involved the regulatory implications of the traditional taxonomical controversies about just how one determines the categories of species and subspecies subject to population declines. On the Pacific Coast, for example, the wood products industry sought to combat the influence of protection of the spotted owl on wood harvest by arguing that the three main subspecies of the spotted owl that were recognized in the endangered species program— the northern, the California, and the Mexican—were in fact all one species, and thus the owl population was far larger than usually recognized and not at all threatened or endangered. This strategy was known in taxonomy as "lumping." NCASI attempted to tackle the "speciation" issue primarily in general terms, but also by sponsoring research on the validity of spotted owl habitat policies in western Oregon. On the whole, NCASI seemed to take up this field of ecological research rather gingerly, and one could predict that in the early twenty-first century it was only in the beginning stages of a long-term commitment.

Through a variety of institutions, of which the National Council for Air and Stream Improvement was the most important, the industry could advance the significance of the research it sponsored as "sound science" and give it considerable political significance in influencing regulatory activities. But this research was more significant for its particular goals, both to advance the primary use of the forest for wood production and, especially in the case of NCASI, to protect its interests from environmental and ecological regulation. In these objectives it played a major role in establishing the scientific views of the wood products industry in competition with the scientific views of the biological and ecological professions. Two groups of scientists emphasizing very different groups of forest resources were advancing quite different objectives in forest management.

The Society of American Foresters

The Society of American Foresters was formed in 1900 by Gifford Pinchot, then head of the U.S. Bureau of Forestry, as an organization to advance forestry as a profession. From the earliest days it focused on wood production and it has continued to do so throughout the years.[16] While national interest in forests has grown beyond that limited emphasis to encompass a wide range of subjects, such as the habitats needed to support biodiversity; old forests; watershed protection; the special value of large, intact, forested areas; human forest disturbances; and forest restoration, the society has remained preoccupied in its initial limited focus. On many occasions over the years, the Society of American Foresters has experienced opportunities to incorporate into its organizational orbit professionals emphasizing interests other than wood production, but it has operated in such a manner as to prompt them to go elsewhere. As a result, instead of evolving into an inclusive organization incorporating diverse contributions to forest science and management from many professional organizations, the society has remained narrow and professionally isolated.

An episode in the society's affairs in the early 1970s revealed these tendencies when Leon Minckler, former director of the branch of the Northeastern Forest Experiment station located in the Shawnee National Forest, attempted to broaden the range of vision of the society. Minckler had been conducting successful experiments in selection cutting on the Shawnee and was highly critical of the decision by the Forest Service to feature clearcutting. In the process of elaborating his opposition to clear-cutting, Minckler broadened his interests to include what he called "ecological forestry" and spearheaded a petition signed by 151 professional foresters and directed to the society, asking that body to establish a special working group, a common practice in the society, on the subject of ecological forestry. The petition was denied, with the argument that since all forestry was ecological there was no need for such a working group. Rebuffed here, Minckler then drew up a series of pamphlets, coauthored by Peter Twight, on ecological

forestry for different forest regions, which were published through the National Parks and Conservation Association. It was at this time that he became
closely associated with the forest reform movement and an advisor to the
citizen drive to work more of the environmental provisions of the Randolph
bill into the Forest Management Act.[17]

Comparison of the rather limited scope of the subject matter of the
Society of American Foresters with the much broader scope of the American
Institute of Biological Sciences is useful, because a number of professional
organizations that might well have established close relationships with
the society became integral members of the institute, instead. By the early
twenty-first century the institute comprised eighty-four organizations, each
quite separate, but each with a common focus on biology. Eighteen of these
were organizations in which a significant number of members had taken up
forest issues.[18] Their publications frequently contained articles of considerable importance in forest science. But all of that took place outside the orbit
of the Society of American Foresters, which seemed to gauge the importance
and value of forest-related research in terms of whether or not it took place
within the context of its main preoccupation with wood production.

From the point of view of public policy, the most significant aspect of
this contrasting course of professional development was the way in which
the agenda of the Society of American Foresters pertaining to the national
forests evolved in striking similarity to that of the forest industry. When
the society took up the issue of forests and watersheds it drew heavily on
the work of the National Council for Air and Stream Improvement. When
it took up issues of forest certification it displayed a strong preference for
the Sustainable Forestry Initiative of the American Forest and Paper Association rather than its competing group, the Forest Stewardship Council, often
thought to be more ecologically oriented.

It adopted arguments similar to those of industry about the citizen
movement for forest reform, with a special emphasis on the severe limitations on deriving forest management policy from the environmental analysis requirements of the National Environmental Policy Act and the implications of the Endangered Species Act. When it reported research monthly
in the *Journal of Forestry*, it focused heavily on research related to wood production, and the reader interested in ecological forestry research found few
items along that line. The SAF sought to restrain the influence of ecological
forestry by objecting, much as did the industry, to the "species viability" requirement of the regulations and to the opportunities for citizens to take up
administrative appeals to forest plan and project decisions. The society and

the industry seemed to go hand in hand in limiting their focus on wood production, and each kept a deliberate distance from ecological forestry.

The National Association of State Foresters

During the early decades of the twentieth century most states had developed state forest programs. While a few of these managed forest land in a manner somewhat similar to the U.S. Forest Service, and some such as Pennsylvania, Michigan, and Washington had very large holdings, most were service agencies that carried out programs such as dealing with pests and tree diseases, fighting forest fires, planting trees, and promoting private, usually smaller scale, wood production. Federal funds to finance these forestry programs prompted the state forest agencies to pay close attention to national forest affairs, especially the relevant committees in Congress, and the state and private forestry branch of the U.S. Forest Service through which the funded programs were administered. By the 1960s, the state foresters formed the National Association of State Foresters (NASF) with a major objective of lobbying both Congress and the U.S. Forest Service in Washington to obtain increases in financial support.[19]

State forest programs faced many of the environmental and ecological influences of the last third of the twentieth century. Issues such as wilderness, air and water pollution impacts of forest management, nongame wildlife, laws pertaining to rare and endangered species, and the environmental review process carried out under the National Environmental Policy Act impacted state forest programs. While a few states had their own statutes which brought environmental and ecological influences to bear on state forest policy, most did not. On the whole the state agencies resisted the federal influences.

The NASF went considerably beyond advancing its own interests in seeking federal assistance for state forest programs into the wider realm of national forest policy and became a major participant in the opposition to environmental and ecological forestry. It took a vigorous stand, for example, in fostering a commodity influence in the national forest regulations drawn up to implement the National Forest Management Act of 1976; it opposed additional federal wilderness designations; it resisted the application of the Endangered Species Act to forests such as in the case of the lynx; it spoke disparagingly of the changes in the policies promoted by the U.S. Forest Service during the Clinton administration, and in strongly positive terms of the changes brought about in the second Bush presidency.

In the deliberations of its annual conventions reported in the pages of its semimonthly publication *Washington Update*, NASF gave little recognition to the new forest objectives such as protection of nongame wildlife and preservation of old growth, or ideas such as the value of mixed-age forests and the adverse impacts of clear-cutting and motorized forest recreation. It was especially vigorous in objecting to actions on the part of EPA to reduce forest-based nonpoint sources of water pollution, which included the impact of forest practices on water quality. And its coverage of events in Washington included many anti-environmental twists that were characteristic of wood production institutions. When these issues took the form of controversies involving contrasting directions in forest-related science, NASF joined with the Society of American Foresters and the Association of Forestry Schools in opposing the policy views of ecological scientists who called for reduced wood harvest in the national forests.[20]

The Forestry Schools

The role of the forestry schools in this complex of commodity forest institutions was far more subtle and complex. After Gifford Pinchot had financed the first forestry training program at Yale University, a number of colleges and universities followed Yale's lead. They obtained financial support from the federal government as part of its support for agricultural education and gradually grew in student numbers, faculty, and institutional support. They came upon the national scene as an organization only in 1981, when the National Association of Professional Forestry Schools and Colleges (NAPFSC) was formed.[21] By the early twenty-first century it comprised sixty-seven organizations and represented university faculty members, scientists, and extension specialists "working to enhance and protect our forests." While the stated purpose of the organization emphasized the interest of members in "providing information for the national budgetary and research planning process," it also expressed a broad interest in "subjects or issues of national and regional concern."

Forestry education became a highly significant part of the gradual development of forestry as a profession in the United States, but its particular influence in establishing the tone and direction of forest affairs through its influence on forestry students is less well understood. Especially marked was the relative degree to which some forestry schools broadened the scope of their training as the broader public context of forestry changed. The changes were quite uneven as some advanced more rapidly and others remained more traditional. A number of schools evolved from an initial focus on forestry to take on wildlife, then recreation, and by the 1970s they had moved into "environmental" subjects. At the University of Michigan, for example, the Department of Forestry established in 1903 became in 1927 the School of Forestry and Conservation (a course in the recreational use of forests and other wildlands was added in 1934) and in 1950 the School of Natural Resources with Departments of Forestry, Wood Technology, Wildlife Management, Fisheries, and Conservation. Many schools of forestry took a similar route and on the advent of the environmental era the trilogy of forestry, wildlife, and recreation had become a standard pattern in most such schools.

The evolving environmental and ecological activities in forest management posed a challenge to then traditional components of forestry school training. Some forestry schools added faculty and curricula that brought new forest-related subjects such as ecology, biology, zoology, geology, and landscape architecture into their programs. More commonly, forestry schools worked with specialists in other schools and departments and generated interdepartmental programs. It was particularly striking when professionals with ecological specializations were appointed as program administrators, though this was rare. At the University of Missouri, Dr. Mark Ryan, a specialist in endangered species with close ties to the Nature Conservancy, was appointed as dean of the School of Natural Resources. Some schools sought to broaden their school's reach with names that indicated a more diverse and expanded curriculum, such as Yale's School of Forestry and Environmental Studies; Montana's College of Forestry and Conservation; Michigan's School of Natural Resources and Environment; Colorado State's program in Forest, Rangeland and Watershed Stewardship; or the School of the Environmental and Earth Sciences at Duke University. Changes in curriculum and faculty were often the direct result of a change in the number of students enrolled, as at the University of California, Berkeley, where a decline in 2003 to two student majors prompted the abolition of forestry as a separate student concentration.

Not all forestry schools went through these changes, resulting in a broad spectrum of responses to the growth of environmental and ecological forest interests. Some schools, especially in the South, continued to emphasize forestry and wildlife, for example, the School of Forestry and Wildlife Sciences at Auburn University in Alabama. The program at Oregon State University in Corvallis remained a School of Forestry with a dominant wood production focus. While the main divisions in the Penn State University curriculum continued to be forestry and wildlife management, the program continued to be called the School of Forest Resources and it sought to carve out a less controversial middle ground by stressing its role in promoting "reason" amid forest controversy.[22] In short, the former forestry schools that had been able to maintain a clear sense of purpose during the growth of interest in wildlife and outdoor recreation were now, in the midst of ecological innovations in forest management, displaying considerable variation in the direction of their programs. While a solid core retained a program of training and research in traditional commodity forestry and thus served as a source of recruitment for Forest Service employees, a few sought to move in new environmental and ecological directions.[23]

Studies of the changing personnel of the U.S. Forest Service identify a division between commodity-oriented and environmental/ecology-oriented professionals.[24] The former were more from agricultural and small-town backgrounds and had training from forestry and natural resource schools; and the latter had more urban origins and came from a broader range of academic disciplines involving a variety of ecology-oriented subjects. Further studies revealed that these social differences within the agency were closely associated with differences between commodity and ecological forest management objectives.[25]

On the whole the forestry schools tended to identify their role in contemporary forest affairs in terms of research and forest science.[26] But in the 1990s they took on quite a different role through their sponsorship of the Seventh American Forest Congress. The congress was organized and directed mostly by academic forestry leaders rather than industry or the agencies. Yet the many choices made in carrying through the congress made clear the preferences of the academic organizers for the commodity side of the ongoing public debate on forest management.[27]

Forest Reform: Pretense but Limited Practice

The environmental era gave rise to a number of new approaches to forest issues that purported to incorporate environmental and ecological objectives but did so primarily in public statements, while largely failing to observe them in practice. Some advocates took on a "green" public presence without much change in on-the-ground management. For the most part, ecological objectives provided an "umbrella" terminology that gave an ecological tinge to varied efforts to foster new approaches to wood production. These instances of reluctant incorporation of ecological proposals are important cases of a type of adjustment of older commodity objectives to ecological objectives in the era of forest reform. Other examples are the Seventh American Forest Congress, the use of conservation easements to restrict development in forest areas, the Forest Certification movement, and varied programs to increase the intensity of management among the owners and managers of forest lands of smaller acreage.

The Seventh American Forest Congress

The Seventh American Forest Congress in Washington, D.C., in 1996 brought together a variety of individuals and organizations whose starting point was the desire to reduce the intensity of public disputes over forest management and to foster a climate of greater cooperation among the contending parties. Rarely did they deal directly with the substantive issues reflected in the public debates, but instead chose to cast their views in terms of the desirability of reducing controversy and "working together."

The first of such appeals was the "Duluth Manifesto," so named because the first steps in shaping the statement were taken by three individuals attending a conference in Duluth, Minnesota, "who believed there is a need to encourage civil debate over forest policy issues confronting the U.S." A discussion draft was circulated among some forestry leaders across the country and, with a foundation grant, a two-day meeting was held in July 1992 to discuss and refine the statement. The revised statement, circulated in March 1994, was signed by eighty-four leaders in forest affairs and expressed this objective: "To articulate and champion principles to ensure the vitality of forests to help sustain the global environment and economy." The principles broadly emphasized the general importance of healthy and sustainable forests to society; the largest number of signers were academic professionals and public resource administrators.[28] No representatives of the forest industry or of either citizen or scientific advocates of ecological forestry were involved, nor were the terms "ecological" or "environmental" in evidence. The general tone of the manifesto was that a middle ground of academic and governmental representatives could steer forest debates in a more constructive direction by emphasizing principles on which all could agree.

This venture had little impact on the world of forest affairs, and its general tone and direction were continued by activities leading up to the Seventh American Forestry Congress held in Washington, D.C., in 1996. The congress grew out of the Nebraska Roundtable, a meeting held earlier at the Arbor Day Foundation in Nebraska City, Nebraska. There, "a small group of people circulated the idea that in spite of the wide range of beliefs regarding how to manage natural resources, individual citizens concerned with America's forests may agree on more aspects of America's forests than they realize." The group comprised fifty-three individuals from a number of organizations who had been leaders in traditional commodity forestry; most were from academic institutions (fifteen), government (thirteen), and industry (nine). Only two citizen groups that had been deeply involved in the ongoing debates had representatives at the meeting, and none came from scientific ecological organizations.

The Seventh American Forest Congress was preceded by a number of roundtables held in each state, which the Nebraska group hoped would produce a broad constituency to give popular legitimacy to the entire affair. Citizens of each state were to meet to formulate general ideas about basic principles on which everyone could agree. The citizen reform groups whose objectives had given rise to much of the controversy over forest policy were not present at these meetings; either they were not invited or were not interested in attending. Forestry and natural resources schools, such as Purdue University in Indiana, took up the responsibility of organizing the roundtables in their respective states, and a central office was organized at the Forestry School at Yale University.[29] The congress, with the widely circulated motto of "Many Voices—A Common Vision," was surrounded by a general mythology that there was a common view about forests that was more fundamental than the existing policy divisions.[30]

As the time of the congress approached, the citizen reform movement throughout the country took a jaundiced view of the entire matter. Few were invited into the organizational circle or to the congress, or showed much interest in it. However, through the initiative of a longtime and highly respected leader of the citizen movement, Brock Evans, a foundation grant was obtained to help finance the presence of a number of such leaders, which was then managed by the National Audubon Society in New York City; this led to the presence of representatives of a number of citizen groups at the congress. While their attendance at the meeting was recognized by the organizers, few of their specific objectives obtained much recognition among the efforts to steer the meeting toward vague statements of generalities. Amid some confusion, some walked out. To them the sharpest irony was expressed when congress members voted in favor of the proposition that old-growth forests were of special social value, but then voted against the proposal that old growth should be protected from elimination through timber harvest.[31]

The organizers of the Seventh American Forest Congress loudly declared it a great success, demonstrating that there was a wide consensus on forest affairs even though public debate might convey otherwise. However, despite efforts to establish a continuing presence for the ideas of the congress, little subsequent organization took place, and the congress soon devolved into insignificance and obscurity. One committee established by those who organized the congress, emphasizing the idea that forest policies should be decided more on the community level, continued to carry out activities, especially in the Pacific Northwest.[32] But amid the debates over forest policy, which continued as vigorously as before, the Washington event was hardly mentioned or even remembered.

Conservation Easements

Conservation easements became a major innovation in land management in the last third of the twentieth century; they played an important role in a variety of land use areas, including forest management. They were frequently described as carrying out significant environmental and ecological objectives, but in fact their objectives were quite varied, and they provided only limited support for ecological objectives. One must approach their ecological implications with considerable caution.

Conservation easements were legal arrangements between private parties that stipulated future long-term or even permanent use of the land. They could state both what the land could be used for and what it could not be used for. In an easement agreement the landowner retained fee simple ownership but usually gave up the right to develop the land, except for limited specified purposes; at the same time the easement stipulated the designated future uses of the land, which could vary considerably, and which were intended to be perpetual. While the fee simple ownership of the land could be transferred to other parties, future owners were bound by the negative restrictions and the acceptable uses in the easement agreement.

The most well-known aspect of conservation easements was their restriction on future development. Less well known and less publicized were the stipulated uses permitted. These uses varied but usually were of three types: wood production uses, agricultural uses, and ecological land uses. The most extensive agreements were those stipulating permanent wood production managed by industrial forest companies, often drawn up through the initiative of organizations such as the Conservation Fund and the Nature Conservancy. The second most numerous conservation easements were carried out by the extensive number of land trusts throughout the country that often acquired rights to the use of land through easement agreements for ecological purposes or open space and agriculture. While both types of easements were financed partially by private funds from foundations or land trust members, significant funding also came from public sources.

Conservation easements became popular in northern New England states largely as a response to major changes in northern forest land ownership.[33] Much of the region was owned by private timber companies, which in the last decades of the twentieth century began to look upon their holdings as more valuable for real estate development than for wood production. An initial sale took place in 1983 to Sir James Goldsmith, a British investor who, in turn, sold to another company that specialized in development. People in the region reacted with great consternation as they visualized a future in which development would eliminate traditional uses of the land for wood production, outdoor recreation, fishing, and hunting. Public funds for the purchase of the lands from the timber companies were not available, and the alternative approach of purchasing only the development rights appeared to be more feasible. As other wood production companies decided to sell, a variety of proposals arose to acquire land use rights in order to maintain traditional uses.[34]

Even conservation easements, however, cost more than available funds; hence members of Congress from New England proposed that federal funds be appropriated to finance them. They were successful, and a program called the Forest Legacy Program was approved. At first the program was focused on northern New England, but it gradually expanded to other states as well. As the program moved into the Midwest, and especially the South, it attracted the support of the timber industry. Studies indicated that much forest acreage in urban regions was being liquidated for development, and sectors of the timber industry in the South took up the argument that this could be slowed down through the Forest Legacy Program in order to reduce the decline of available forest land and hence timber supply.

Use of conservation easements grew rapidly within the context of preserving timberland as a desirable social goal. Announcements of successful agreements to establish easements to maintain forest lands for the future were greeted with enthusiasm. However, their popularity seemed to be confined to their negative implication, that is, what the land would not be used for—development—when, in fact, the meaning of conservation easements, what the land would be used for, attracted little attention. In northern New England one heard much of the retention of "traditional uses" through the easements, but there was also the question of what ecological and environmental objectives would be guaranteed. Would old-growth forests be retained or restored? Would riparian areas be protected, and if so, what would be their width and would they include intermittent as well as perennial streams? Would biodiversity protection be limited to rare and endangered species or be extended to sensitive species? In only a few cases were such implications brought into the public discussion.

As time passed and easements covering large acreages were approved, they came under increasing scrutiny and skepticism because of the secrecy of their negotiation, the limited public supervision of the agreements despite the use of public funds to obtain them, the stipulations that permitted the landowners to exclude public use of the land for recreation, and the restrictions on the application of environmental protection laws to the land. Many aspects of the agreements were considered to be privileged information in the order of trade secrets and not available for public scrutiny and influence. In the early stages of the development of conservation easements in New England, these complicating issues received little public attention, but in the early twenty-first century, the largest proposal yet, the West Branch project comprising some 340,000 acres of forest land in Maine, brought them to light and resulted in a more extensive public debate. The ensuing publicity and controversy seemed to shatter the aura of enthusiasm which conservation easements had earlier enjoyed. By 2004 one could conclude that the future of large-scale conservation easements in New England was somewhat problematical.[35]

Certification

The movement to "certify" forests as "well managed" involved a more complex relationship to ecological forestry.[36] While the effort arose from the Rainforest Alliance, a citizen environmental group, it had continual difficulty in embracing and advancing many ecological objectives. It arose in an international context, was shaped by objectives in international forest affairs, and then, often in awkward ways, sought to make itself relevant to conditions within the United States. Reformers abroad and reformers at home found considerable difficulty in coming together, especially with respect to ecological forest objectives and practices. Forest certification has its own inner history that is difficult to ferret out because of continual attempts to ignore specifics in forest management objectives and enforcement, and major difficulties in practicing ecological forestry, amid the media rhetoric of "good forest management" with which the proponents attempted to convince the public of the significance of its ambitious goals.

After becoming well established on the international scene with an organizational headquarters in Mexico, the certification movement in the United States, through the Forest Stewardship Council located in New England, sought to establish standards of "good forest management" in the United States and enhance the marketability of wood products by "certifying" that forest practices conformed to those standards.[37] In this way consumers could choose wood products knowing that they were produced under environmentally acceptable conditions. The program was intended to copy the market-based program that had developed successfully in organic foods. In this case, consumer preference had created a new market when consumers were convinced that their purchases were, in fact, grown under organic conditions. The approach attracted a number of free market theorists and foundations, who argued that this mobilization of market forces was a preferable alternative to governmental regulation of forest practices. Citizens, through their market choices, rather than regulation and the many disputes it generated, could bring about acceptable standards of forest management.

While the certification movement generally enjoyed the support of the leadership of several of the more prominent environmental citizen organizations such as the Sierra Club and the World Wildlife Fund, it was not able to strike roots in the many citizen organizations which had arisen after the 1976 Forest Management Act and which had, over the years, developed strategies in interaction with public forest managers. At issue were forest practice standards: a comprehensive biodiversity program including sensitive as well as rare and endangered species; the protection and restoration of old growth; a comprehensive and diverse habitat program of classification and management; the preference for selection cutting rather than clear-cutting; silvicultural systems to enhance the creation and maintenance of forests of mixed rather than even age and mixed species rather than monocultures; a watershed program to establish wide riparian areas based upon cumulative effects of forest management on intermittent as well as main stem streams. While certification advocates seemed to be content with publicizing their program in terms of generalities such as "good forest management," they bypassed the standards of the citizen reform movement, which were cast in terms of specific forest practices.

The key elements in the certification movement were the process by which forests were deemed to be "well managed," and how forest practices arising from the certification agreements would be implemented and enforced. Two certifying groups were identified by the Forest Stewardship Council (FSC) as its vehicles for this process: Scientific Certification Systems, an organization that supervised certification of acceptability in a variety of economic fields, and Smart Wood, which was more specialized in forest certification and which was sponsored by an environmental group, the National Wildlife Federation. The certifiers were instructed to work in the context of principles established by the FSC, but from the very start this presented major problems. First, different certifiers applied the standards stated in general principle in different ways on the ground, and second, those practical applications led to wide variations in standards from region to region in the country. As a result, the FSC established standard-setting committees in eleven different regions, which entered into a long and laborious process of making the standards more regionally specific and more workable. These committees became the heart of the issue of just how much the FSC would be able to embrace ecological forestry as the standard of forest management. The overriding reality was that certification was a market-driven process in which the objective was to create markets for identified wood products, and hence that objective could readily retard the contrary objective of enhancing the ecological objectives of forest management.[38]

Difficulties soon arose in applying the certification structure to forest management. On the most general level, the forest industry became alarmed about the effect of certification on its activities and especially its public image. Through its major trade organization, the American Forest and Paper Association, it established its own certifying agency, the Sustainable Forest Initiative (SFI), and entered into a vigorous competition with the Forest Stewardship Council. SFI standards were much weaker than those of the FSC, and the SFI relied on self-certification, that is, the statements of its member industries that their practices were within SFI guidelines; compliance was not subject to independent verification. Acceptability often was in terms of "process" standards, that is, the establishment of an office within the forest owner's headquarters to deal with the relevant problems, rather than "substantive" standards, that is practices in the woods.[39]

The FSC certification program seemed to stumble along with varied degrees of success, but without sustained widespread confidence in its effectiveness.[40] There were continual criticisms of the objectivity of the certifiers and the general FSC program of implementation, with a special focus on the fact that the FSC was quite willing to certify a forest on the basis of what its managers promised to do rather than what they actually did.[41] There was resistance from forest managers on the grounds that the standards evolving from the regional standard-setting committees were too stringent and thus too expensive to implement. In response, Scientific Certification Systems announced that it would establish its own, separate certification program that would be more lenient in its standards and its implementation procedures. And amid its major objective of mobilizing the public as consumers of "well-managed" wood there was little evidence that the public was much aware of the entire program at all. The boycotts of major distributors of wood products such as Home Depot and Staples, intended to persuade those firms to cease the purchase of old-growth wood, in fact attracted far more attention.[42]

Forest reform groups hesitated to become too closely involved, and several incidents that led to an impasse between them and the FSC personnel had made clear that forest reform objectives would have trouble striking roots in the council deliberations. It appeared that while the council seemed to be willing to simply require that the laws with respect to species protection and water quality be followed, the reformers wanted to go further, for example, from threatened and endangered species to the wider realm of sensitive species, and from the rather rudimentary requirements of voluntary "best management practice" programs in water quality to more mandatory watershed protection programs. At the same time the reformers' rejection of clear-cutting and many features of industrial forestry such as the use of pesticides, short-term rotations, and area management became sticking points in forming the regional standards. Since many reform groups were also local branches of the Sierra Club, this often led to tension between the club's formal association with the FSC at the national level and the forest strategies at the local level. In fact, there was a tendency for forest reformers to support the policy of ending the production of timber in the national forests rather than to work with the FSC, an organization that was committed to wood production and even sought to extend certification to the national forests.

An equally divisive problem arose with the procedures developed in certification to implement the standards. Certification agreements inevitably created problems of just how they could be implemented, and especially because many of them certified forests provisionally with the stipulation that certain changes in forest practices would be required in the form of conditions of certification, with the threat of decertification if those conditions were not met. This inevitably led to continued negotiations between the FSC-sponsored certifiers and the forest land managers in a manner not much different from the tension between regulators and the regulated in a more formal public governing process. Observers of the process from the environmental community also objected that the forest landowners were not abiding by their agreements. In 2002 the international body Rainforest Alliance, which had initiated the entire certification movement in the first place, published an independent evaluation of the international program arguing that the certifying bodies were ignoring widespread violations of the certification agreements on the part of the timber companies. By the early years of the twenty-first century, therefore, it was quite apparent that pressures from the market had undercut much of the certification program as to both standards and enforcement.[43]

The history of this still very young certification venture makes clear that it had considerable difficulty in advancing the objectives of ecological forestry. If one takes the standards that made up ecological forestry as the test, the certification movement seemed to be satisfied with simply following what the law required and gave little evidence that it sought to move those standards forward in a progressive fashion, as was the case with the citizen reform organizations or the ecological forest scientists. At the same time, if one judges the movement in terms of its influence in moving the private forest industry toward improved standards of ecological forestry, one can readily conclude that it mostly functioned to give a stamp of approval to forest landowners who either had already moved in that direction or were in the process of doing so through their own momentum. One could not rely on certification as a process that could spread ecological objectives in forest management.

The Smaller Forest Owner

The vast majority of forest lands in the East were owned not by corporate wood production firms but by owners of small woodlots, who sought to carve out a niche for themselves amid the wider field of forest affairs that was dominated by the industrial wood products giants. Together they tended to focus on longer-range management rather than the shorter-term strategies of the forest industry, to emphasize high-quality lumber production for value-added wood products manufacturing rather than the pulp and paper market, and to emphasize knowledge gained through personal experience in the field. They came onto the scene amid the new interest in environmental and ecological objectives, seeking at times to give themselves positive visibility through the expression of those objectives, sometimes under false pretenses. They constitute a useful set of cases through which to examine the impact of ecological forestry on the wider forest scene.[44]

THE FEDERAL STEWARDSHIP PROGRAM

Small privately owned woodlots remained after the decline of agriculture in the region or were purchased by urban dwellers for weekend retreats or even more permanent homes after World War II. These lands were called Non-Industrial Private Forests (NIPF), and it had long been known that their owners were far less interested in wood production than in environmental amenities—the wildlife, cleaner water, cleaner air, and aesthetic values of their lands. Owners' limited interest in wood production had long been deplored by state and national forest agencies as well as the forest industry, who urged the owners to add to the nation's wood production resources. Hence, often with the hopes that they could find the clue to change the attitudes of NIPF owners, professional foresters and their allies conducted frequent public opinion surveys to determine just how that could be done. The resulting surveys only confirmed the strong environmental values and the very low interest in wood production associated with the purchase of these holdings. This gave rise to a number of organized activities carried out with public pretension of ecological forest objectives but with only partial actual implementation.

For some years the forest industry had sponsored a Tree Farm Program that gave formal recognition to woodlots managed on a long-term silvicultural basis. As time went on, however, state wood production leaders urged that a more extensive promotional program be instituted with federal funding. Begun in 1977, this involved programs organized through the state extension service and county foresters under legislation known as the Forestry Incentives Program.[45] Limited results with this program led to a more extensive effort in 1990 known as the Stewardship Incentive Program. This provided funds to private woodlot owners, under the direction of county foresters, to draw up and implement plans for long-term forest management. However, while the Tree Farm Program and the Forestry Incentives Program had stressed wood production as a management objective, now amid the environmental climate of the times the stewardship program authorized a broader set of objectives, such as soil protection and wildlife habitat preservation. In 2002 Congress replaced the stewardship program with a new version known as the Forest Lands Enhancement Program, which added a few objectives such as riparian protection, but was administered also through the established state agencies dominated by those with wood production rather than ecological objectives.

On the whole one could describe this effort as an attempt to facilitate wood production, with a modest set of environmental and ecological objectives added to enhance the program's public acceptability. Hence the term "stewardship" and the aesthetic photography of ecological resources used to advertise the program. But the program was firmly controlled by the state wood production institutions, the state forest agencies, and the forest branch of the state extension services, with influence on the ground by the county foresters. The cases of true ecological forest management were relatively rare, represented by only a few states, and the great majority of programs were shaped by a core commitment to wood production on small woodlot holdings. They constituted updated versions of the older Tree Farm Program, with only minor and occasional additions of ecological objectives.

FOREST STEWARDS GUILD

The Forest Stewards Guild, an organization of professional foresters with strong roots among smaller forest landowners and with a more explicit interest in things ecological, sought to distinguish itself sharply from both the dominant wood products industry and the Society of American Foresters.[46] The guild grew out of a successful community forest program, the Forest Trust, which was active in the area around Santa Fe, New Mexico. The Forest Stewards Guild, with a membership slightly less than five hundred, soon carved out a niche for itself and played a distinctive role in forest affairs more closely attuned to ecological objectives.

The guild was composed of field foresters, whose starting point in the world of forestry was experience in forest holdings much smaller than those of the large industrial firms. In many respects they were the traditionalists amid extensive and radical changes in the forest world, espousing time-honored silvicultural practices that carried a forest from seedling to timber harvest by thinning and pruning to provide the space for the growth of trees. They objected strenuously to modern industrial forestry in which "foresters must remove all trees and start over again to make the forest productive . . . which justifies the familiar clearcut, burn and plant regime." They derided the assumption that "natural forces are inherent under-producers" and instead argued that the natural processes constitute the basic elements of forest development with which the forester must work. Those natural forces, rather than the "regulated" forest of human manipulation, were the fundamental beginning of sound forest management.

Two focal points of the guild's approach stood out. One was the constant attack on "high-grading," the notion that one practiced forestry by removing the larger and more marketable trees and leaving the rest as relatively worthless residue. Instead, they took seriously the traditional silvicultural wisdom that the first emphasis in forestry was not on what was taken but what was left, because what was left would shape the future forest. Whereas the market gave a single-minded stress on removing timber that the market wanted, the forester as silviculturist emphasized the long-term future and was concerned first with the beginnings of new growth, removing only that which could be spared from the requirements of the forest-to-be.

Thus, the guild's statement of principles read, "The forester's first duty is to the forest and its future." But this was followed with the implications for the forester, "When landowner direction conflicts with the mission and principles of the Guild and cannot be modified through dialogue and education, the forester should dissociate." This first duty principle was a powerful identifying feature of the guild and emphasized its basic concern as care for the land in the manner of Aldo Leopold's land ethic. The sharp difference in orientation between the focus of traditional silviculture on the resource conditions of the forest, on the one hand, and market pressures, on the other, was continually underlined by discussion of the "first duty" of the forester. Thus, "intensive silviculture associated with plantation forestry should seldom occur at the expense of natural forests."

The Forest Stewards Guild came into the world of forest affairs from a vantage point quite different from the ecologically oriented citizen reform groups and did not work closely with them, but they seemed often to run a parallel course. Thus, the guild complained that "the pages of the Journal of Forestry regularly conveyed increasingly angry invectives about environmental extremism and sinister threats to God given private property rights, family and the American way." Or "the Society of American Foresters is currently in a state of denial. Its president articulates a vision where commodity production is all. In his distaste for 'preservationists', he goes to the other extreme and idealizes human domination of the ecosystem." "In recent years, with the growth of the environmental movement and changes in science, the mechanistic view of the forest has hindered the ability of forestry to provide solutions that are relevant to contemporary values and perspective."

The guild defended the importance of the National Environmental Policy Act, the Endangered Species Act, and the National Forest Management Act. At the same time, while the guild brought into the forest debate a strong emphasis on traditional silviculture in contrast with market domination and in this way adopted significant elements of ecological forestry, it did not give as strong an emphasis to biodiversity objectives. Hence its acceptance of ecological forestry, while significant and far more extensive than was the case with the federally sponsored stewardship program, was not as comprehensive as was the case with the attempts to apply ecological forestry to the public forests.

THE MENOMINEE FOREST

Those who espoused a sustainable and conservative silviculture often cited the Menominee Forest in Wisconsin, managed by the Menominee tribal government, as a model forest program.[47] Over the years of the twentieth century, this forest on the Menominee Reservation had had a checkered career, extending from the clear-cutting days of the latter years of the nineteenth century to various attempts at selection harvesting under the auspices of the Bureau of Indian Affairs. In 1970, however, the Menominee Tribe obtained control of the forest and was able to establish a more complete version of long-term forest silviculture, which involved a relatively high volume of wood production, but under a more firm commitment to management practices that provided a major role for future as well as contemporary production.

Hence, interested visitors who came to the Menominee Forest to observe its forest practices experienced a multi-aged forest of some 150,000 acres that was managed on conservative harvest practices with ample room for retaining smaller and younger trees for future long-term growth and selection harvest. The forest managers, Menominee Tribal Enterprises, maintained its own mill but directed harvest in terms not of the needs of the mill, or the overall profitability of the enterprise, but of the silvicultural requirements of long-term wood productivity. Many of the controlling factors in management rested upon the division of the forest into over a hundred management units; in each of these a Continuous Forest Inventory (CFI) provided a continuous accounting of growth, which then governed harvest levels.[48] Fundamental to this process was a cultural perspective in which tribal members thought of their forest's role in their long tribal history as well as their responsibility for later tribal generations. The federal and Wisconsin state arrangements under which the forest was managed also eliminated state property taxes. The conditions under which the Menominee Forest was managed freed it from the pressures of both the market and state tax liabilities to enable it to practice long-term sustainable wood production.[49]

The Menominee management also affirmed the importance of including both wildlife and water considerations in forest management. But while these seemed to accompany the multi-aged forest, they did not receive as firm management attention as sustained-yield wood production. Tribal leaders expressed a concern that "not enough data exists on either riparian or forest biodiversity" to enable this facet of ecological forestry to be placed on a par with wood production. With respect to these objectives, Paula Huff, the first director of the College of the Menominee Nation's Menominee Sustainable Development Institute, "often points out that the reservation's database is far from adequate." It is not yet clear how extensive the application of ecological forestry will be on the Menominee Forest, even though the commitment to a multi-aged forest and extensive site-specific management provide a far firmer basis for those objectives than does industrial wood production.

Ecological Forestry in the U.S. Forest Service

Management of the national forests by the U.S. Forest Service contrasts markedly with the cases analyzed in the previous pages as an example of the impact of ecological forestry. Left to its own internal professional dynamics, the agency might be expected to have retained a wood production emphasis as strong and uncompromising as the Society of American Foresters, which grew up alongside the agency. The traditional training in wood production offered by forestry schools placed its firm stamp on the values of the agency's personnel. But the agency could not escape the effects of changing values about forest lands expressed in the wider society or the growth of ecological forest science, and it was confronted with these influences expressed through the environmental impact analyses required by the National Environmental Policy Act and the Endangered Species Act, and the specific standards and planning process in the Forest Management Act of 1976. Soon the agency was both expressing the need for change and facing the legal requirements imposed upon it. This led to tension between the old and the new within the agency.

The Forest Service was quite aware of the changing values in the society at large concerning the role and importance of forests. For while the earliest public opinion surveys about such matters were conducted by other institutions, such as the 1977 survey sponsored by the American Forest Institute, an industry organization, the Forest Service soon took up surveys on its own. Such surveys consistently indicated that to the public the forests were of the utmost importance for watershed protection and wildlife habitat, that old growth and wilderness were very highly valued, and wood production and motorized outdoor recreation were at the low end of the value scale. In a more recent survey sponsored by the Forest Service, conducted as part of the planning process for 2002, the agency reported that 87 percent of those surveyed agreed that protecting ecosystems and wildlife habitat was "important," 72 percent had the same view for watershed protection, 77 percent agreed that a wilderness experience was "important," while only 19 percent felt the same for motorized off-highway vehicles. These rankings of values were consistent with the results in many surveys of statewide rather than national scope.[50]

The Forest Service was even more immediately aware of values expressed by that segment of the public who took a direct interest in national forest affairs by participating in forest planning in the 1980s and 1990s.[51] The agency was required to establish alternatives in its planning decisions and then to provide reasons for its choices. These choices were frequently organized on a scale so as to represent variations of the balance between production objectives and ecological/environmental objectives. Moreover, the impact analysis stipulated by the National Environmental Policy Act required the Forest Service to identify in an "interdisciplinary and searching" manner the effects of its actions, such as timber harvest, and in so doing it was made continually conscious of the new values being brought to bear on forest management. In the numerous administrative appeals by the public from both planning documents and project proposals, which frequently criticized the agency for not giving more attention to environmental and ecological objectives, it became painfully aware of the steady gap between public desires and agency performance. .

Forest Service managers were none too happy with this new state of affairs, as the requirement that they defend their planning decisions forced them to think in new ways. While they customarily thought in terms of trees that produced wood fiber for the market, they were now asked to go beyond their training and experience and think in terms of forest ecosystems composed of a multitude of species and ecological processes. They tended to blame these new requirements on the society at large and more directly on the people who were forcing them to change how they looked at "their" forests, who were seen as interlopers on "their" turf.

These ecological influences brought a new stage in a long-standing process, whereby the Forest Service's inability to adjust to new circumstances led to externally imposed restrictions on its administrative autonomy. Limitations on the agency's freedom of activities now became more extensive and, to the agency, more irritating.

One result was the loss of influence in the scientific aspects of forest management. One of the most significant features of the history of the U.S. Forest Service was the establishment of its forest experiment stations, which for many years defined the course of forest research. But as forest management faced a marked expansion of ecological objectives, independent scientists at a wide range of institutions were also conducting pertinent research. This network of researchers generated a body of work in forest science that supported new directions in forest management, and their research was brought to bear on forest decisions by citizen reform organizations as well as by scientific bodies specializing in biology and ecology. Moreover, many scientists now within the Forest Service tended to forge links with fellow scientists outside as well as inside the agency. This entire process came to constitute a scientific influence in forestry well beyond the influence of the agency and the traditional forest profession. In a subtle and informal way it led to the loss of agency control over the direction and use of forest science.

In a similar way, the Forest Service reluctantly had to face studies about agency activities conducted by external institutions, primarily because agency statements were often considered to be questionable. The first such case involved the work of Peter Morrison of the Wilderness Society, who directed the Northwest Office GIS and Remote Sensing Project. Using aerial photographs, he challenged the agency's standard wisdom about the extent of ancient forests in the region, arguing that the acreage had been greatly overestimated. This information was widely convincing, and the agency was compelled to accept it. In a second case, dealing with agency administrative appeals involving fire prevention proposals, the Ecological Research Institute at Northern Arizona University challenged the agency's report as to the number and sources of appeals, when it found that the agency had no reliable data on which to base a sound conclusion, and compiled its own competing appeal data. A third case involved the activities of the Wildlands Center for Preventing Roads, which sought to obtain information about the progress of the road reduction initiative instituted by the agency in the year 2000 and, in the absence of available agency compilations, constructed its own based on reports drawn up by individual national forests. The institutional infrastructure maintained by citizen organizations and academic institutions had grown to the point of being able to challenge many of the agency's own assessments about its affairs, which greatly weakened both its credibility and its capability.

The persistently skeptical, even negative attitudes of Forest Service personnel to the scientists and the citizen organizations that were pressing for ecological forest innovations constituted a roadblock to effective collaborative efforts between the agency and the public. This situation was addressed in a special issue of the *Journal of Forestry* devoted to the subject of "Appeals, Litigation and Forest Policy." In describing collaborative approaches to forest policy, Nancy Manring's article in this symposium, "Democratic Accountability in National Forest Planning," focused on the problem. She stated that "collaborative efforts may be constrained by what some agency officials have referred to as a longstanding paranoia—an absolute distrust of the public and environmental groups by line officers and most management."[52]

The agency's response to the challenges of the ecology movement was easily observable in its changes in word use, a cosmetic strategy that generated more cynicism than confidence in its activities. For example, the customary "logging" was replaced by "harvest," and later by the words "vegetative management." The agency claimed to reject "clear-cutting," which, it argued, it no longer practiced because it had developed cutting practices with a few "leave trees" (even though, it was often argued, these minor changes had much the same consequences for the ecologically defined forest).

The agency became even more adept at taking the language of ecological forestry and giving it traditional commodity forestry meanings. Thus, it accepted diversity as a desirable goal but defined it in terms of tree species and ages rather than the much more inclusive range of species that the ecologists included, or it drew up lists of "management indicator species" but defined the indicators in terms of game rather than biodiversity categories. To those advocating ecological forestry, these instances of "forest double-speak" seemed to be ways in which the agency tried to convince itself and the public that it was responding to the winds of change while it continued past ways of on-the-ground management. Forest doublespeak became a hallmark of the culture of mutual suspicion and distrust that reflected the gulf between the old and the new.[53]

The tension between old and new in forest affairs also involved differences within the agency. Those professionals with biological expertise beyond wood production, a minority within the agency, increasingly made themselves heard, so much so that the agency financed studies of the backgrounds and values of its own personnel. The most significant such study found a clear distinction between an older, commodity-oriented group of professionals who were heavily male and rural in background, with degrees in traditional resource-based subjects, and a newer and younger group, with a larger proportion of women, more urban in background and representing a wider group of specialized professions, such as botany, zoology, ecology, nongame wildlife, hydrology, and landscape architecture. The continual interplay of the old and the new within the agency, in fact, gave rise to distinctive groupings known within it as "silviculturists" and "ologists."[54]

This agency-wide split was visible in the selection process of the first chief forester in the Clinton administration. Rumor had it throughout the agency that the administration's preferred choice was a wildlife biologist, Jack Ward Thomas. In response to the rumor, a considerable number of forest supervisors wrote a joint letter to the administration objecting to the possible choice. In counter to this initiative, an agency employee from the Monongahela National Forest, Tom DeMeo, prepared an e-mail petition to urge that the next chief be a professional with a "non-traditional" background. The petition signers, whose names and affiliations were attached to the petition on the Internet, were drawn heavily from the ranks of agency "ologists." The episode indicated the way in which broad innovations in forest values had become important not just within the American public and the world of biological science, but within the Forest Service itself.[55]

Two distinct groups within the agency are the line officers, those involved directly in the management of specific national forests, and the staff officers, those from other sectors of the agency who influence the line officers with a broader perspective. Staff officers may work in the Washington office, some in the regional offices, some in the experiment stations, and a few even within each national forest. The distinction between line and staff officers has rarely received as close attention as has the identification of values within the agency, but it has been spelled out on several occasions by agency observers, for example the former chief Jack Ward Thomas, who wrote of the different degrees to which line and staff were responsive to the Northwest Forest Plan. The most common idea is that line officers were intensely preoccupied with on-the-ground management and hence skeptical about outside suggestions that they divert budget and their own time from customary practices to new ones. Moreover, these activities traditionally were organized around wood production so that the line officers resisted changes in the elementary tasks of inventory, management, and monitoring that were rooted in that central preoccupation.[56]

In the late twentieth century this tension between old and new in the agency took a new and somewhat larger turn, the creation of an organized group to challenge the wisdom of the line officers. Over the recent past a number of issues had arisen in which the technical staff of individual forests had felt that their scientific judgments as professionals had been ignored or overridden by forest supervisors. The Forest Service Employees for Environmental Ethics not only took up the cause of employees who felt similarly overridden, but became a critic of agency policies. In 1998 it led to the creation of a new publication, *Forest Magazine*, which became an important source of information and analyses independent of the agency and its closely associated wood production allies.[57]

The regional offices of the Forest Service served as a potential avenue through which new ecologically based ideas could enter the agency. These offices usually included a staff with a much broader professional training and background than was the case with the individual national forests. Here one could find ecologists and nongame wildlife specialists, hydrologists with a watershed perspective, landscape architects, and a variety of professionals who found a receptive home because of the role of the regions in seeking to bring constructive change to the more limited perspective of the line officers.

While this kind of analysis of the relationship between the old and the new within the Forest Service is relatively easy to obtain, it is more difficult to chart the "winds of change" over time and how rapidly change has occurred or, more important, how gradually, as the twists and turns of innovation and resistance to innovation veered back and forth. At almost every year along the way, one meets the assertion by agency personnel that the "agency is changing." Although this statement is true in terms of the changing professional backgrounds of the staff, it is far more difficult to chart changes in day-to-day management. That the agency needed to "think in new ways" was a major theme in the advice by service chiefs from the 1980s onward. But strategies to develop an evaluation of the results of such advice on management practices have not yet been worked out, and the conclusion that the tension between the line and the staff remains vibrant seems, at this writing, quite convincing.

Varieties of Response to Ecological Forestry

The firmly rooted values that sustained and drove the application of an ecological perspective in forest management generated a wide range of responses in both individuals and institutions long associated with commodity forest objectives. In this chapter I have organized these into three broad groupings: one that unabashedly defended commodity objectives from ecological inroads, a second that took a similar course but that was sufficiently aware of ecological goals to clothe their commodity objectives in environmental and ecological language while retaining their commodity commitments, and a third that felt compelled by law and by scientific and public opinion to take the emerging ecological culture more seriously and apply it to forest management. In this format one can track the slow but persistent pressures that commodity forestry advocates felt and to which they responded with varying degrees of glacial change often mixed with defiance and desperation.

The precise focal points of tension between old and new in forest affairs can be elaborated more fully through state forest activities. Each state had its own cluster of forest institutions, well-established commodity forest organizations and newer citizen and scientific ecological groups that were only emerging and seeking to influence state forest affairs. In the next chapter I describe several of these in greater detail, selected from among the fifty states to reflect varying ways in which old and new confronted each other. This adds more specific state-level insight to the broader-based analysis of national trends. The tension between old and new in forest affairs had its dramatic moments in the nationwide media, but its significance lay less in these dramas and more in the long-term slow and steady impact of change on older ways of thinking that the events often obscured. The state-level focus of the next chapter elaborates further the varied and intricate ways in which this historic encounter was taking place, often more quietly but with equal significance.

CHAPTER 4

Ecological Forestry
in the States

Commodity forestry was far more deeply entrenched in the state forest agencies than in the national forest system. Tomas Koontz has elaborated on this in *Federalism in the Forest: National versus State Natural Resource Policy*. He emphasizes two factors: the greater dominance of commodity objectives at the state level, and the far less frequent citizen involvement in forest decisions through which ecological forest objectives might well exercise more influence. I have already observed the general isolation of the National Association of State Foresters from ecological forest activities, in support of Koontz's conclusions. His observations, however, do not provide the detail necessary to work out the many and varied ways in which resistance to ecological forestry takes place. In this chapter I explore the impact of ecological objectives on state forest affairs, with respect both to the management of public lands and the regulation of forest practices on private lands.

The Alaskan Forests: State and Federal Links

State forest administration in Alaska has a distinctive relationship with the management of national forests. Personnel of the state's Department of Fish and Game have provided major expertise concerning big game habitat on both the state and national forests. Matthew Kirchoff of the Alaska Department of Fish and Game was the agency's leading deer researcher for many

years and contributed enormously to knowledge about the relationship between black-tailed deer and forest management policies in Southeast Alaska.[1]
When the Alaska Department of Natural Resources (ADNR) reviewed permits for logging on state lands, it was required to seek advice from the Department of Fish and Game before approving them. Extractive industries in
Alaska had long chafed under this role of the Department of Fish and Game
and had sought to change it.[2] Their objectives were rewarded when in 2003
the new governor, former U.S. senator Frank Murkowski, greatly reduced
the role of Department of Fish and Game professionals in both federal and
state forest management by transferring their investigative division to the
Department of Natural Resources, thereby placing them under the control
of an umbrella agency with primarily extractive objectives.[3] A closely related move to redirect the objectives in Alaskan state forest management was
the decision of the state legislature to change the primary purpose of the
two state forests from multiple use to timber production, thereby prioritiz-
ing wood production over other uses in forest management.[4] An extractive
resource culture dominated state forest affairs in Alaska.

Washington: State and Private Forest Policies

The Pacific Coast states have developed the most elaborate program to establish desirable forest practices for private forests, and among these the
Washington State program is currently one of the most complex and contentious. In the mid-1980s the state land commissioner administered both
state-owned "trust lands," which were managed primarily for public school
revenue, and the legally mandated "forest practices" required on private
lands. Both these forest administration programs stimulated considerable
public debate on forest issues and led to a continuing interest in that policy
on the part of a handful of statewide environmental groups and a number
of more regional and local groups. The state's forests generated an extremely
diverse set of policy issues that were intensely debated, and the outcomes
reflect the limited impact of ecological objectives on state forest affairs.[5]

The first forest practice act in Washington was adopted in 1974. Initially
it was devoted to traditional objectives such as requiring replanting after
harvest, and only gradually was it influenced by ecological and environmental issues.[6] These later objectives made their mark on private forests in Washington primarily through the environmental analyses required by SEPA, the
state environmental impact statute, and the application of the federal endangered species act on private forests, for example in protection programs
for the spotted owl and the wide range of species dependent on old growth

that the spotted owl represented. Anadromous fish, especially salmon and
steelhead trout, played a significant role in debate over the effects of timber
harvest on the water quality of Pacific Coast streams. Declines in salmon
populations were attributed to declining stream quality, especially to the
deterioration of aquatic habitat by deforestation. Intense argument ensued
over the causes of salmon decline and proposals for recovery and led to
many issues in both private and public forest management.

The Washington Environmental Council, the oldest statewide organization with an ecological bent to take up forest issues, tended to focus on the
decisions of the Department of Natural Resources that pertained both to the
management of trust lands and the regulation of private forest lands. Early
in the 1980s the council had taken the lead in attempts to modify the strong
commodity orientation of the Public Lands Commission by advocating that
the commissioner be elected rather than appointed. Voters approved the
proposal.[7] During the tenure of the first two commissioners under this arrangement, Brian Boyle and Jennifer Belcher, the program seemed to be
receptive to ecological forest objectives, but amid political jockeying in
management disputes with respect to both trust lands and the regulation
of private forests, a working coalition between the administrators and the
industry seemed to emerge as the dominant influence in state forest affairs.
A new commissioner, Doug Sutherland, seemed determined to reverse the
previous direction.[8] Intense disputes over the state's "forest practice acts"
had led to a new legislative program, the Timber, Fish and Wildlife (TFW)
program, which provided funds to finance joint committees to deal with
problems such as wildlife and riparian management. This arrangement included financing for joint field investigations in the case of controversial
issues.[9] TWS deliberations seemed to pit environmental groups and Native
Americans against the private forest industry. The effort led to an increasingly complex set of proposed rules and regulations in which the issues
often hinged on disputes over the assessment of available scientific information, such as the data to support narrower or wider riparian buffer areas.
The industry rejected the view advanced by the environmental participants
that studies argued for a 250-foot buffer.[10] In the course of the proceedings,
the environmental participants came to believe that the industry exercised
far too much influence and withdrew from the entire venture, which left
the regulators and the industry to negotiate with each other.[11]

The complex political forces that shaped the Washington forest practice
program can be illustrated by the Teanaway River case involving U.S. Timberlands and the lawsuit brought by the Audubon Society concerning the
programs of both the state and the company and their effect on spotted owl

habitat. When the previous owner of the timberlands, Boise Cascade, felt that the logging rules were too restrictive to make the operation profitable, it sold the tract to U.S. Timberlands, which now was under considerable temptation to "mine" the existing timber in order to pay off the debt acquired to finance the purchase. It chafed under Washington Department of Natural Resources (DNR) restrictions that required the protection of forest land around owl nesting areas. The two parties argued over the certification and decertification of "owl circles" and whether or not particular timberlands would be available for harvest. In the ensuing controversies both the citizen environmental community and the Washington Department of Fish and Wildlife complained that the concessions granted to the company by the DNR to "bring it to the table" rendered the tract "unsuitable for spotted owls for years to come." And as the environmental groups became highly critical of the resulting DNR actions, and the Audubon Society engaged the Washington Forest Law Center to bring court action against the agency, the DNR became publicly hostile to both the society and the center. The case illustrates the complex of interacting pressures involving the logging company, the regulating agency, other agencies "at interest," and the role of citizen groups.[12]

After withdrawing from the forest practice proceedings, the Washington Environmental Council shifted its activities to focus primarily on state trust land administration, with an emphasis on preserving old-growth forests from harvest and improving wildlife habitat as major elements of a sustainable forest program. It gave special attention to the proposal that the state lands in western Washington be reviewed for certification as "well managed" under the program of the Forest Stewardship Council.[13] The reviewing team recommended that certification be approved and that "conditions" be applied prior to certification. These conditions gave a clearer expression to ecological forestry objectives than had yet been advocated seriously for the state lands, including an extension of cutting cycles from 60 to 75–80 years, wildlife and habitat inventories, and the protection of old-growth areas as permanent reserves, all of which required additional field biologists and law enforcement. The certification report gave rise to a serious problem for the DNR, since some degree of public involvement in follow-up action could not be avoided. Hence the department sponsored a series of six meetings throughout the state to determine the appropriate response. It then set out to construct a new "sustainable forest" model for some 40,000 acres of trust land in western Washington, with the rationale that it was "seeking a sustainable blend of trust revenue, healthy ecosystems and other benefits for the people of Washington." One might well predict that the certification process in Washington was heading toward a more complex version of a quiet confrontation between reviewers and the regulatory agency.[14]

Oregon: Salmon and the Tillamook Forest

The evolution of forest practices in Oregon took much the same turn in its earlier years as was the case in Washington. The basic law in 1971 established requirements for the "continuous growing and harvesting of trees and maintenance of forestland." The law arose from concerns by leaders in the forest industry and was administered by a board composed entirely of industry representatives. In response to the evolving environmental climate of the times, demands arose to broaden the public role in state forest affairs, as had been done in Washington. In 1987 the legislature reduced Board of Forestry membership from twelve to seven and required that no more than three of these could hold financial interests in forestry. New rules were developed dealing with riparian protection, including retaining specific numbers and sizes of conifer trees in riparian areas in western Oregon. The 1987 legislation required "site-specific protection for state and federally listed threatened and endangered species; sensitive bird nesting, roosting and watering sites; wetlands, and ecologically and scientifically significant biological sites."

Over the next few years, in the 1990s, the state focused on fish, especially salmon, their decline, and the role in that decline of changing forest watershed cover. Policies to foster the recovery of fish populations came to exercise a highly influential role in forest affairs.[15] The decision of the National Marine Fisheries Service to require changes in the forest practices of Pacific Coast states in order to protect and improve coho salmon habitat faced Oregon with a challenge to modify its own forest practice requirement in order to forestall federally imposed restrictions. This led to initiatives by Governor Kitzhaber and formal action by the legislature to adopt "The Oregon Plan for Salmon and Watersheds." At first this program focused on the coastal areas, but in 1997 it was expanded by executive order of the governor to include water quality, "watershed health," and native salmonids statewide.

The resulting activity was financed in part by funds from the state lottery approved by a popular referendum, Ballot Measure 66, in 1998. The Oregon Watershed Enhancement Board then allocated these funds to projects throughout the state. This program was influenced significantly by the role of an Independent Multidisciplinary Science Team (IMST) established by the legislature in 1997 to advise all sectors of the state government on matters of science related to the Oregon Plan, including relevant forest practices. The IMST was to make specific recommendations to state agencies arising from its scientific reviews, with the requirement that the agencies were to respond in writing to its recommendations and that both recommendations and replies were to be made public.

The provisions of the Oregon Plan brought a broad context to bear on forest practices by relating them to the role of forest watersheds in fish habitat. The context in which disagreements about scientific issues were worked out differed from that in Washington. While in Washington disagreements involved quiet negotiations between industry and agency as to which science was to be preferred, in Oregon they were to be a product of judgment by a multidisciplinary team of scientists, whose recommendations the agencies could not effectively dismiss because they were continually exposed to public view. The broadly interdisciplinary context of the IMST created a perspective much akin to that required by federal environmental impact analysis. Yet by the early twenty-first century, the fruition of this potential remained to be seen.

The extensive interest in salmon in Oregon gave rise to a comprehensive and integrated salmon recovery program within the Department of Forestry. The program combined science, watershed restoration, and financial support activities and shaped much of the department's forest practices around ecological objectives. At the same time, however, the department enjoyed some independence and autonomy in which, left to its own devices, its more traditional commodity-based programs dominated. Some of these pertained to water quality. For example, in Oregon the state's water quality standards for forest practices, which normally would be administered by the state Department of Environmental Quality, were defined in terms of the Department of Forestry's "best management practices." What the Board of Forestry adopted, the Department of Environmental Quality was required to accept as its own. In another instance, the Board of Forestry declined to accept responsibility for administering the federal watershed forest requirements associated with the restoration of endangered species and chose instead to assign that responsibility to the private forest manager.

The clearest case in which the Department of Forestry adhered to commodity forest objectives and rejected ecological forestry came in connection with the evolving forest plan for the Tillamook Forest.[16] This involved the management of a forest tract of 720,000 acres in Tillamook and Clatsop counties, which developed following extensive fires in northwestern Oregon, the first in 1933 covering 250,000 acres, with subsequent smaller fires in the same areas in 1937, 1943, and 1946. Following the fires, the timberland owners abandoned their holdings and ownership reverted to the counties, which experienced a sharp drop in income from property taxes. The counties then approached the state, offering to convey the land to the state in return for the state agreeing to replant the area and manage it. A popular vote approved the arrangement. The result was that the state Forestry Department now was responsible for 720,000 acres of land, quite different in origin and administration from the 120,000 acres of state "school lands" that had been conveyed to the state by the federal Congress on admission of Oregon to the union, and which were under the jurisdiction of the state land board.

Replanting the Tillamook Forest was carried out successfully, and a half century of growth followed, so that by the 1990s the Department of Forestry was prompted to develop a plan for management.[17] Under the provisions of the legislation providing for the transfer to the state, the lands were to be managed for their "greatest permanent value," a sufficiently vague and general overall guidance to open the way for considerable debate over management objectives. In the first stages of planning the department adopted wood production as the primary objective and proceeded to work up a forest plan built around that central goal. The plan also included some collateral environmental objectives, at that time conventional, such as outdoor recreation and the protection of wetlands and endangered species. However, over the same span of years the Tillamook Forest area, located just southwest of Portland, had become a major location of outdoor recreation and, at the same time, of ecological interest, so that an influential body of opinion had evolved that the area was a major environmental and ecological asset in the backyard of the city and other nearby urban areas. At the same time an "environmental economy" had grown in the Tillamook Forest area, giving rise to a large number of small business enterprises oriented to tourism and outdoor recreation.

These two sets of influences, one from the Department of Forestry, well supported by the Oregon wood production establishment, and the other from the environmental organizations and their environmental business community allies, now defined the conflicting directions of plans and policies for the Tillamook Forest. The environmental groups organized the Tillamook Rainforest Coalition and sought to shape the objectives of the department's plan in an ecological direction, but failed. As the draft of the department plan neared completion and was ready for public presentation, the Rainforest Coalition devised its own alternative plan and prepared to take it to a public referendum. The coalition proposal was known as the 50/50 plan, because it provided for a wood production program for half of the tract and an ecological forest program for the other half, based upon the zoning of ecological forest areas that emphasized a range of ecological objectives such as watershed protection, wild flora and fauna resources, and nonmotorized outdoor recreation.[18]

A major point of contention was the department's proposal to organize forest management around what it called a "structure-based" forest plan. This plan was an attempt to establish a set of different-aged stands, each one uniform, in place of the mosaic of integrated ages throughout the forest, which was the mode advanced by ecological forest advocates and which seemed to be the more "natural" pattern of forest evolution. The department argued that older forests were undesirable because they were more susceptible to natural catastrophes like stand-replacement fires and insect infestations; its silviculture management program would avoid those risks. Ecological forestry advocates in Oregon countered this with a report of a Scientific Panel on Ecosystem Based Forestry Management drawn up under the sponsorship of the National Wildlife Federation. Panelists included Reed Noss, a leading conservation biologist, and Professor Jerry Franklin, the most prominent old-growth forest researcher in the Pacific Northwest. The report argued that "structure-based management" was not supported by the research and that old forests were, in fact, more resistant than younger forests to both stand-replacement fires and insects and parasites. Logging, they argued, tended to increase the severity of both fires and pests. The proposals of the Department of Forestry tended to sharpen further the debate over old-growth forests in Oregon, with special reference to the Tillamook Forest.

Protection of watersheds and especially wild salmon played a major role in the coalition proposal. Ecotrust; Oregon Trout, the state branch of Trout Unlimited; and the Wild Salmon Center were leading participants in the coalition.[19] They had been active in compiling scientific research on the role of forest harvest in the decline of wild salmon and the need for forest habitat in stimulating its restoration. These groups had jointly developed a proposal to create salmon "anchor habitat areas" in which productive spawning areas were to be protected, watershed functions restored, old-growth forest characteristics recovered, and landslide risks minimized.[20] They calculated that 17.9 percent of the Tillamook Rainforest contained critical anchor habitat areas, and that because of the detrimental effects of timber harvest and roads on salmon, some 31.4 percent of the state forest land should be protected for salmon fisheries alone. The coalition argued that headwater non-fish streams were as important in restoring salmon habitat as were the fish-bearing streams, that they comprised over half of the 330 miles of stream on the Tillamook and Clatsop state forests, and that the department did not require a desirable review of alternative methods of logging such as cable-yarding across non-fish streams.[21]

The coalition proposal was firmly rooted in a wide range of ecological and economic analyses, which by this time had become well established in ecological science and community economics. The proposal incorporated the ecological work of two prominent conservation biologists, Reed Noss and Allen Cooperrider, who had written an important book, *Saving Nature's Legacy*, using the Oregon Coast Range as a case study.[22] After citing the major disturbances in the history of the area, they concluded that managing around 50 percent of the Coast Range (which included the Tillamook Forest) for conservation, in addition to establishing multiple-use buffer zones, would enable native species to be restored and sustained for the long term.[23]

To this work rooting the Tillamook Rainforest proposal in ecological science, the coalition added an economic analysis under the direction of Thomas Power, chair of the Economics Department at the University of Montana at Missoula.[24] For a number of years Power had spearheaded the argument that forests in the Northwest constituted major regional economic assets when managed as wild and undeveloped ecological areas. Power stressed the multiple roles of such areas in attracting incoming migrants (including older people who brought with them pensions and investments to play an important role in the regional economy), in the tourist and out-door recreation economy, and as attractive settings for "footloose" indus-tries, which prized natural environments for their location. Power brought his analytical experience and skills to bear on the Tillamook Forest to argue that the proposal would be of considerable economic benefit to the region. This added a significant economic context to the ecological context of the Rainforest Coalition's proposal.

By the end of 2003 both the Department of Forestry and the Rainfor-est Coalition were geared for a vigorous confrontation, as the department firmed up its Landmark Plan and the coalition gathered signatures to put its proposal on the ballot as a referendum in the 2004 election. That referen-dum failed, winning only 39 percent of the popular vote. It remained to be seen if the entire episode would have any effect on the plans of the Depart-ment of Forestry.

California: Competing Water and Forest Agencies

California displayed still another variant of the relationship between forests and waters amid a three-part state agency complex including the California Department of Forestry and Fire Protection (CDF), the Department of Fish and Game, and the regional and state water boards. Over the last third of the twentieth century the California environmental community had given considerable attention to the Department of Forestry and its governing body, the Board of Forestry, raising issues about forest practices and the effects of wood production on fish, wildlife and water quality.[25] These issues involved the relative ability of the two non-forest agencies responsible for fish and game and water quality, both independent of the Department of Forestry, to modify timber harvest permits in the light of their own program objectives. The ecological forestry community continually sought to strengthen the hands of the two agencies vis-à-vis the Department of Forestry, which they felt was too committed to wood production.

In 1988 the State Water Board signed an agreement with CDF and the Board of Forestry that assigned those agencies responsibility for assuring that logging operations would not harm fish habitat, water supplies, and other natural uses of rivers and streams. At the same time, the Water Board, noting that there were many deficiencies in the rules of both the CDF and the Forestry Board, made the agreement subject to significant reforms in the near future. Fifteen years later, in 2003, neither CDF nor the Forestry Board had dealt with the issues identified, including analysis of cumulative impacts, provisions for water quality monitoring, and excessive logging in stream buffers, issues that had been debated and highlighted for many years. Hence in the summer of 2002 a coalition of conservation and fishing groups, farmers, and residents from around the state, led by the Environmental Protection Information Center of Garberville in the state's northwest coast and the Sierra Club, petitioned the State Water Resources Control Board to revoke the CDF's sole power to approve logging operations.

By the latter years of the twentieth century these issues had come to the fore, especially around the effect of timber harvest on aquatic habitat for salmon and the conditions imposed by the CDF on harvest permits. The resulting public debate focused on the Headwaters forest, which comprised the watershed of rivers flowing into Humboldt Bay near Eureka and Arcata, and the role of the timber company Sierra Pacific Industries in logging the Headwaters forest watershed.[26] California water quality regulations were administered by regional water boards under the supervision of the State Water Board. These agencies had continually sought to influence harvest permits toward water quality objectives. Two issues especially came to the fore. One involved whether or not the timber companies would be required to monitor streams both before and after harvest in order to determine the effect of the harvest on water quality, a practice that the CDF agreed to require but Sierra Pacific Industries refused to undertake.[27] The other proposal was that water quality would be based on the cumulative effect of harvests throughout the watershed over time rather than one harvest at a time, a policy the department declined to institute.[28] By the early years of the twenty-first century these long-simmering issues had led to considerable support for some new legislative mandates to institute regulations and require that their enforcement be carried out by the water boards rather than the CDF.[29]

California offered a more fertile ground for action about such issues than did Washington. The organization of water quality administration around water boards in California gave a sharp focus to an alternative agency through which those wishing to enhance water quality could exercise leverage. Moreover, while the forest industry had a similar degree of influence in the boards and departments of both states, the industry's influence on the public and in the legislature differed. In Washington the Weyerhaeuser Company, the main private forest firm, had considerable prestige because of its century-long role in the state's economy and its early interest in long-range sustained-yield wood production, a major innovation in the face of the short-term "cut and run" tactics that had long prevailed in the timber industry. But in California the dominant timber industry, Sierra Pacific Industries, was a relative newcomer and was associated not with long-term timber management but the short-term financial manipulations of the Maxxam Company owned by C. J. Hurwitz. Hurwitz had acquired the California forest lands through the issuance of junk bonds and now intended that the debt would be financed by rapid harvest of the redwood timber. In this way the Maxxam Company opposed both the California public's interest in a more conservative approach to forest management and the state's legal requirements for the management of private timberlands. Hence Sierra Pacific Industries was vulnerable to regulatory action in the state legislature.

In October 2003 the California state legislature enacted new legislation requiring that the California Water Board review and approve each timber harvest permit issued by the Department of Forestry for its acceptability in meeting water quality objectives. The legislation also required that applicants for permits provide maps indicating the location of previous harvest areas and future planned ones so that calculations could be made about cumulative effects. Many state forest administrations had problems in sharing authority with fish and wildlife agencies and water quality agencies over approval of timber harvest proposals. In most cases the forest agency held the upper hand, though at times the affected agencies were granted opportunities to review timber harvest decisions made by the forest agency. But this case in California of "sign off" authority granted to the water board was unusual.

Southern Private Forests

During the last third of the twentieth century forest affairs in the South were marked primarily by the steady advance of the private forest industry, with an emphasis on growing trees rapidly for pulp and a plantation-style management program similar to forestry in such places as Central America, Chile, and New Zealand. This involved considerable emphasis on replacing hardwoods with pine, well suited for pulp production, and intensive cultivation through genetically improved seeds, fertilization, and control of competing vegetation through use of herbicides. This style of wood production received considerable support from state forest agencies in the region, but at the same time it aroused increasing concern from both scientists and the public about the impact of massive clear-cutting on water quality and the effect of even-age monocultures on wildlife and wildlife habitat. State governments warded off these challenges with a vigorous defense of this vibrant industry, which constituted an important new element in the region's economy.

The most widespread debate concerned water quality. The southern pulp industry became organized around "chip mills," which carried through the first stage of the manufacture of wood into pulp. These gathered clear-cut-harvested logs from surrounding areas, leading to denuded watersheds and, so the critics argued, to unacceptable soil erosion and water pollution. Amid these criticisms there developed a series of best management practices (BMPs), some drawn up by private organizations and some in the form of legislation, which were intended to modify logging practices to deal effectively with both erosion and its effects on water quality. The resulting controversies were much like those on the Pacific Coast, but in the South, as well as in the eastern United States generally, the development of regulations to control forest practices was in its infancy, in contrast with the West. In the context of these early beginnings of a regulatory forest regime, both ecological forest reformers and the complex of wood production advocates staked out their claims.[30]

The most extensive beginnings of a state program to regulate forest practices pertaining to water quality was in Virginia, where in 1975 some initial best management practices were adopted emphasizing sedimentation control to protect streams, and a state Board of Forestry was set up to administer the law.[31] The statute provided for enforcement that was limited and ineffective. The leader of each harvesting project was required to notify the State Forest Agency about the project within at least three days after it began, an action that supposedly enabled the agency to inspect to see that the logging project met the sedimentation requirements. Virginia Forest Watch, a coalition of twenty different citizen groups in the state, convinced that the program was ineffective, took up the task of monitoring harvests to determine if the projects met the requirements. It found that most of them did not.[32] It reported that, according to its investigations, no notification was provided in more than half the cases. Publicity about the data gathered by Forest Watch generated sufficient media attention to provide some momentum for a change in the law to establish a fine for lack of notification. This, it was later argued, brought most operators into the regulatory system.

In 2002, all nine members of the Virginia Board of Forestry were closely associated with the forest industry. Forest Watch singled out two members as owners of timber companies that had failed to comply with the law, although they had been certified under the Sustainable Forest Initiative of the American Forest and Paper Association, which required compliance with all applicable state forest laws. While this exposure momentarily enlivened the debate over forest practices, the proposal of Forest Watch that these two individuals be dropped from the board was ignored, and there was no change in board representation to make it reflect broader public interest in the state's forests.

The chip mill problem in Virginia greatly broadened the issue of the state's forest practice program and at least briefly led to more extended debate. The chip mill industry obtained visibility beyond ecological forestry because of its potential adverse effect on the state's more traditional wood products industry, which used lumber to manufacture furniture and building material. Now pulp and paper manufacturing was becoming more influential, and a divergence in objectives was emerging between the larger industrial wood pulp firms and the smaller Virginia lumber operator. Which was preferable for the forest economy of the state? The legislature established a commission to investigate this problem; four out of the ten appointees to the commission were friendly to the forest reform groups. While the commission's report concluded that the chip mill industry presented no substantial threat to the state's forest economy, the four issued a minority report that gave rise to short-term media attention to ecological forest objectives.

This visibility was greatly enhanced by the role in these affairs of Rupert Cutler, a professional forester who had been associated with environmental organizations and was assistant secretary of agriculture during the Carter administration. Cutler had lived for a while in Virginia, had become involved in several land trust projects, and served as an advisor to Virginia Forest Watch. He was appointed to the chip mill commission, and because of his media visibility he was asked to speak to the Virginia branch of the Society of American Foresters. In his speech, Cutler proposed extensive reforms in the supervision and regulation of Virginia forests, almost all of which the Virginia SAF voted to disapprove. The entire episode led to no substantive results for forest reform, and it displayed in dramatic fashion the political strength of the wood production industry in resisting ecological forest objectives.

Proposals to establish state supervision over best management practices arose in a number of southern states; West Virginia, Tennessee, and Missouri were the main cases.[33] In West Virginia the debate concerned a law that was weakly administered; in Tennessee and Missouri it involved rejection of proposals to establish regulation in the first place. In most cases public regulation was rejected.

The issue took another turn when an investigating committee representing federal and state agencies, the Southern Forest Resource Assessment, concluded that "States report generally high rates of implementation" of BMPs.[34] Studies of North Carolina and Missouri, however, both sponsored by the assessment project, raised doubts about the availability of data on which to base sound conclusions about cumulative effects, that is, the accumulated consequences of many harvests on a given watershed.[35] The entire problem became even more confused when the federal EPA included forest harvests as an important element in nonpoint source water pollution, while the assessment reported that "State water pollution laws are the backdrop for regulation, but silviculture is exempt from the permit requirements of those laws in every state studied."[36]

The effect of "industrial forestry" on watersheds and water quality was the most important ecological forestry issue in the South. Its wider effect on habitat and biodiversity was hardly mentioned. The early conversion of hardwoods to pine in the South was one of the important reasons for the appearance of the diversity clause in the 1976 National Forest Management Act. As time went on, however, the interest in species diversity or biodiversity grew as these issues became pervasive in national forest administration. Little of this, however, spilled over into the management of private forests until attempts were made to carry out the mandates of the Endangered Species Act, which applied to private as well as public forests, and some actions in the South were taken with respect to habitat for signature species such as the red-cockaded woodpecker.

The Southern Forest Resource Assessment had, for the most part, ignored the changing values on the part of southerners, which were frequently described in surveys of public attitudes toward forest management.[37] In dis-

cussing sustainability of forests, the report emphasized almost exclusively
sustained-yield wood production with little attention to ecological sustainability. Its discussion of biological factors was limited to the traditional
"forest health" topics of plant diseases, exotic plants, and exotic pests, not
of ecological conditions. In emphasizing the commitments of the region's
industries to "good forestry," the assessment noted industry participation in
the Sustainable Forest Initiative sponsored by the American Forest and Paper
Association and did not mention the more ecologically preferable certification program of the Forest Stewardship Council. While the assessment was
quite positive about the future of intensive pine monoculture in the South, it
ignored the ecological alternative: mixed-age and mixed-species forest with
a richer and more complex association of plants and animals amid selec-
tively harvested trees. And while some of the technical reports on which the
assessment drew seemed to provide some opening for a larger perspective,
the report itself seemed to close firmly that open door.[38]

The New England Context: The Focus on Maine

The forests of Maine gave rise to a long-standing debate over forest practices.
Most of Maine's forests were privately owned and for years had been dominated by large industrial companies that produced pulp for making paper.
At the same time, two-thirds of the central and northern parts of the state
were still "unorganized territories" (that is, not organized into counties),
which came under the direct jurisdiction of the state and specifically of its
Land Use Regulation Commission. In the last third of the twentieth century,
ecological forest advocates were increasingly active in the state, serving as
vocal critics of the industry on a variety of issues, including clear-cutting,
the use of pesticides and herbicides, water quality, and wildlife. This led to
a series of legislative proposals and public referenda in which public support
for many facets of ecological forestry was expressed but a comprehensive
and firmly based forest practice regulatory system was not instituted.[39]

The Maine Forest Practices Act (MFPA) was adopted in 1989 and implemented in 1991. It grew out of public objection to some very large clear-cuts
of 2,500 acres and more following a spruce budworm outbreak in the 1980s.
The initial rules established limitations on the size of clear-cuts, established
"separation zones" of various sizes, time limits on regeneration, and reporting requirements that varied according to the sizes of the cuts. While the
immediate public concern to which these requirements responded was the
visual impact of clear-cuts, a variety of other ecological objectives, such as
wildlife habitat and water quality, were close behind. As a result the MFPA

gave rise to a wider public debate, which led to a proposal to the legislature that it submit an "Act to Preserve Productive Forests" for approval by the voters. This would have banned clear-cutting in the unorganized territories and established standards as to the amount of wood that could be cut over a ten-year period on other forest lands. The legislature turned the proposed referendum into a study to determine the effects of the existing MFPA and evaluate how well it was working.

Because the 1994 referendum proposal had not brought about a change in policy, a new citizen-sponsored referendum was proposed in 1996 to carry out objectives similar to the 1994 proposal. This aroused serious objections from the industry and, in response, a governor-appointed panel consisting of both major landowners and some environmental groups drew up a competing measure, "A Compact for Maine's Forests," which would toughen current standards but not abolish clear-cutting. In the 1996 election the compact received 47 percent of the vote, the referendum 30 percent, and 23 percent of the voters chose neither. The compact, without the referendum, was submitted again in 1997 and still received only 47 percent of the vote, missing the necessary majority. The vote was split along north-south geographic lines, and the widespread concern over clear-cutting and overcutting was interpreted by the Maine Forest Service to express a desire "to ensure the long term health of forest ecosystems and to provide sustainable ecological and economic benefits." This concern did not go away, and in the year 2000 "An Act Regarding Forest Practices" was proposed, which would require a permit for all clear-cuts and defined cutting levels for lands subject to the tree growth tax law; but it, too, failed to pass.

Vigorous debate continued over a wide range of contending forest policy proposals, and though none seemed to reach a majority, a few were able to get a "foot in the door" as serious developments. One was an industry proposal called "Outcome Based Forestry," which would provide exemptions from the Forest Practices Act for those tracts that enrolled in the program and met performance standards and periodic performance audits, neither of which were specified in the proposal. The proposal was accompanied by a cloud of suspicion because one of its major advocates argued that stream buffers of no more than twenty-five feet were needed and frequently none at all were required. Another was the issue of "liquidation forestry," the practice of woodlands being sold and then cleared of timber in order to pave the way for permanent development. There seemed to be widespread agreement that liquidation should be stopped, but the major debate was over how this could be accomplished. Another issue debated was certification. The programs of both the Forest Stewardship Council and the Sustainable Forest Initiative of the American Forest and Paper Association had active proponents in the state; the Maine Natural Resources Council was the major advocate of the first and the industry of the second. In an attempt to resolve the problem the governor embraced both systems.

Amid these contending approaches to the future management of Maine's private forest lands, the most vigorous actions came from large funding sources such as the Nature Conservancy and the federally sponsored Forest Legacy Program, which provided for conservation easements to ensure permanent prohibition of development and allocation of land to wood production. Some areas of more ecological significance were also acquired by the state to be managed as ecological reserves. These were usually thought of as core areas surrounded by active wood production areas, much in the order of the customary core-buffer strategy of ecological land management. But since management of the core and the buffer were usually in different hands, they were not integrated. Thus, in the West Branch case a "reserve" area was managed by the state and the conservation easements on the surrounding lands were supervised by a completely different body, the Forest Society of Maine, a wood production organization.

An exception to this general practice, fostered by the Nature Conservancy, stood out. In the Katahdin Forest Project the Conservancy purchased 41,000 acres in the Debsconeag Lakes region, adjacent to Baxter State Park, which it proposed to manage as a firmly protected nature reserve. At the same time it acquired a conservation easement on 200,000 additional acres surrounding the Debsconeag reserve, ownership of which was retained by the Great Northern Paper Company. Thus the Conservancy was able to coordinate in one management scheme both reserve and easement so as to protect the reserve and enforce effective implementation of the easement. This arrangement constituted a significant practical experiment in core-buffer ecological forest management, made possible because the Conservancy both owned the reserve and supervised the easement within a general policy of ecological forest management.[40]

Biodiversity and Habitat in the Lake States

The states of the upper Great Lakes—Michigan, Wisconsin, and Minnesota—displayed their own distinctive context for charting the incorporation of ecological forestry into the management of the region's public and private forests.[41] This area was blanketed by a thick and extensive cover of white pine forests at the point of European settlement, which came under intense deforestation as Lake States forests were harvested rapidly to feed the nineteenth-century development of the urban Midwest. This forest was eventually replaced with a second growth of aspen and other relatively short-lived early successional trees that provided the raw material for the pulp and paper industry. It also provided early successional habitat for browsing animals such as deer, grouse, and turkey. The combination of industry and game hunters resisted serious attention to a broader range of wild resources and measures to create a habitat of mixed-aged, old growth, wetlands, and riparian areas that was the hallmark of ecological forestry.

Michigan

Michigan contained some 2.5 million of acres of state-owned forest land, a result of tax reversions of abandoned cut-over pine land to the state in the early part of the twentieth century. The timber industry was highly influential in the management of these lands and enjoyed a legislative mandate that the state conduct a minimum level of 63,000 acres of timber harvest each year.[42] At the same time the game hunters enjoyed a position of great influence in state forest affairs, where management was dominated by preference for short-lived trees that guaranteed a maximum amount of early successional habitat for deer, turkey, and browse game animals. Ecological advocates, on the other hand, sought to restore some of the earlier white pine forests as part of an old-growth initiative.

In the late twentieth century this drama took the form of proposals to allocate state forest lands to old growth. In the 1980s a new forest planner for the Michigan Bureau of Forestry sought to carve out a modest amount of old-growth forest on the state lands, a proposal that met the opposition of both the industry and the state's hunting advocates.[43] Decision on a formal proposal was continually postponed. It had not achieved results even by 2005 and only seemed to arouse extravagant fears about the eventual complete loss of early successional habitat. A proposal by the Huron-Manistee National Forest, the one national forest in the lower peninsula, to allocate 20 percent of its lands to old growth met equal resistance.[44] The combination of these two old-growth proposals seemed only to stimulate opposition from game advocates, and the entire process became stalemated.

Ecological forestry advocates took up a different line of action emphasizing a wider range of wildlife than game by challenging the U.S. Fish and Wildlife policies of distributing monies from the national Pittman-Robertson fund, derived from a tax on firearms, without providing an accompanying environmental impact analysis (EIS).[45] Distribution of federal grant-in-aid funds, the argument went, should undergo an EIS analysis to determine environmental consequences, but the Fish and Wildlife Service (FWS) had not done so. After some years of negotiating the issue unsuccessfully with the FWS, the Michigan chapter of the Sierra Club brought a lawsuit to require an EIS. The court rejected the Sierra Club's claims for past violations, but ruled that in the future both the Department of Natural Resources and the FWS must provide project environmental reviews annually. Game advocates widely described this lawsuit as an attack on hunting, while the state Department of Natural Resources recognized the significance of the ruling for future federal grants; to avoid the problem, it reorganized its funding to finance the activities in question with state funds.

Minnesota

The setting for the interplay between ecological and commodity forestry in Minnesota was somewhat different than in Michigan. For in Minnesota, while some tax-reverted lands had wound up in state forests, distinctive historical circumstances had resulted in almost twice as much acreage being owned by the counties. Third in size was forest land in private non-industry ownership and fourth was industry land. The 1970s and 1980s brought to the management of this mix of ownerships the usual cluster of environmental and ecological objectives, and the usual defense by advocates of commodity objectives. This led to the decision by the Department of Natural Resources (DNR) to commission a massive study of wood production potential on the state's forests, which in 1994 produced a "Generic Environmental Impact Statement on Timber Harvesting and Forest Management in Minnesota" (GEIS).[46] The GEIS concentrated primarily on the analysis of an expanding wood production industry in the state; gave almost no attention to such current ecological issues as clear-cutting, even-age management, or fragmentation; and outlined only briefly the adverse effect on forest biodiversity that accompanied those disturbances.

The Sierra Club sought to emphasize the consequences of the amount of harvest predicted and its ecological effects by an extensive analysis of forests in the fourteen northern counties through aerial photographs.[47] This analysis identified cutting that had occurred recently and emphasized that the most extensive was on lands under private nonindustrial, industrial, and county ownership, with less cutting on state and federal holdings. The study warned that the rapid growth of aspen harvest was leading to a short-lived monoculture in the relatively near future and noted the extensive degree of fragmentation that seemed to be quite acceptable to the wood production powers that be. The report focused sharply on the GEIS prediction that at an annual harvest of 5 million cords, "Half of the forest-dependent bird species studied (69 species) would be harmed including hawks, owls, woodpeckers and warblers. A large conversion from conifers to aspen would occur, resulting in decreased biodiversity and negative impacts for conifer-dependent wildlife species." Few of these ecological concerns were emphasized in policy and management actions to which it gave rise.

In 1995 the Minnesota legislature passed the Sustainable Forest Resources Act, which created the Minnesota Forest Resource Council to implement the provisions of the act. The most important were the "Timber Harvesting and Forest Management Guidelines," which the Forest Resource Council developed and finalized in December 1998. The council was composed of some twenty individuals, almost all of whom were drawn from industry-related groups; there was one representative of "environmental interests" and one specialist in "game species management." The resulting forest practice provisions were overwhelmingly dominated by commodity objectives. They established "timber harvesting and forest management guidelines" that were purely voluntary, gave only minimal recognition to forest ecological objectives or policies, and established an "oversight" scheme in the form of periodic monitoring that was equally dominated by commodity objectives.[48]

Amid this larger commodity focus of the GEIS, the Department of Natural Resources undertook a pioneering thrust toward an old-growth program under the guidance of Kurt Rusterholz.[49] This policy was shaped to establish and maintain old growth in each of the state's forest regions. In order to facilitate the project maps were prepared of the state's ecoregions as of the time of the first white settlement and the initial U.S. land surveys. These then were printed in conjunction with maps of current land use so that the two could be compared, and the maps were made available to the public. An old-growth policy was adopted in June 1994 after two years of round-tables that led to publication of a DNR Old-Growth Forests Guideline and a program to identify and protect old-growth "candidate stands," pending the final selections, which were completed and announced in 2003.

The forest industry in Minnesota accepted this old-growth program, but apparently made clear the limits of its support. When the state Department of Natural Resources embarked on the old-growth policy in 1994 and finalized it in 2003, Wayne Brandt, executive vice president of the Minnesota Timber Producers, affirmed the support of his group for the old-growth protection plan and objected primarily to the "long delay" in forming it. But Keith Wendt, a DNR planner who headed the Old-Growth Forest Committee, affirmed that the industry support was limited, observed that the 40,000 acres in the plan fell short of the 56,000 acres recommended in 1994, and noted that this smaller amount was "about what we could do considering the controversial nature of old growth."

Wisconsin

While in Michigan tax delinquent lands reverted to state ownership, in Wisconsin they ended up in county ownership, giving rise to twenty-nine county forests with a total of 2,341,789 acres, the largest bloc of forest land in the state.[50] Forests owned by the state, arising from the same economic circumstance, the failure of marginal cut-over pine lands to produce a viable farm income, were acquired primarily in the 1930s largely through federal funds; they were managed by the state Division of Forestry in the Department of Natural Resources. Finally there were privately owned forest lands that were subject to programs established by the state legislature. Above and beyond these formal programs, the Division of Forestry exercised a general leadership in the state's forest affairs by assessing public views, establishing desirable but voluntary guidelines for forest practices, and developing plans that had, for the most part, only voluntary implications. This varied mix of forest lands and programs provided a number of opportunities for the inclusion of ecological forest objectives and management programs such as resource inventories, protective and restorative activities, and monitoring, but these opportunities were not realized.

The county forests had considerable leeway to formulate their own objectives under the guidance of a statewide county forest law, which carried considerable weight because of state financial support and restrictions that land could not be withdrawn from the forests and returned to the tax rolls. This resulted in considerable attention to outdoor recreation, but very limited attention to ecological objectives. The collective interests of the county forests were represented by the Wisconsin County Forests Association. One of its objectives was to exclude some environmental clauses written into the county forest law at its last revision in 1998, but the association was reluctant to push too hard for this for fear of jeopardizing its financial support from the state. The 1998 environmental clauses were supported by the environmental community, and their adoption was interpreted as a result of the industry decision not to fight them. The private nature of these proceedings tended to obscure both support and opposition for the role of ecological objectives in the Wisconsin county forest program.

An extensive private forest program in Wisconsin, the "managed forest program," has a history dating from the 1920s. As was the case in many eastern states, forest landowners, faced with property taxes based on assessed land valuation, frequently harvested timber before it was mature in order to pay their taxes.[51] As a result, programs arose to reduce or forgo property taxes on forest land with the stipulation that an ad valorem tax be imposed at harvest. Landowners had to agree to foster tree reproduction and growth by fencing the land and keeping out grazing animals such as cattle, and, in Wisconsin, to harvest their timber only under permit and the guidance of a professional forester. By the early twentieth century this Wisconsin program encompassed 25,000 landowners and 2.5 million acres of land. The latest version of the Managed Forest Law stated that forestry under the law "means managing forest lands and their related resources, including trees and other plants, animals, soil, water and air," but it is not apparent that these ecological objectives have been applied.

Ecological Initiatives in the States

The resistance of state forest agencies to ecological forestry provided opportunities for new institutions to develop that were far more receptive to ecological objectives. While the scope of these land management initiatives went beyond forests, forests were often included, and forest administrations could not remain oblivious to them. They acted as gadflies, continually challenging conventional forest leaders to justify their policies and programs in terms of ecological acceptability. They also served as a firm base from which ecological initiatives could influence land management in the state.

Natural Areas

The earliest of these activities were the state natural area programs that came into being around 1970, arising first in the midwestern states of Illinois, Indiana, and Ohio.[52] These budding programs focused on the protective management of areas of unique geological, biological, and landscape features. In search for an administrative home for these new ventures, their advocates proposed that natural area management be brought under the jurisdiction of state forest agencies. The response was negative. As a result the Nature Conservancy negotiated with a number of states to establish separate state natural area management agencies, each with its own sources of funding and its own professional personnel. The starting points for these programs were surveys of natural features—plants, animals, wetlands, and streams—that gained distinction in contrast with the more highly urbanized and developed landscapes around them. Frequently surveys arose out of earlier inventories of such areas conducted by academic professionals, which after a few years had acquired a public constituency of citizen naturalist groups. While some became organized into privately supported and managed institutions, the public programs involved more areas, far more funding, and greater accumulations of professional and managerial skills. By the twenty-first century, natural area programs had become integral parts of state government.

The natural area programs throughout the nation have not yet received their historian, and it would be impossible to describe many of them here, but one of the oldest, in Wisconsin, serves as an example of the direction of their evolution.[53] In 1938 a group of scientists at the University of Wisconsin, one of whom was Aldo Leopold, first urged communities in the state to "conserve wild flowers as a natural resource." In 1945 the Wisconsin Conservation Commission, responding to a motion by Commissioner Aldo Leopold, established a Natural Areas Committee to acquire natural areas of distinctive value. In 1951 the legislature gave the program a new twist by establishing a State Board for the Preservation of Scientific Areas. In 1956 the legislature authorized a budget for program management, and in 1969 a pilot program was established to inventory natural areas by county. This first round of inventory was completed in 1983 under a periodic reinventory program at ten-year intervals. Discovering that areas already designated were being lost to development, the program acquired federal funds for land acquisition. In 1985 a Natural Heritage Inventory program was established under the Natural Heritage Act within the DNR's Bureau of Endangered Resources, and a stronger permanent program was established through legal dedication. By the 1990s the program broadened from saving relatively small areas to assessing large landscapes. This focus on larger ecological processes facilitated emphasis on restoring degraded areas located between protected ones and establishing connecting corridors between them. By 2002 this continually evolving program had led to the creation of 333 areas, now called State Natural Areas, and to increasing attention to protective management.

An even more intriguing focus for ecological land management, with a more recent history, was the Chicago Wilderness program.[54] This was promoted by a network of 172 landholding organizations in the Chicago area that managed 200,000 acres of land and cooperatively worked on natural lands management, much in the spirit of natural area programs generally. The goal was "to study and restore, protect and manage the precious natural ecosystems of the Chicago region for the benefit of the public." The organization's quarterly publication, Chicago Wilderness, was established in 1998 and a Web site was begun on the Internet. The organization fosters a wide range of standard ecological management strategies including inventory, protection, restoration such as fire ecology, and monitoring. It also fosters an extensive nature education program that includes field experiences, as is customary with such organizations, as well as the history of the region's natural environment. Since land protection activities of the many organizations in the group have their own histories, the organization serves to emphasize their broader regional significance.

State Parks

The popularity of natural areas affected the already existing state park programs.[55] State parks had "taken off" in the 1920s. They were assisted by the Civilian Conservation Corps program of the New Deal and continued to grow after World War II. For many years they were heavily oriented toward outdoor recreation in a natural setting, with limited emphasis on the natural world itself. Some, with Kentucky as the most notable example, developed resort-type accommodations under the pressure from the legislature to become self-supporting. But most tended to respond to the interest in outdoor recreation and evolved into complex recreation programs. By 1998 the fifty state park systems were managing 7,899,808 acres that were classified as parkland, 1,452,811 as recreation areas (such as reservoirs for boating, fishing, and swimming), and 1,235,312 acres classified as natural areas.

This last category of parkland had evolved slowly over the years. For a while it was not even identified as a separate category of parkland, but in the mid-1990s it appeared in the annual compilation of park statistics as a separate item, and one began to hear park agencies report more frequently about their natural area activities as a distinctive program. In 1998 the 1,235,312 acres of natural areas represented 9.78 percent of total acreage managed by state park agencies, compared with 11.50 percent managed as recreation acres and 61.55 percent as park acres. The natural area acreage had grown 71 percent since 1990, when it stood at 803,133 acres, but still was confined to only thirty-one of the fifty state park programs. By the 1990s the category had received a distinctive definition: "Areas where a clear emphasis is placed on protection; management and interpretation of natural resources or features might include wilderness areas, nature preserves, natural landmarks, sanctuaries, etc." These statistics should be qualified, however, by the fact that three of the largest state parks of the country are not included, Baxter State Park in Maine, the Adirondack Park in New York, and Custer State Park in North Dakota, because they are managed not by state park departments but by separate agencies.

These programs administered a range of natural areas: wetlands, pine barrens, nongame fish/wildlife/bird habitats, ecological reserves, natural rivers, areas of distinctive biological diversity, habitats for indicator species and keystone species, habitats for rare and endangered species, as well as the more traditional category of unique geological features. They also involved a variety of administrative arrangements and cooperative relationships between public and private agencies. These ranged from Pennsylvania, where the Bureau of Parks, like the Bureau of Forestry, confined its designations to its own holdings and did not attempt to acquire additional acres, to Colorado, where a "Natural Areas Initiative" worked solely to identify areas that private owners sought to designate as protected natural areas, and where by 1998 the acreage in these reached almost as much as the areas owned and managed by the park agency.

These distinctive units of the state park systems display a somewhat mixed role in the overall picture of the impact of ecological land management in the modern United States. Rather than to identify them as fully committed to those objectives one could best describe them as "maturing" and currently only in the adolescent stage. They exist in only thirty-one of the fifty states and are in agencies that are still dominated by an outdoor recreation ethos, which overshadows the biodiversity initiatives in ecological land management. They do not yet appear to have taken on as full a commitment to ecological objectives—ecological terms and concepts appear rarely in their literature—as is the case with the more formal natural area programs described previously. And while they conduct nature education and protection activities, they do not display a resource-oriented approach in which the maintenance and enhancement of natural conditions and processes is their major objective.

Land Conservancies

In the last quarter of the twentieth century natural area programs became overshadowed by "sister" institutions in the form of the privately organized land conservancy.[56] These also were inspired by professional biologists and the Nature Conservancy but took the form of privately organized institutions to save more natural lands from development. They became a major source of ecological land management. The number of these organizations grew rapidly in the last twenty years of the century and by the early twenty-first century had reached over fifteen hundred in number, with land holdings under their ownership and control of well over five million acres. They devised a number of different techniques to acquire land that could be divorced from the pressures of the private land market and popularized "less than fee" holdings of conservation easements. Land conservancies, known popularly as "land trusts," emerged in the Northeast in the 1970s and expanded to the Pacific Coast States, the Midwest, and even to the states in between. In 1984 they began to come together in the Land Trust Alliance to help with initial organization and continued management.[57]

The ecological management objectives of these conservancies were far more extensive than the natural area programs and were often expressed through the term "open space," since one of their main objectives was to provide more natural and open uses of land in contrast with the developments that were springing up around cities. These conservancies expressed a variety of land use objectives, reflecting the range of objectives in the ecological impulses throughout the nation. In the following list the Land Trust Alliance tabulated the varied types of land and land uses that they encompassed with the percentage of the organizations that featured each use.

Wetlands 52%

River corridors 51%

Watersheds/water quality 47%

Farm/ranch land 46%

Nature preserves 45%

Open space 43%

Habitat of rare or endangered species 42%

Scenic views/scenic roads 34%

Trails 27%

Historic/cultural sites 24%

Cultural resources 18%

Urban open space 10%

While many organizations acquired older tracts of woodland, they did not include wood production among their objectives, but spoke of preserving woodlands rather than harvesting them. They were far more closely associated with those state parks that managed woodlands without wood harvest than with the forest management agencies.

Spreading Ecological Land Objectives in the States

The activities of the state natural area programs and the land conservancies, both of which had a strong state-based perspective and a state-oriented role in ecological affairs, served as a focal point for ecological land objectives that forest agencies had abdicated. A wide range of ecological land practices were sustained and strengthened in the natural area and land trust organizations, and these served as a continual source of alternative ideas, skills, and strategies that the forest agencies could not ignore. In some states, such as Pennsylvania, the forest agencies had limited the range of influence of these programs by confining them to state-owned lands, but in others, especially in the Midwest, they became more active contributors to the larger ecological land management environment within which state forest agencies had to work. These inroads can be traced in the development of nature interpretive programs, the broader focus of the Forest Legacy Program in some states, and the gradual development of biodiversity zoning in state forest lands.

Much of the significance of the emerging role of natural areas and land trusts arose from the relationships that they established with the general public. The protected areas organizations developed an interested clientele by sponsoring public involvement in their nature-oriented activities, such as museum displays in their nature centers, nature-oriented products sold there, and field trips through their protected lands. The forest agencies at times carried out similar activities, but these were more frequently oriented toward educating the public about timber-harvesting objectives, while the ecological organizations were more focused on nature appreciation. The ecology groups were more successful in maintaining ties with people of many generations and combining on-site informal education with nature appreciation.

The older and more established forest and game agencies developed a distinctive set of educational activities built around the development of formal educational materials. Agencies and organizations created educational materials that carried different messages. For the Forest Service, the preference was "Project Learning Tree," which carried a wood production message and was sponsored by the wood products industry.[58] The game and wildlife agencies sponsored "Project Wild," which included much more of a wildlife focus but which tended to concentrate on vertebrate animals with less emphasis on plant and invertebrate biodiversity, much in the spirit of their agency objectives.[59] Still a third environmental education program targeted at school teachers was the Aldo Leopold Project, headquartered at the Leopold farm in Wisconsin and promoted and financed by the hunting organization, Pheasants Forever. It focused less on specific land management issues and more on the promotion of a general "land ethic" much in the style of Leopold's own writing.[60]

Another program had a more distinctive ecological context. Produced by the Forest Service Employees for Environmental Ethics (FSEEE), it was composed of several educational units dealing with biodiversity, soils, wood decomposition, and organisms associated with soil building.[61] These aspects of ecological land circumstance were generally absent from either of the two more well-known curricula. Another curricular program titled "Eastern Forests and Biodiversity" drawn up in more informal learning segments, was distributed by the Biodiversity Project of Madison, Wisconsin.[62] And still a third was a curriculum authored by Fred Powledge, which grew out of the International Biodiversity Observation Year of 2002 but as of this writing was not yet published. This curriculum was rooted far more in plant ecology than the two more popular ones fostered by the resource agencies.[63]

These curricular materials fostered quite different connections with their "learning clientele." Project Learning Tree and Project Wild were directed specifically to school teachers, and their materials were available only to teachers who attended their varied conferences. The FSEEE materials, on the other hand, were freely available on the Internet. The nature centers and the land conservancies were oriented less toward a formal curriculum and more toward hands-on, on-site, informal education in which the direct experience in the field or with a field ecologist was the preferred method of contact with family visitors. While the agency curricula focused on formal classroom education, the nature centers and conservancies worked to create continuing ties between the public and the centers in the form of ongoing, periodic visits; memberships; and nature-oriented product sales.

The close ties between the public and the nature centers and conservancies played a major role in the continuing popularity of public strategies to raise money for nongame wildlife generally, and natural land purchases specifically. Fundraising became popular beginning in the 1980s in such forms as sale of license plates with a natural image for a higher than normal price to support nongame wildlife activities, but even more extensively in the public referenda that began to take off in the early 1990s. In each election during the 1990s and in the early twenty-first century some sixty to seventy referenda for such purchases received strong support; while the earliest ones emphasized funds for state programs, increasingly during the 1990s they were focused on county and local open space purchases. These publicly supported land acquisitions completely bypassed the federal and state forest agencies; the purchase of forest land for wood production was not among the purposes of the referenda. The forest agencies were preoccupied less with attempting to follow the changing public interest in wildlands, biodiversity, and wildlife, and more with trying to persuade the public about the value of their activities related to wood production.

The federally funded Forest Legacy Program carried with it the potential of land protection measures that were far broader than were the more widely known measures in northern New England. While the program was a part of the State and Private Forestry department of the U.S. Forest Service, funding for Legacy-sponsored conservation easements was determined by state committees, and these varied state by state in their composition and, therefore, in their ideas as to what land use objectives should be protected.

Some Legacy projects, for example in Wisconsin, protected large commercially based forest lands, while others protected smaller conservancy lands with broader ecological, open-space, and heritage purposes. Other projects included a wide range of objectives such as protection of riparian environments, scenic vistas, recreational opportunities, and non-game as well as game wildlife, from which the applicant could specify permissible uses of the land under easements financed by federal funding. It remains to be seen, however, how much of this potential will be realized by this as-yet young federal program.[64]

Biodiversity zoning was a third window of opportunity for the entry of ecological objectives into state forest management. The natural area and land conservancy programs only directly influenced their specific properties, whether state natural areas or conservancy lands. But as awareness grew that a wide complement of plant and animals species were crucial ingredients of nature management and as action focused on their inventories, it became obvious that the forest agencies could not remain free from public interest in biodiversity. Soon action emerged to go beyond inventories to the protection of significant clusters of plants and animals whose populations were not entirely viable.

An approach quite like the traditional form of forest zoning began to appear to identify areas of concentrated biota distinctiveness. These were called "hot spots" or "important areas," as in "important bird areas" or "important mammal areas." Together they gave rise to an increasing recognition that species protection required action beyond the protection of nesting sites, foraging areas, or den trees for individual species but called for the protection of specific areas of distinctive clusters of species populations.

The first approach for this type of "species zoning" was gap analysis, pioneered by botanist Michael Scott. Based on his research on Hawaiian species, the program was organized into a state-by-state project.[65] Gap analysis arose from the belief that species protection, which was associated in the 1970s with "threatened and endangered" species, should be extended to species that were not in such dire straits, but that could become so if not provided special protection. Under the slogan of "Keeping Common Species Common" the project aimed to "assess to what extent native animal and plant species are being protected by identifying those species and plant communities that are not represented by existing conservation lands." These lands were the "gaps" in protection programs that the project identified.

One of the most well developed of similar approaches were the "Conservation Opportunity Areas" that were worked out for Oregon's ten ecological regions through a joint project of the Defenders of Wildlife, the Nature Conservancy, and the Oregon Natural Heritage Program, which was instituted in 1994. "The strategy," the project reported, "is designed to protect native flora and fauna and thus reduce the risk of future endangered species designation." The "opportunity areas," around 18 percent of the state's land, included federal lands and hence involved federal agency management, as well as private lands, which "are not well represented in the existing conservation network." The report, therefore, called for conservation incentives for private landowners as well as public management. In the year 2001 the Oregon legislature passed HB 3564, a bill that expanded existing conservation incentive programs for private landowners. But the report also called for additional protective action for "opportunity areas" on state and federal public lands.[66]

These projects sought to identify areas that would be singled out for special attention through a zoning process, much as recreational and wilderness areas had been given attention as special management areas on the national and state forests. While they identified clusters of species and their habitat requirements, several attempts emerged to provide the same kind of special protection for particular groups of plants and animals. In the early twenty-first century the National Audubon Society promoted the identification of Important Bird Areas for protective ecological management. The first of these was in Pennsylvania, where a technical committee identified seventy-three Important Bird Areas in the state, comprising one million areas of public and private lands.[67] The range of areas included in the selection reflected the degree to which the concept of "habitat" had gone far beyond the more limited traditional focus on nesting areas. It included "migrating staging areas, winter feeding and roosting areas, prime breeding areas for songbirds, wildland birds and other species" as well as "critical habitat such as spruce-fir bogs, tidal salt marshes, bottomwood hardwoods, swamps and open grasslands."

These ventures at identifying crucial habitats for clusters of species carried significant implications for land managers, for to allocate lands to habitat required that land management for traditional extractive purposes would have to be adjusted to the requirements of species habitat. Most of the attempts to allocate habitat lands for clusters of species were not specific to any particular category of land ownership. But they were especially significant for state land and presented a special challenge to state forest agencies, which managed a considerable portion of state public lands. In this way, the issues that the state forest agencies had earlier tried to distance themselves from now came full circle, as the agencies were under increasing pressure to pay closer attention to their biodiversity resources and develop management programs for them.[68]

This review of responses to ecological forestry makes clear that not only were innovations in forest policy widely expressed from region to region, but that resistance to them was also. While some episodes of resistance were described in the media and became subjects of public debate, many occurred in the less visible and quieter realms of state administrative decision making. Because this drama was often unrecorded, much of it is beyond the reach of those who seek to understand it more fully. During the twentieth century, resource issues increasingly became matters of behind-the-scenes administrative politics—not just how legislative decisions were implemented but even more how policy choices of the greatest consequence were made by the administrative agencies themselves.

In the next chapter, devoted entirely to the state of Pennsylvania, I focus more extensively on administrative politics in order to understand more precisely the resistance to ecological forestry on the part of those involved in commodity forest institutions. I approach this as a case in which a series of opportunities arose in the form of ecological forest initiatives that the state's forest establishment could have taken up but, instead, rejected in favor of continuing their traditional preoccupation with commodity forestry as the "dominant use" to which they devoted their time and energy. Much of this interplay was carried out in the quieter realms of administrative choices in a variety of venues in which I took part over a period of thirty years, participating in many discussions and collecting documents about matters that remained out of sight of the public media and removed from public debate.

 CHAPTER 5

The Pennsylvania Story

Missed Opportunities

Travels of a Participant Observer

Pennsylvania constitutes one of the nation's most celebrated cases of state forest management. The Pennsylvania Forestry Association, organized in 1875, was the oldest such state organization in the United States. The state legislature established the state forest system in the late 1890s; its first state forester, Joseph T. Rothrock, is acclaimed as one of the nation's pioneers in forest conservation. By the 1970s the state forests totaled over 2 million acres, along with Michigan and Washington comprising the largest state forest systems in the country, and by the 1980s the state planning system had made considerable progress. These achievements, however, were deeply rooted in a commodity wood production culture that proved to be remarkably resilient to change amid the new winds of environmental and ecological forestry. Hence, while the state's forestry establishment sought to acquire the outward trappings of the new developments swirling around it, it resisted them quietly and effectively, and its actions can be characterized as missed opportunities for innovations in forest affairs.

I came onto the Pennsylvania state forest scene in the early 1970s, just as a new stage in the evolution of environmental and ecological forestry was taking shape. My active involvement began in 1972, when on behalf of the Pennsylvania chapter of the Sierra Club, I undertook a review of unit and resource plans and then of the first forest-wide plan by the Allegheny

National Forest (ANF). After developing a forest plan for off-road vehicles on the ANF, I returned in 1982 to analyze a second forest-wide plan.

Gradually, I also became involved in state forest activities, and, in addition to analyzing state issues, I took part in a variety of groups. My experiences included participation for five years in a joint forum involving a range of "stakeholders" in state forest affairs called the Forest Issues Working Group, co-sponsored by the Pennsylvania Hardwood Council and the Extension Division of the Penn State School of Forestry; invited attendance at meetings called by the state Bureau of Forestry to assist in developing forest plans; participation as both speaker and audience member in several annual Forest Forums sponsored by the School of Natural Resources of Penn State University; participation in eastern old-growth forest conferences, which included the presentation of a paper analyzing the way in which each of the eastern national forests had implemented the 1989 old-growth directive issued by Dale Robertson, chief of the Forest Service; participation for four years as a member of the Ecosystem Management Advisory Committee established by the Bureau of Forestry; production of two critiques of environmental education materials developed by the state's commodity forest leaders; and an extensive critique of the assessment of the state forests by Scientific Certification Systems. In many of these activities I wrote documents involving ecological forest proposals, and in others I wrote follow-up accounts of the meetings attended.[1]

These experiences involved the management of both federal and state forests in Pennsylvania. They highlight the degree to which the competition between ecological and commodity forestry has been quite similar on both types of public ownership. While the contest between old and new in forest affairs works out differently depending on the various historic and physical circumstances of each venue, it involves common objectives and common tensions. In this chapter I summarize my personal observations of the "wars in the woods" as they evolved in Pennsylvania.

From Watershed Protection to Wood Production

The initial objective in Pennsylvania state forest management was watershed protection. Over the years this objective was modified considerably, first by the administering bureau and later by administrative code and statute, much in the same way that the U.S. Forest Service modified its objectives first through administrative action, some changes of which were incorporated into the Multiple-Use Act of 1960. The Pennsylvania Administrative Code of 1929 identified watershed protection as the primary purpose of the state forests, giving only secondary and peripheral importance to wood production. But in the revised code of 1952, wood production was first in the list of objectives, and recreation, which had not been mentioned before, was now included.[2]

In 2003, in presenting its new forest plan, the Bureau of Forestry stated that "The state forest system was first established in 1898 for the purpose of providing a continuous supply of wood products, protecting watersheds and providing opportunities for outdoor recreation."[3] On the contrary, neither the objective of providing "a continuous supply of wood products" nor "opportunities for outdoor recreation" became major state forest objectives until some fifty years later, after World War II. This statement of objectives substantially rewrote the history of the establishment of the state forest system. A similar misreading of forest history was conveyed in speeches by former chief forester Jim Nelson, who stated simply, "Because of the destruction of the forest by fire, the Bureau of Forestry was established," without mentioning the primary focus on watershed protection.

The original objective of the state forest was much in the spirit of the times. Watershed protection was the underlying rationale for acquiring eastern national forest land under the 1911 Weeks Act, including the Allegheny National Forest in northwestern Pennsylvania, and was uppermost in the minds of legislators as they established the Pennsylvania state forest system. The New York state program for protecting the Adirondack watershed was held up by the lawmakers as a model to be followed in Pennsylvania. When the legislature authorized the acquisition of forest lands, it required that the purchases be concentrated in the headwaters of the state's three major rivers, the Delaware, the Susquehanna, and the Allegheny.[4]

The close connection between forests and waters in these early years was reflected in the new title that the bureau adopted in the 1920s, the Bureau of Forests and Waters, and in the appointment of its head as one of five members of the State Sanitary Board, which had charge of the state's water quality program. But after World War II, wood production began to emerge as the central feature of Pennsylvania state forest management. Land began to be classified in relation to the requirements of wood production; data collection was concentrated in terms integral to wood production: tree species and rates of tree growth and regeneration. Each round of planning led to increasing detail and quantity of this kind of data. There was little thought of classification or description in terms of other forest elements such as plants other than trees; animal species, whether vertebrate or invertebrate; older forests and their characteristics; the role of forests as habitats; or the potential of lands and vegetation for watershed protection. Such forest elements were not high on the list of federal foresters, either; they had long since believed that such inventories were only of limited importance in their profession.[5]

As foresters in Pennsylvania, as well as in the nation at large, turned increasingly in the direction of wood production, they were, at the same time, rejecting involvement in more varied forest resources and uses. By the 1990s one did not hear of watershed protection as the top objective of management, but instead of the municipal water supply systems that drew upon state forest landholdings and especially from underground water supplies. By this time the Bureau of Forestry had reduced considerably its interest in watershed affairs in the face of a newer agency formed to administer state and federal water quality programs, the Bureau of Water Quality in the Department of Environmental Resources. The most significant aspect of this change was that the Bureau of Forestry greatly reduced or even seemed to drop its interest in "high-quality waters." In the 1920s there was considerable interest in both protecting high-quality streams and upgrading those that were degraded. Two of the members of the five-member State Sanitary Board, which at that time administered the state's water quality program, had a direct interest in maintaining the high quality of forested streams, namely the head of the Fish Commission and the head of the Bureau of Forests and Waters. But after World War II, the Bureau of Forestry deferred an interest in the water quality of state forest streams to the Bureau of Water Quality, which after 1970 administered both federal and state water quality programs, and it deferred to the Fish Commission its former interest in the separate program for high-quality waters.[6]

The narrowing of the range of interest in forest resources to wood production by the Bureau of Forestry extended to a variety of programs that were initiated in the early twentieth century but soon dropped. The first state chief forester, Joseph T. Rothrock, believed that exposure to the cleaner air of forests fostered recuperation from lung diseases. He established a tuberculosis sanitarium at Mt. Alto in one of the first state forest reserves in south central Pennsylvania.[7] The Mt. Alto institution remained for a number of years as a distinctive contribution of the Bureau of Forestry to public health, but it was later abandoned as irrelevant to the bureau's primary task, and an interest in air pollution as an integral aspect of forest management did not reappear even amid the extensive impact of acid rain in the last decades of the twentieth century.

Similar initial ventures in wildlife and parks were later dropped. In the early years of the twentieth century, game preserves protected from hunting were identified on state forest lands to foster the reestablishment of game in

Pennsylvania.[8] It is not at all clear from the historical accounts just how this effort was abandoned, or whether the initiative came from the wildlife or the forest leaders, but by the 1920s the experiment came to an end when the legislature provided that the Game Commission would own and manage its own lands for the benefit of game, a decision that led to an extensive system of game lands reaching well over a million acres by the year 2000. At the same time, however, the Game Commission was responsible for game management on all state lands, including the state forests. In earlier years the Bureau of Forestry had excluded grazing by farm animals from the state forests in order to concentrate on its major objective of wood production, but deer, beyond its direct jurisdiction, later presented the bureau with a more serious problem.[9] As the deer herd grew to extensive proportions in the last half of the twentieth century, it began to create serious harm for tree regeneration in the forests, and the bureau took up the strategy of fencing regenerating areas to protect them from deer.

The state parks were also carved out of the initial state forest holdings but remained within the jurisdiction of the Bureau of Forestry much longer than was the case with the game reserves. In 1945 a new Bureau of Parks was established to administer those lands. This reflected the steady rise of outdoor recreation in the 1920s and thereafter. In the 1950s and 1960s under the direction of Maurice Goddard, who administered the state's resource programs, the state park system expanded, reaching 273,000 acres in 104 parks by 1970.[10] But that growth did not continue and by 1995 state park acreage was even slightly smaller than in 1970. During the 1990s the Bureau of Forestry took a more active interest in recreation but still thought of its responsibilities as custodial—to protect forests from recreation users—rather than expanding its outdoor recreation program to include a wider range of natural environmental uses, as was taking place in many states of the country.[11]

This historical evolution of the management of Pennsylvania's state forests left two dominant legacies by the year 2000. One was that the Bureau of Forestry, along with its personnel and management infrastructure, focused narrowly on wood production, so that it was poorly prepared to accept newer environmental and ecological values and science. Forestry personnel tended to respond to these changes largely by considering them as strange and undesirable and by ignoring them as best they could. A second legacy came from the fractured organization of multiple specialized natural resource agencies, which gave rise to suspicion and competition between agencies as they faced a host of overlapping issues. All of this hampered almost every effort to foster cooperative and integrated action. This resulted

from the evolution of the Bureau of Forestry as the agency remaining after specialized administrative programs developed in fish, wildlife, parks,
water, and air quality. While the U.S. Forest Service by statute had been
required at least to consider multiple forest values, the Bureau of Forestry
simply assigned responsibility to another agency.

Resource administration became more fractured over the years. The
steps toward integration that had taken place when the Department of Environmental Quality was organized in 1970 came to a halt in 1996, when
natural and environmental resource administrations were separated by Governor Tom Ridge. A few new responsibilities along the way had given some
hope for a broader perspective on the part of the Bureau of Forestry itself.
One new proposal, taken up under the authority of the 1970 act establishing
the department, sought to establish a Pennsylvania Biological Survey; it fell
apart under the pressures of interagency competition. Another new venture, arising from the Pennsylvania Natural Biodiversity Report, produced
by an interagency effort in 1995, seemed to provide more hope but as of this
writing has done little to overcome interagency rivalry. The Wild Resources
Conservation Fund, financed through a tax write-off and sale of a special
license plate, produced some cooperation, but was limited to a joint process
of distributing research funds rather than substantive interagency managerial action.

Pennsylvania Forest Institutions

The Commodity Forest Enterprise

The limited perspective of the Pennsylvania Bureau of Forestry that took
shape over the course of the twentieth century was reinforced by the general conservation climate of the state. The state forest scene was dominated
by a network of interacting institutions including the forest industry, the
forest profession, state forest managers, consulting foresters, and forest academics, all of which gave only weak or no support to environmental and
ecological forest activities. This influence had been responsible for the continued reinforcement of wood production as the dominant objective in state
forest management and for restraining the incorporation into state policy of
the values and science of modern ecology.

In advancing these objectives the forest establishment faced little resistance from a weak public. Forest users such as hikers and bird-watchers,
who valued nature highly for recreation purposes, found it difficult to extend those values to broader questions of public policy. This was markedly

evident in the limited presence of some of these groups such as the Audubon Society, the Pennsylvania Wildlife Federation, and the Chesapeake Bay Foundation in Bureau of Forestry planning meetings. In the meetings held around the state in 1998 on the proposed forest plan, the Sierra Club was the only significant citizen group participant to advocate ecological forest policies. But even within the Pennsylvania chapter of the Sierra Club, identified nationally for its interest in ecological forestry, attempts to stimulate such interest in the state met with only minimal success.[12] And the Pennsylvania Environmental Council, a private organization that appealed to the state's institutional leaders rather than the general public in its programs, occasionally took up some forest issues but they were almost wholly within the context of the interests of the state's forest establishment.[13]

The relative lack of interest in ecological forestry on the part of Pennsylvania citizen environmental organizations contrasts sharply with the attitudes of the general public, which when surveyed expressed great preference for natural values in forest management. In a survey undertaken in 1995 by the Forest Extension program of Penn State University, the public ranked clean water, clean air, wildlife habitat, and sediment control as its top priorities in forest management and placed wood production at the bottom. Hence it is not so much that forest values in Pennsylvania differed from those held by the national public at large, but instead that the public lacked organizational mechanisms to activate their objectives.

The Western Pennsylvania Conservancy, headquartered in Pittsburgh, played a distinctive though peculiar role in the state's forest affairs. In the 1960s and 1970s it provided critical leadership by acquiring forested lands that were then transferred to the Bureau of State Parks; in so doing it was instrumental in the expansion of the state park system under the leadership of Dr. Maurice Goddard. In the 1980s the Conservancy provided crucial help in establishing the first wilderness area, the Hickory Creek Wilderness on the Allegheny National Forest, by brokering the federal acquisition of the area's mineral rights. In the 1990s, however, in attempting in similar fashion to broker acquisition of the Presidential Oil Tract in the northwestern part of the state, which was planned to become a part of the state game lands, the Conservancy met resistance from rural communities and their state legislators in that part of the state. Much of the problem lay in the fact that while it attempted to work out a program for long-term silviculture for the tract, the Conservancy had no expertise or experience in forest management on which to draw. By the early twenty-first century this led to the Conservancy's active participation in promoting conservation easements for the permanent protection of commercial timber land. Through this convoluted history the Conservancy had shifted from potentially contributing to ecological forest affairs in Pennsylvania to a pragmatic association with the state's commercial wood products industry.[14]

The most influential sector of the state's forest establishment was the wood products industry itself, with the Hardwood Council of Pennsylvania, made up of member companies, as the major player. The council had direct access to the office of the governor in successive Democratic and Republican administrations and had considerable influence with the legislature. The council received ongoing financial support in the state budget and carried on a variety of activities to enhance forest industry in the state. It sought to extend its reach when it promoted the Forest Issues Working Group, intended to bring together diverse individuals interested in forest issues but serving more to establish working relationships between the industry and public resource administrators. A few representatives of environmental organizations were invited, but few attended when they discovered that the interests of the wood products industry shaped the agenda.[15]

The most comprehensive wood production organization in the state was the Pennsylvania Forestry Association.[16] Formed in 1875 with a wood production focus, this group brought together many elements of the forestry establishment on its board of directors. These included the forest industry, Bureau of Forestry officials, leaders of other state natural resource agencies such as the Game Commission and the Fish Commission, the leadership of the School of Forestry at the Pennsylvania State University (Penn State), and citizens closely associated with programs sponsored by these groups such as the Tree Farm Program and the Stewardship Program. When new ideas about forest management arose in the 1960s and thereafter, the Pennsylvania Forestry Association did little to reach out to their advocates and, in fact, rejected the few efforts within the organization to do so.

The Pennsylvania Landowners Association was a major contributor to an overall tone of hostility toward public land objectives. Its base was northwestern Pennsylvania, and while it originated around issues of wetlands and biodiversity inventories, it displayed continued opposition to public land ownership and management in general. The association was considered to be a major element of the eastern wing of the more western-based "wise use" movement. Wood products industries were important financial contributors to its work and one of its more vocal supporters was the Unified Sportsmen of Pennsylvania, a breakaway hunting and fishing group from the Pennsylvania Federation of Sportsmen, with a program critical of the environmental bent of that federation.

The School of Forestry at the Pennsylvania State University played a significant role in this complex of establishment forestry institutions, assisting in sustaining a climate favorable to wood production and skeptical about newer environmental and ecological forest objectives.[17] While its curriculum and its faculty included a range of specializations, wood production remained at the core of its program with environmental and ecological affairs at the periphery, and those few faculty members with ecological inclinations displayed a marked reticence to express such opinions when participating in seminars and working groups. The Extension Service of the School of Natural Resources established a program to assist smaller woodlot owners, such as in the more recently established federal stewardship program.[18] The program carried with it a veneer of ecological objectives, but it was administered by consulting foresters with commodity forestry training and objectives whose income came primarily from advising woodlot owners as to marketable wood harvest, and who were only peripherally knowledgeable about the wider objectives that the federal stewardship program ostensibly sought to implement.

The overwhelming but informal influence of this complex of forest institutions was modified for a brief period in the 1980s by the presence of Steve Thorne in the Goddard Chair at the School of Forestry. A major responsibility of holders of that chair, who had three-year renewable appointments, was to bridge the gap between the academic programs of the school and wider public policies. Thorne sought to pursue that objective seriously and did so at first with considerable vigor. As his initial task when he took up the post, he took an extended tour throughout the state and became acquainted with members of the public interested in forest affairs. Included in his visits were meetings with those active in citizen environmental affairs, a type of outreach that was highly unusual. Thorne had been not only a professional forester but also an official of the Nature Conservancy in Minnesota and was quite open to taking ecological forest concerns seriously. In contrast with the state's current forest leaders, he was genuinely interested in a vigorous public and regretted that it was not larger and more active in the state's forest affairs.

Steve Thorne's major accomplishment while Goddard Professor was to successfully promote the production of the Pennsylvania State Biodiversity Report, drawn up by a representative group of state natural resource administrators. The report contained an excellent biodiversity analysis and a clear set of biodiversity objectives for the state. However, Thorne did not take up a renewal of his academic appointment and returned to Minnesota, and implementation of the report languished.

Despite all this I look back on the three years when Steve Thorne was in the Goddard Chair as the only time in my some forty years of experience with forest affairs in Pennsylvania when I felt a significant degree of openness on the part of the state's leaders to considering even a few elements of the ecological forest agenda. At a lower level of the forest hierarchy there were others, but of considerably lesser influence, who often conveyed the impression that they were reluctant to take the risk of speaking out amid a cultural climate distinctly hostile to environmental and ecological objectives. After Thorne's departure the reaction to such objectives among the state's forest establishment remained, as before, one of stony silence, firm opposition and, in a few cases, direct confrontation.

Forest Words and Their Meanings

Through exposure to discussion and debate concerning forest affairs over the years, I was made continually aware of the distinctive words used by ecological forest advocates, on the one hand, and commodity forest advocates, on the other. Commodity forest advocates, for example, were loath to use the words "ecological" and "ecological forestry"; ecological terms such as "disturbance," "recovery," "restoration," "focal and keystone species," or "fragmentation" did not appear in their vocabulary. The significance of words and their meaning in the forestry debates of the time was sharpened in an article entitled "Forest Terminology" in the newsletter *Pennsylvania Woodlands*, published by the Cooperative Extension Service of the Pennsylvania State University. It read, "Because forestry is a specialized field of study, it has a vocabulary all its own," and listed some 160 terms with definitions.[19]

I drew up a similar list of ecological forestry terms, and when the two were compared I found only a handful of terms that were on both lists. Here were two worlds of forestry quite far apart; even on the level of basic vocabulary little of the world of ecological forestry had entered the world of commodity forestry. Later I ended a talk to a group of professional foresters with this example, and argued that when the two groups could agree on a common set of terms with which to talk about forests it would constitute evidence that a middle ground was emerging, but at the same time, because such a common terminology was not in evidence, it identified the gulf between the two.[20]

The advocates of commodity forestry with whom I had frequent conversations and exchanges over these forty years seemed to be quite aware that something new was stirring in the world around them to which some response was required, and this, in turn, called for some new words, arguments, and phrases. The term "new forestry" extensively used in the West did not seem to take hold with forest leaders in Pennsylvania. The words that were emerging on the part of the Bureau of Forestry were "ecosystem" and "ecosystem management." The new forest plan evolving in the late 1990s declared that future state forest management would be guided by "the principles of ecosystem management," and the bureau established a new "Ecosystem Management Advisory Committee" that was to assist in that venture. However, there was not much talk of what this meant in terms of specific objectives in forest management, or the practices adopted to carry out those objectives.[21]

Then in 1995 the Penn State Extension Service held one of its biennial conferences called Ecosystem Management: Putting Concepts to Practice.[22] The audience was composed primarily of forest professionals in the state and federal agencies, as well as academics and others with commodity forestry interests, and the conference was intended to be a short course that offered professionals credits toward continuing education requirements. The lead speaker in the conference was Susan Stout, head of the U.S. Forest Experiment Station at Warren, Pennsylvania. Her talk, "Overview of Ecosystem Management," was cautionary in the extreme.

Stout's talk was far less an elucidation of "ecosystem management" and more an attempt to reassure the audience that the term involved no change in forest management practice. It was, so said Stout, merely a new term to describe what foresters had been doing for many years, and was "neither a thundering management concept nor the next stage in forestry." At the most it might involve some "process" innovations in how decisions were made, but not in their substance. As she identified specific "ecosystem management" problems she focused primarily on deer overpopulation as a threat to forest regeneration, a problem on which Stout had long been an articulate speaker but that was now in her mind a crucial example of a new piece of forest terminology. Most of the specifics brought up in the conference were of this kind, long-standing issues now dressed up with a new term, rather than new issues for which ecological management now required the attention of foresters. Yet the fright caused among the professional foresters by a new word made rather clear the emotions at stake in the values implied.

Another concept of broad implications was "biodiversity," a term with which the Bureau of Forestry apparently desired to be associated, but with a distinctive twist. My first acquaintance with some rather novel innovations came on a field trip when the chief forester, Jim Nelson, introduced us to a "biodiversity cut," a distinctive method of timber harvest in which a select number of diverse tree species were to be left at the time of a timber harvest so that the mix of species regenerated would be similar to those that were the mix of the harvest. The problem, so Nelson explained, was that otherwise the new mix of species was somewhat unpredictable and not exactly what the foresters wanted. He insisted on describing the process as a "biodiversity cut" with the clear meaning that to him biodiversity involved diversity of tree species, and not of a wider range of forest species.[23]

I sought to make this meaning more precise when I asked the district forester present if an inventory of forest plants other than tree species had been made prior to the cut that we were observing so as to compare the post-harvest species with the pre-harvest ones. His reply was "No, I am not a botanist and we don't have funds to hire a botanist to make such surveys." In our evening discussion associated with the field trip I noted to Nelson that ecologists spoke of biodiversity usually with the term "native biodiversity" with the idea that an objective of forest management should be to restore an earlier diversity of plants and animals. He made clear that he rejected that interpretation and that the object of management should be to retain an existing diversity and not to restore an earlier one.

The bureau's interest in using the term "biodiversity" to sustain an ecological image without applying biodiversity policies on the ground became clear at a joint meeting of the Forest Issues Working Group and the Forestry Task Force of the Pennsylvania Legislature on "Pennsylvania Biodiversity Issues" held on October 15, 1996, at Harrisburg, Pennsylvania. At this meeting, representatives of the Fish Commission, the Game Commission, and the Bureau of Forestry reported on the biodiversity activities of their respective agencies.[24] Representatives of both the Fish and Game Commissions were candid as to the meager support given by their agencies to the subject. In 1995 only one half of one percent of the Game Commission budget and only .19 percent of the Fish Commission's budget was devoted to rare and endangered species. Cal DuBrock of the Game Commission noted that existing state wildlife law did not mention biodiversity, and hence the agency had no policy on the matter. Both he and Andy Shields of the Fish Commission emphasized the unfavorable institutional context in which they worked.

Dan Devlin, chief planner of the Bureau of Forestry, however, maintained no modesty in his presentation and asserted that a wide range of bureau programs were products of the agency's strong interest in biodiversity. Most of these programs had no connection with a biodiversity strategy and were in fact programs established with other objectives, which were included in the cluster of programs that the bureau now described as biodiversity programs. The bureau's designated wild areas, for example, were established primarily as "quiet areas" for outdoor recreation in which no motorized vehicles were allowed but which were subject to timber harvest in a one-hundred-year rotation to create wildlife openings. Devlin's presence at the meeting was curious, since a "biodiversity coordinator and chief of ecological services," Robert Hill, had recently been appointed in the bureau and would have been expected to be the bureau's representative at such a meeting. But Hill was usually more candid about agency policy and practice. Later he wrote in a report about biodiversity affairs in the Department of Forestry that it (the department) "should candidly and unabashedly explore the differences between what is said" and "what is done" across the agency in its biodiversity affairs.[25]

Issues of the Early 1970s in Pennsylvania

Wilderness and clear-cutting were the environmental/ecological issues that dominated debates in the United States over national forest policy in the 1970s prior to the National Forest Management Act of 1976. They were present in Pennsylvania as well. There were wilderness proposals for both the Allegheny National Forest and the Pennsylvania state forests, and the state's leading forest professionals played an active part in defending clear-cutting.

Throughout the East, proposals to add eastern areas to the national wilderness system arose in every state where there was a national forest; eastern members of the Sierra Club organized new state chapters around such issues. Members in western Pennsylvania identified and mapped three wilderness proposals for the Allegheny National Forest, raised them for public discussion, and submitted them to members of the Pennsylvania delegation in Congress.[26] The opposition, led by the state's forest industry, succeeded in excluding the Pennsylvania proposals from the 1974 Eastern Wilderness Act, but one area was included ten years later. Wilderness proposals for the state forests were taken up by a relatively new branch of the state's environmental apparatus, the Citizens' Advisory Council, an advisory body to the Department of Environmental Resources established in 1970. The council drew up a proposal to establish wilderness areas on the state forests entitled "Clear Fragments of a Whole."[27] But it met the vigorous opposition of the state Bureau of Forestry and was dropped, never to be revived.

As the clear-cutting issue emerged on the national level with the threat of an executive order by President Nixon to restrict it, a group of deans of forestry schools throughout the nation arranged for a defense of the practice to be published in book form. Forestry leaders of Pennsylvania took up the challenge on their own and produced still another defense, *Clearcutting* in *Pennsylvania*, published by the School of Forest Resources, College of Agriculture, the Pennsylvania State University.[28] Its twenty-three contributors were drawn primarily from the state's natural resource agencies—the Game Commission, the Fish Commission, and the Bureau of Forestry—the Northeastern Forest Experiment Station at Warren, Pennsylvania, and the School of Forest Resources. The perspective of the booklet was overwhelmingly that of commodity forestry. I wrote a critique, published in *Econotes*, a newsletter of the Department of Environmental Resources, where I described clearcutting as "of importance for forest policy in Pennsylvania from an environmental and ecological viewpoint."[29] *Clearcutting in Pennsylvania* became a part of "inside" forest policy making in the state when it was used to persuade the Citizens Advisory Council to withdraw its criticism of clear-cutting in its document, "Clear Fragments of a Whole."

Some years later I was involved in another clear-cutting episode when the Pennsylvania State Bureau of Forestry and the Pennsylvania Forestry Association jointly published a booklet, "Let's Talk About Clearcutting: A Forestry Book for Youth," a defense of clear-cutting directed at children. The booklet was considered as an "official" document from the bureau. Five out of the nine acknowledged as "reviewers" were staff of the bureau. The pamphlet was placed on the bureau's Web site and in his preface, James B. Grace, state forester, made clear that it was directed toward children whom he hoped would "share" it with "their parents." The booklet soon became controversial, led to letters to the bureau that criticized its financial support of the publication, some of which were derived from federal funds. This was followed by a decision by the bureau to remove it from its Web site and an explanation by Grace that their decision was because of "misinformation" about the pamphlet. My review of the episode for the Sierra Club newsletter, the *Sylvanian*, placed it in the context of the current controversy between the advocates of commodity forestry and ecological forestry and pointed out that the pamphlet said nothing at all about the negative results of clear-cutting on the forest as an ecosystem.[30]

Two other issues in Pennsylvania during these years had close connections with ecological forestry. One involved off-road vehicle use, primarily in the Allegheny National Forest (ANF).[31] Off-road vehicles (ORVs) then were mainly two-wheeled motorbikes and snowmobiles; three- or four-wheeled all-terrain vehicles had not yet made their appearance. But the ANF was having difficulty in controlling their use. The issue presented two alternatives. Should areas be signed "open" to ORVs, mandating that the vehicles be prohibited elsewhere, or signed "closed," permitting them to be used anywhere outside the signed areas? This was an early version of the problem of ORV use on the public lands, which has grown over the years. Administrators of the ANF preferred the "signed open" policy, which would enable them to contain and thereby police the use of ORVs more effectively.

The natural areas policy of the state Bureau of Forestry made a positive contribution to an ecological component in the state forest program. While most forest agencies spurned opportunities to administer statewide natural area programs, Pennsylvania took a different tack and in the early 1970s, under the leadership of Jim Nelson, then the chief planner in the Bureau of Forestry, the agency expanded an earlier program identified as the protection of "natural monuments"—unusual geological formations and large, old trees—into a broader program involving "natural areas." These were typical of natural area programs evolving elsewhere but were confined to lands managed by the Bureau of Forestry. The bureau did not take up the opportunity to expand this program into the type of statewide natural areas program that was developing in many states.[32]

Biodiversity

Biodiversity objectives run through the entire gamut of ecological forest policies throughout the country; they also have been present, though in limited fashion, in the affairs of the Pennsylvania Bureau of Forestry and the Department of Conservation and Natural Resources (DCNR) of which it is a part. Some early beginnings were brought to a head in a joint effort on the part of several natural resource agencies to formulate a plan for the state. This appeared in 1997 in the document *Conserving PA's Biological Diversity: A Heritage for the 21st Century*, which was drawn up by an interagency resource committee under the leadership of Steven Thorne.[33] Thorne's successor, Robert McKinstry Jr., attempted to take the biodiversity issue further by organizing the Third Annual Goddard Forum sponsored by Penn State University on the theme of "Biodiversity: Addressing a Global Issue Locally." The proceedings of this forum were published later in the volume *Biodiversity Conservation Handbook: State, Local and Private Protection of Biological Diversity*, which gives special emphasis to the Pennsylvania experience.[34] Most of the chapters on Pennsylvania were written by state resource administrators, whose accounts consisted of favorable public statements about their agencies, quite different from the real world of resource administration under which the emergence of a state biodiversity program labored. Details related here supplement and modify these authorized statements. While it is a fair conclusion that some significant strides in biodiversity have been made in Pennsylvania, these have been limited to plans far more than action, and the task of turning plans into active programs still meets severe roadblocks. Their relevance for state forest management remains uncertain.

An action that had the potential of more effective results was the appointment in 1996 of a biodiversity coordinator within the DCNR, who initially was to serve as an advisor to the department secretary on such matters. Over the course of the next six years, however, the position was reduced in significance to serving primarily the Bureau of Forestry, and then only as manager of its Division of Ecological Services. Bob Hill held this position for six years until he resigned in 2001, at which time, at the request of DCNR secretary John Oliver, he produced a report of his six-year experience, with suggestions for changes in the position. His suggestions were bold: An Office of Science Advisement should be established, managed by the biodiversity coordinator, with equal status to other offices in the department. It should serve as "an umbrella science/research unit designed for cooperation and decision-making, and would assist in policy-formulation, funding support, and sustainable management of the state lands under DCNR's trust." Each bureau within DCNR should establish an ecological services unit with a liaison to the Office of Science Advisement to coordinate biodiversity conservation. Hill urged that the secretary and all of the agency's staff should "assume bold roles in articulating and promoting biodiversity conservation in all that the agency undertakes."[35]

While Hill in his report made concrete policy suggestions, he also dealt with the bureau's lack of interest in the issue. "The Bureaus of Forestry and State Parks have strong undercurrents that privilege resource extraction, recreation, and at times seemingly anti-environmental sentiments over strong ecological alternatives." A cultural climate pervaded the department, Hill argued, that severely inhibited staff with strong ecological views, who "openly acknowledge resistance to speaking an ecological point of view because they read the overall organizational culture as otherwise." "There is the feeling," he related, "that to raise unsheltered questions about certain projects, or herbicide application, or bioreservation, or motorized use, or old-growth policy is to invite silencing, marginalization or scorn." Moreover, he argued, the DCNR's response to the "Green Certification" sustainable forestry report (discussed further below) demonstrated the agency's "resistance to foster an unbridled ecological approach. . . . Rather than seriously addressing most recommendations, they have been met with rhetoric or silence."

One of the bureau's programs that was part of its "biodiversity mix" involved an index of rare, endangered, and featured species called the Pennsylvania Natural Diversity Index (PNDI); it was housed in the Bureau of

Forestry.[36] This involved an informal arrangement with botanists in various institutions in the state, universities, museums, and botanical gardens who searched out and identified such plants, information about which was then placed in a computerized index. The group was collectively known as the Pennsylvania Biological Survey but had little formal organization and no official standing; individual specialists worked together to do what they could to enhance a focus on biodiversity within the state. The computerized information was used largely to provide a readily available source of data that both private and public developers could consult so that they could know the potential adverse ecological effects of their proposed projects.

The bureau provided a home for the PNDI, and staff was devoted primarily to conducting computer searches for proposed projects submitted to it. But, in contrast with programs in a number of other states, the Pennsylvania staff provided no leadership in statewide natural diversity affairs and provided no services to private landowners who might wish to protect areas of ecological importance or attempt to identify lands that should be protected through public programs and to promote public acquisition for that purpose. A more vigorous potential "natural heritage" program was inhibited not only by DCNR lethargy but also by the fact that two private natural area organizations had long been active, and even rivals, in such affairs in the state, the Nature Conservancy in the eastern part of the state and the Western Pennsylvania Conservancy in the west. DCNR officials, instead of using their limited influence to bring the two separate groups into a unified state program, tended to perpetuate that regional division.[37]

The bureau took an equally jaundiced view toward a program that the legislature had established in 1983 to develop a system of "plant sanctuaries." The legislative history of this program seemed to confine it primarily to preventing private extraction of plants on public lands, but it clearly had the potential to become a major ingredient of a state biodiversity program. But by the end of the century, while the bureau had taken some internal action to implement the program, it had taken no publicly announced action and was still talking about plans to identify and protect such areas, yet boasting of its authority to do so as evidence of its biodiversity commitment.

By the early years of the twenty-first century, biodiversity matters in Pennsylvania had given rise to many affirmations of interest and assertions of viable programs, but little on the ground result. While one might add the lethargy of the state legislature to this mix of indifference on the part of the state agencies, the DCNR, and the Bureau of Forestry in particular, one should note a report of the Forestry Task Force of the Pennsylvania General Assembly in 1997, which included a proposal for more long-term research, for opening DCNR lands for experimentation in each of the forest types found in Pennsylvania, for sustained investigation of the state's biological diversity, and for designation of buffers and areas of future old-growth forest. Here was an invitation to DCNR, with some detail, to take up the issue, but there was scant evidence that it chose to do so.[38]

THE ECOSYSTEM MANAGEMENT ADVISORY COMMITTEE

In 1996 the Department of Conservation and Natural Resources appointed an Ecosystem Management Advisory Committee (EMAC), which was touted as the group on which the Bureau of Forestry would rely to carry out its declared policy of using ecosystem management principles as guidance for the agency's policies. It was composed of thirty-five members selected by the DCNR, who were identified less by their knowledge of ecological forestry affairs and more by the degree to which they represented the various interests in state forestry matters. Its initial meetings displayed an "assertive, independent, challenging and courageous agenda," as Bob Hill noted, but over the course of a couple of years it adopted a "more domesticated" one. At its start eight members reflected ecological or quasi-ecological views about forest management and made several unsuccessful attempts to establish an ecological beachhead in the committee's deliberations. The meetings became dominated by state agency and Penn State School of Forestry personnel, and the ideological climate was confined largely to the Bureau of Forestry's primary goal of resource extraction and utilization rather than ecological management and sustainability. The observer mentioned above then queried, "Has EMAC misplaced its inspired discourse for a more 'safe' one?"[39]

Several ecological initiatives, while promising at their outset, soon evaporated into insignificance and helped to shape the group's lethargy and declining interest. The idea of an inventory of ecological resources by the bureau arose in the very first meetings. Bureau representatives presented their proposals for additional resource inventories that would be an integral part of the new forest plan, proposals that were devoted almost entirely to perfecting knowledge of wood fiber resources. This prompted a protest on the part of some half dozen members that there was a sufficient amount of such knowledge and that new inventory resources should be devoted to greater knowledge about species other than sources of wood fiber. The bureau personnel seemed somewhat taken aback but promised to return at the next meeting with a revised inventory schedule that would reflect this concern. But instead they simply provided a list of research projects that ecological scientists had conducted on the state forests. The issue continued to come up at subsequent meetings, though amid an increasing sense of resignation, and it soon evaporated amid the quiet but persistent insistence of bureau personnel to increase knowledge about wood fiber resources and refusal to divert inventory resources toward knowledge of forest ecology.[40]

Two years later an affirmation of ecological objectives by the Ecosystem Management Advisory Committee took on a new twist with a committee position paper, "Special Roles for Pennsylvania's State Forests and the Pennsylvania Bureau of Forestry." It was built around the question as to the "special roles" that public forests should play "by virtue of their being publicly owned forests." An elaboration of this set of objectives contained a quite comprehensive list of ecological forest activities: "inventories of species of concern, plant communities and ecosystems"; "design and implement a system to address issues of fragmentation and connectivity"; "establishment of a system of reserves, buffers and connectivity zones"; conduct long-term scientific studies on the effects of silviculture on the functioning of ecosystems; and monitor the impacts of human influences in different ecoregions. The paper stated, "it is primarily to public land that we must look for the long-term management stability needed for the establishment of bioreserves or diversity." In a final paragraph the document acknowledged the wider significance of its message by referring to the certification report, which I will describe in the next section of this chapter, submitted subsequent to the committee discussion, which "touches on many of the issues with which EMAC has been wrestling, and serves in large measure to emphasize further the importance of many of these special roles recommended for the State Forest system."[41]

This was a remarkable document that went through a number of revisions as it wound its way back and forth between the EMAC as a whole and the group that drafted it. A keen observer could have noted that bureau personnel seemed to be caught between a high level of skepticism about its contents and a sense of resignation that the bureau could not take a frontal assault against the process as it unfolded. But the bureau had the last word. Although the document was approved it was simply "accepted" by the agency and shelved, not to see further light of day. In retrospect, one is struck by the breadth of its ecological scope and the significant changes in bureau policy that would have been required had the agency taken it seriously. But the strategy of the bureau's response was typical. As occurred in so many cases, the bureau simply refused to refer to it further and in effect denied that it existed.

The main ecological forestry program to which the EMAC devoted its most serious effort was the proposal to establish bioreserves within the state forest system. This had been a featured proposal of the Pennsylvania Biological Diversity Report of 1997 and had seemed to gather support from a number of quarters as the main element of a biodiversity policy. The question remained, however, as to just how this objective would be accomplished: how many reserves, how large, and where would they be located? This could have been done rather quickly had the objective enjoyed firm commitment from the bureau, but it could take a considerable amount of time if the bureau procrastinated by promoting extensive and exhaustive deliberation over the basic questions. As it turned out, the Bioreserves Subcommittee of EMAC, which worked on the task under the direction of Wayne Myers, a specialist in remote sensing, produced a well-thought-out system for mapping possible bioreserve areas. But as of yet, this format has not been translated into an active, ongoing bioreserve management program.[42]

After only a half dozen years, the early promise of the Ecosystem Management Advisory Committee seemed to evaporate into obscurity as a result of quiet Bureau of Forestry resistance, still another example of how existing forest institutions with a commitment to wood production can artfully resist the inroads of new ecological forest management objectives. But the demise was as much a product of the composition and interests of the members of the committee, who seemed to be most interested in their own separate worlds and concerned about how the committee proposals would affect them in their activities back home.

The entire experience of EMAC activities over a period of four years only reinforced in my own mind the insularity and traditionalism among Pennsylvania forest leaders and the way in which that perspective shaped their inability to express more than lip service to the objectives of ecological forestry.

Certification

Pennsylvania and Minnesota were the first two states to undertake a certification review for their state forest lands. Such reviews were conducted under the auspices of the Forest Stewardship Council (FSC), and their objective was to identify "well managed" forest lands so as to inform consumers of the most environmentally desirable choices to make in purchasing wood products. Proponents of certification hoped that it would provide an alternative to public regulation of forest practices and lead to a circumstance in which "market forces" would guide improvement of those practices. Private forest lands were the initial objective of the FSC, but its limited success with private landowners prompted the organization to extend its proposals to public lands as well, and an invitation to states with public forest lands brought Minnesota and Pennsylvania into the program.

Very early, the work of the FSC came to the attention of the Forest Issues Working Group (FIWG) in Pennsylvania, and as I was more than curious about its program, I took up the task of investigating it in detail and drawing up several reports to present to the group. At the same time the leader of the FSC program spoke to the FIWG and a report was presented to the FIWG by an official from Kane Hardwoods, which at that time was the only private forest industry in Pennsylvania to have been certified. These sources of information made clear that there were two crucial aspects of certification. One was the set of standards to be used on which to base a judgment that a forest was "well managed," and the other was the arrangement put into place to implement and enforce those standards. With respect to the standards, while the FSC had a set of principles that it sought to apply, they were so general and vague that the crucial factor was the personal views of the individuals who inspected and reviewed forest practices on the ground. These could and did vary from project to project, and much would depend on who was selected for the inspection team. With respect to enforcement, since there was no force of law involved in implementation, much depended on private arrangements that might foster compliance and especially whether changes in forest management would be made before certification approval, or if approval would be made with promises of improvement thereafter.[43]

The inspection team was comprised of three individuals, one for each of three general categories of review, timber management, wildlife, and available economic resources. For ecological forestry the wildlife program was most crucial. The wildlife expert of the Pennsylvania team was Bryon Shissler, a consulting wildlife biologist. I had known him casually for some time and had considerable confidence in his independence of judgment; at times he had held his ground well in disagreements with the Bureau of Forestry. As I discussed the project with him I was pleased that he had persuaded the reviewers to add an external peer review to the project, and I was further pleased that Shissler was planning to invite Jerry Franklin, one of the nation's best-known forest ecologists, to join the peer review team.

I was also concerned about the problem of enforcement. Since the certification involved no legal enforcement, the only clout that the certification might have was twofold: management improvements would be required before certification was granted, not as post-certification promises; and decertification could be instituted if promised improvement were not forthcoming. The reviewing team approved the Pennsylvania state forests as "well managed" while stipulating that ten "conditions" should be met, all of which would be required post-certification with the proviso that if they were not carried out certification would be revoked. To these were added fifteen "recommendations" that were not requirements, but which the bureau was urged to implement. While some of these conditions reflected important ecological forestry objectives, their inclusion as post-certification requirements would, in my mind, only shift them to a continuing ongoing tussle between the regulators and the regulated, no different from a governmental regulatory process. The Bureau of Forestry could easily outlast the relatively weak clout of the certifiers, and successfully resist changes in its practices.

The reviewing document and conditions expressed several important ecological policies, including the requirement that the agency shift from its dominant even-age management program to one involving more mixed-age management; that it develop a program to reverse fragmentation and establish connectors and corridors between fragments; that it create a significant bioreserve system; and that it devise a more limited and targeted use of herbicides with subsequent monitoring as to their effects on forest organisms. A number of the certification conditions were quite similar to the recommendations in the document approved by the Ecosystem Management Advisory Committee, "Special Roles for Pennsylvania's State Forests and the Pennsylvania Bureau of Forestry."

The bureau displayed a mixed reaction to certification and its conditions. On the one hand, it immediately publicized that it had been approved by the FSC as having a "well-managed forest" and used this as an aid in seeking new markets for wood produced from the state forests, including a trade mission to England, led by the secretary of the Department of Conservation and Natural Resources. On the other hand, it made no mention of the conditions attached to the certification in publicity statements or in the twenty-seven public meetings that it held throughout the state concerning the draft of the state forest plan. At EMAC meetings the conditions were mentioned as problematical circumstances, and chief of the bureau referred disparagingly to some of the adverse comments of peer reviewers as the reviewers' "personal agendas." As I anticipated, the annual assessments made by FSC reviewing teams of whether or not the conditions had been met were based not on performance but on bureau "statements of progress," with little suggestion of decertification either then or in the future.[44]

The most ecologically significant suggestion made by the certification team that continued to play some role in bureau affairs was the proposal for biodiversity reserves. As it turned out the main effect of certification was the media advantage to both FSC and the DCNR that a large acreage of state forest in Pennsylvania was approved by FSC as "well managed."[45]

Old Growth, Old Forests

In the 1980s the issue of old growth or ancient forests emerged with considerable force in the Pacific Northwest and Alaska; in the 1990s interest in "old forests" began to emerge in the East. This was fueled partly by the search for old trees and small stands of them in several of the eastern national forests, primarily in the Southern Appalachians, always amid the recognition that while in the Northwest some old forests remained, in the East they had been systematically destroyed, first in New England, then in the Mid-Atlantic and Great Lakes States, and finally in the South. In a few places, such as the Boundary Waters in northern Minnesota, the Upper Peninsula of Michigan, the southern Adirondacks, and the Southern Appalachians, there were medium-sized forests of a hundred years of age or more. But for the most part it was well recognized that the possibility of old-growth forests depended largely on the decision to create them by letting current forests aged eighty years or more become still older.[46]

The interest in old growth took the form of a number of eastern conferences of both citizens and scientists interested in the subject, the first one in western North Carolina, then at Williamstown, Massachusetts; Fayetteville, Arkansas; and Clarion in western Pennsylvania. Books appeared that identified existing old growth, most in small tracts of forest land scattered throughout the region. In 1989 the chief of the U.S. Forest Service directed that each national forest develop an old-growth policy, a directive that set off a variety of types of action and inaction. I took up this interest with a special focus on Pennsylvania, attended the Williamstown conference, and then conducted a survey of all the national forests in the East to determine what action each had taken in response to the directive.[47] Soon I was writing an analysis of the state of old growth in the Pennsylvania state forests and seeking to increase interest in the issue among both administrators and citizens in the state.[48] The experience was instructive, and placed the old-growth issue on the list of ecological forest objectives about which there was limited interest among the state's citizen environmental organizations and both indifference and opposition in the Bureau of Forestry and the Department of Conservation and Natural Resources.[49]

When the fourth eastern old-growth conference held at Clarion University in northwestern Pennsylvania was announced, I urged Bob Leverett, the eastern guru of old growth, to invite John Oliver, secretary of the Department of Environmental Conservation, to give the keynote address. I thought that this might give a nudge to the department to complete its old-growth policy statement.

The strategy produced no positive results. In his opening remarks Mr. Oliver affirmed the strong interest of the department and the bureau in a vigorous old-growth policy and cited two actions that reflected that interest. One was the bureau's natural area program in which big, old trees had been a part of the initial "natural monuments" policy established in the 1920s and continued since then. This, of course, followed the interest in the 1920s in "big trees," in which different states, encouraged especially by the American Forestry Association, gloried in the fact that they contained the biggest of this or that species. It reflected little of the newer interest in old forests rather than old trees, and the interest in their ecological composition. The second action that Mr. Oliver cited was the bureau's "wild area" policy that established forest areas to be managed primarily for quiet recreation with motorized vehicles being prohibited, even though the areas would be available for wood harvest to create wildlife openings. In establishing wild areas initially in the early 1970s there had been no thought that they would have any particular ecological or age rationale or value, nor had there been any ecological addition to that rationale since then.

The 2003 draft of the state forest management plan took a partial but significant step toward protecting old growth when it stated that 20 percent of the state forest acreage would be managed as old growth. This was further specified in an old-growth symposium in the April/May 2004 issue of the *Journal of Forestry*, which devoted one article to the Pennsylvania plan. The specific areas devoted to old growth would comprise three tracts: the already existing natural areas (85,000 acres); wild areas (149,000 acres); and limited resource zones (321,000 acres), which were identified as "forestlands of limited operability," a rather ambiguous category that presumably meant rocky mountaintop areas, steep slopes, and other areas where geological conditions rendered normal forest operations impossible. This selection, based on existing administrative categories rather than potential for old-growth forest, seemed to bypass the long-standing contention that old-growth designations should proceed cautiously so as to make them scientifically credible.

The article provided no rationale as to old-growth objectives, either aesthetic, scientific, or ecological, or whether or not the designated areas would be subject to future wood harvest, but did give some inkling as to bureau perspectives by identifying three categories of old-growth management. These involved management actions to foster tree regeneration of desired species; methods of fostering "stand structure," both horizontal (tree spacing) and vertical (uneven tree heights); and techniques to increase "biological decadence," that is, "dead wood on the forest floor, standing dead snags and logs and branches in streams." This elaboration of Pennsylvania old-growth objectives incorporated almost no ecological content, either in identifying the rich species content of old forests, or long-term ecological processes of forest aging. The management rationale, stipulated as an attempt to speed up natural processes through human intervention, seemed to express frustration at the slow pace of those natural processes and called upon human intervention for faster action toward silvicultural old growth rather than more effective realization of ecological forest objectives.[50]

Forest History

Issues such as biodiversity and old growth made clear that the historical context for ecological forestry and commodity forestry differ markedly. While the benchmark for ecological forestry was an earlier time, the time of white European settlement, that for commodity forestry was the more recent time at which the current second-growth forest had begun. For ecological forestry the desired goal was "restoration" with that earlier time in mind; for commodity forestry it was "regeneration" with an emphasis on instituting an entirely new pattern of species that was geared far more to what the contemporary market wanted rather than an older pattern of species. While to ecological foresters the task of restoration involved the entire forest, to the commodity foresters it was more limited to the trees rather than the forest as an ecosystem. Thus, while ecological foresters sought to place the context of their actions as a current phase of an evolutionary process over the years, commodity foresters sought to establish a forest that broke from the past to create something entirely new; thus, they rejected old growth. The continuity with the past reflected in old-growth thinking required a wrench in their values against which they rebelled with intensity.

My experience with this set of values in commodity forest history was sharpened rather dramatically by watching on several occasions a slide show about "forest history" which had been put together and presented by Jim Nelson, chief of the Pennsylvania Bureau of Forestry. Its backdrop was the cutover land in Pennsylvania of the last part of the nineteenth century, the bare and often burnt hillsides from which timber had been cut and floated down the Susquehanna River to the mills around Williamsport. From that historical beginning point, with most of his presentation involving not the forest but the lumber industry, regeneration had taken place, depicted by aerial photographs of the new greenery of that section of Pennsylvania. There was no presentation of the species composition of the earlier forest at white European settlement, no description of the earlier intact forest now fragmented over the course of history by roads and power lines, no identification of species that had been extirpated over the years or now were endangered or threatened, no mention of changes in the quality of soils due to lumbering or farming or acid precipitation. The show created the vision of a forest and forest managers cut off from the past with no thought of even a partial return.[51]

The image from the Nelson slide show was repeated toward the end of the 1990s when I was asked by the state chapter of the Sierra Club to review a proposed environmental and ecology forest education curriculum that had been drawn up by representatives of the Pennsylvania commodity forest community under the auspices of the state Department of Education. In the only historical section in the proposal, "Human Influence on Pennsylvania's Forests: Then and Now," the emphasis was entirely on the history of the forest industry rather than the history of the forest. My comment read: "More appropriate subjects would be the impact of these human-induced changes on the destruction of the older forests, widespread forest fragmentation, the destruction of wildlife species, changes in wildlife through changes in forest habitat, and biochemical changes in soils through the impacts of the chemical wood industry, clearcutting, fires and atmospheric deposition."[52]

The role of the past as an influence on the present in forest management, an issue of some interest in ecological forestry, was wholly absent from consideration by Pennsylvania advocates of commodity forestry, who seemed to give the impression that all aspects of wise forest management could be resolved with current "inputs." A number of examples of the influence of the past kept cropping up. Land management practices that became prevalent when farming replaced forests in the Northeast still were influential in later years when forests once again replaced farming. One of the displays at the Harvard Experimental Forest near Petersham, Massachusetts, shows a soil profile created by farm plowing in the nineteenth century that remained almost unchanged a century later in the now-regenerated forest, an example of the permanence of earlier soil disturbance.[53]

Through these experiences I came to the conclusion that ecological forestry provided far greater attention to the role of biological disturbances over the long run and sought to temper a potential enthusiasm for human management with a firm understanding of ecological context, while commodity forestry deliberately sought to cut itself off from that context with a confident conviction that human management could be carried out safely with little provision for ecological circumstances. Ecological forestry fostered openness to the complexities of ecological evolution and circumstance, while commodity forestry expressed a firm confidence in human management and manipulation imposed on ecological processes. Two quite different conceptions of the role of forest history were closely related to quite different conceptions of the proper role of human management.

Watersheds, Water Quality, Deer, and Acid Rain

Several specific issues that recurred over the years reflected the way in which the Bureau of Forestry shied away from an ecological forestry approach in favor of a commodity approach. Watersheds had been a central focus in the establishment of the public forests of the state, but interest in watershed management had declined over the century. The emerging forest plan in the 1990s departed extensively from those early watershed policies. In it the bureau presented no focus on watersheds as such or in their identification, inventory, and management, but instead confined its program to one of granting permits to municipalities for water extraction from sources on state forest lands.

Pennsylvania did participate in multistate efforts to tackle nutrient pollution in the Chesapeake Bay, a significant part of which stemmed from runoff into the Susquehanna River and its tributaries. An important part of this program was the effort to establish forested buffer areas along a significant portion of tributaries to the bay to reduce the flow of nutrients into the bay. The Bureau of Forestry included a buffer program in its 2003 Forest Resource Management Plan, which included two-to-three-hundred-foot widths, a rather advanced program amid controversies over the appropriate size of such protective buffers. But a buffer protection program was not considered by Chesapeake Bay leaders to be a fully developed watershed protection program and was thought only to "help to mimic the function of a larger forested area." For many years municipalities had acquired watershed lands, not just stream buffers, to control runoff in the search to protect their water supplies, and it seemed simply conventional for modern water quality programs to do the same.[54]

The bureau took a more confused position in a private debate over the designation of "exceptional value" waters on state forest lands. In the 1920s the state water quality program had divided streams into three quality categories for administrative purposes, with the highest quality designated in later years as "exceptional value" streams. But despite provisions in the regulations that all streams flowing through the state's public lands should be examined for their exceptional value, the bureau had not done so and in fact had limited that designation to streams that the Fish Commission had identified as "wilderness trout streams." The Sierra Club sought to include other eligible state forest streams in the "exceptional value" category but met resistance from the bureau. The Bureau of Forestry maintained that such initiative rested with the Bureau of Water Quality, and, in turn, the Bureau of Water Quality maintained that it rested with the Bureau of Forestry. Despite a decision by the secretary of the Department of Conservation and Natural Resources (DCNR) that the responsibility lay with the Bureau of Forestry, that bureau refused to act, and when confronted with this problem in one of the planning sessions, chief planner Dan Devlin simply said that the issue would have to be resolved by the courts.[55]

In the last decade of the twentieth century, excessive deer population became an issue of overriding importance on the state's forest lands. Both public and private forest managers argued that deer were eating tree seedlings and hence were destroying forest reproduction. Deer "exclosures," which fenced reproducing forest areas, produced a marked difference between the growth of vegetation inside the exclosure and the lack of it outside. The state's average deer population was approximately thirty per square mile, while to guarantee adequate tree reproduction, so the argument went, it should be brought down to twenty. To reach that figure, the annual deer "harvest" should be increased primarily by increasing the number of doe licenses, which would reduce the overall population.

Ecological forest advocates, however, were bringing into the deer issue research that demonstrated that deer harmed forest flora, such as wildflowers, at population levels much lower than twenty per square mile. The most convincing research, conducted by botanists at the University of Wisconsin, identified harm at levels of ten to fifteen deer per square mile. Much more was at stake than tree seedlings. If one were take a biodiversity approach, one would call for a reduction in the deer population to a figure much lower than twenty per square mile. Yet neither the Game Commission nor the Bureau of Forestry publicized the results of that research and when queried made clear that the overwhelming interest in the issue in protecting tree seedlings precluded any focus on plants other than trees. In fact, Game Commission representatives argued that the long-standing connection between browse food supplies and deer populations, which had been advanced by Aldo Leopold in earlier years, had now been "decoupled." The certification report about the state forests took this issue so seriously that it placed its solution as the top priority of ten conditions that the bureau would have to meet to retain certification. In the certification board's review of progress, however, it accepted the bureau's statement that it was taking part in interagency discussions about the problem as sufficient evidence of compliance.[56]

Still a third issue of considerable interest in ecological forestry to which the Bureau of Forestry gave little attention was acid precipitation.[57] Pennsylvania bore the brunt of the effects of acid precipitation, and the extent of the problem was identified by a set of measurements made under the auspices of the Penn State School of Natural Resources starting in the 1970s and continuing through the rest of the century. Evidence from a dozen monitors across the state clearly identified the pattern of acid precipitation on the state forests. And while the accuracy of this data could not be denied, the effect of acidification was in dispute.[58]

The issue was dramatized for the state because two researchers at Penn State drew opposite conclusions about it. John M. Skelley, a plant pathologist, conducted research on the effect of ambient air pollutants on tree foliage and via foliage on trees themselves. He argued that the case for significant harm could not be demonstrated. Biochemist William Sharpe had studied the impact of acid deposition on streams in the Laurel Mountains of western Pennsylvania and had worked out the relationships between acid deposition on the one hand and the neutralizing quality of stream chemistry on the other as a result of limestone rock through which the stream flowed. He also demonstrated the mobilization of aluminum in the acidified streams and its detrimental effect on fish. He now used that format to examine the effect of acid deposition on forest soils and tree reproduction, emphasizing the same process by which acidified soils mobilized aluminum to create a toxic subsoil environment that was detrimental to tree growth.

A dramatic episode in this debate, in which one scientist emphasized the role of ambient air acidification on tree foliage and the other the role of soil acidification on tree nutrition, took place when the Forest Issues Working Group hosted a presentation by both. In this session, while Skelley spent much of the time attacking the scientific competence of European researchers who had pioneered in studying the impact of air pollution on tree growth, Sharpe devoted his lecture to the research on soil chemistry and seedling growth and development. Bureau of Forestry leaders maintained that they could not decide between the two positions and hence would not take any action at all with respect to acidification.[59]

A year later Sharpe organized a conference at Penn State on acidification, inviting a team of European scientists to speak at the conference and first to tour some of the state's forests that were undergoing considerable decline in growth and report on their findings. One of the European visitors, Babette Munzenberger of the Institute for Microbial Ecology and Soil Biology of Eberswalde, Germany, presented a talk on the effect of acidification on soil mycorrhizae, which was the first such presentation I had heard in Pennsylvania. However, the bureau and the DCNR displayed little

.interest in the meeting; none of the top officials of either agency and only a few of the lower-level staff attended. The conference was not mentioned in the meetings of the Ecosystem Management Advisory Committee and was covered only in *Pennsylvania Wildlife*, not in *Pennsylvania Forests*, the magazine of the Pennsylvania Forestry Association. There was considerable interest among ecological foresters in the Southern Appalachians in the effects of acid rain, in marked contrast to the relative indifference and lack of interest in Pennsylvania.

In each of these issues—watersheds, water quality, deer overpopulation, and acid rain—the views of the Bureau of Forestry were biased toward commodity forestry; wood production seemed to determine how the bureau reacted, what it thought, and what it did. These issues simply support the conclusions I reached, as a participant in a wide range of forest affairs in Pennsylvania over four decades, about the controlling commodity views of the Bureau of Forestry.

The Bureau and the Public

As management of the state's forests evolved in the last third of the twentieth century, a significant gap emerged between views about forest policy on the part of the general public and the course of policy by the Bureau of Forestry. Statewide surveys of public attitudes toward state forests undertaken in the early 1990s illuminated this divergence. The first of these was sponsored by the Stewardship Program and put together by Jim Finley and Steve Jones of the extension service in the School of Natural Resources at the Pennsylvania State University. Two publics were surveyed, residents of the state as a whole and woodland owners. The most significant of the questions concerned views about the benefits provided by state forests. Both groups of respondents gave a similar ranking: clean air, clean water, habitat, and soil protection were at the top of the list, and wood production was at the bottom. Another survey conducted by a Penn State sociologist produced similar results, but added several other questions, including one that showed that both the general public and the woodland owners disapproved sharply of clear-cutting as a forest practice.[60] Some members of the state's forest establishment took these results seriously, and the surveys seemed to provide a firm basis for developing a forest policy that had strong public support. But the most striking result of the surveys was the rapidity with which they were dropped from the agenda of anyone in the forest establishment. On several occasions, such as at one of the Penn State biennial conferences and in an article in the pages of *American Forests*, Finley and Jones sought to give considerable significance to their findings on the grounds that they reflected a state of public opinion to which the forest establishment should pay serious attention. They ended one presentation with the following: "As we carry out our role as professional stewards, we must consider the feelings and attitudes that the general public and landowners have toward the forest. . . . Perhaps it is time to stop insisting that we need to educate the public, and take time instead to educate ourselves. We must be enlightened managers of a public trust." Despite this rather remarkable statement about the importance of public attitudes in forest affairs, the initiatives of Finley and Jones were momentary. The Pennsylvania forest attitude surveys were never publicly mentioned in the affairs of the Bureau of Forestry; neither Finley nor Jones carried their message further. It received no media publicity and soon it was all but forgotten.[61]

Beyond holding "listening sessions" to hear reactions to the draft forest plan, the bureau made no significant efforts to improve its relationships with the public. On this score it differed somewhat from the public participation fostered by the Allegheny National Forest, which applied mandatory and predictable agency procedures. The Bureau of Forestry had no such requirements. For it, public participation was purely a matter of agency discretion. The rules of the game were ad hoc, at times dependent on invitation by the agency and at times subject to formal organization with attendance at public initiative; agendas were set by the agency and the results of citizen input were subject to rather narrow circulation, primarily within the agency itself. While the bureau's public stance was one of extensive public participation, its actions served to limit that participation to listening to the public rather than mutual give-and-take.

The certification report on the state forests provided another opportunity for the bureau to establish closer relationships with Pennsylvania citizens by discussing publicly the conditions and suggestions made by the certifying team that identified state forest management deficiencies. A frank reporting of these "conditions" and "suggestions" seemed to be called for, especially in the public meetings organized by the bureau to obtain public reaction to the draft forest plan, held shortly after the certification report was released. The format of these meetings involved first a statement by Dan Devlin, the bureau's chief planner, followed by a series of small group meetings at which the public expressed its reaction to the draft plan proposals. The bureau's presentation did not mention the certification report or the management problems identified there, and when the conditions and recommendations were raised by attendees they were simply dismissed as inconsequential. The bureau publicized widely that the state forests had been certified as "well managed" but declined to discuss, or even to mention, the management deficiencies identified by the certifiers.[62]

While the surveys of public opinion identified public support for ecological forest objectives in Pennsylvania, the planning meetings across the state brought out few citizen participants with ecological objectives. It seemed rather clear that a reciprocal relationship existed between the limited opportunities for the expression of ecological forest views by the public, the limited interest of the state's citizen environmental organizations in such matters, and the easy dismissal of their importance on the part of the state's forest establishment.

Events early in the twenty-first century had some potential in modifying this pattern of relationships between the public and the bureau, but at least initially they did not. Several initiatives from citizen groups appeared that, together, presented a more forceful agenda for citizen reform than in previous years. One involved the growth, increasing experience, and successful litigation by the Allegheny Defense Project, which in 2003 led to the completion of a major land use plan for the Allegheny National Forest that was well documented and widely available.[63] Another was the Pennsylvania Wildlands Recovery Project, more recent in origin, which produced an extensive and well-documented analysis of the 2003 State Forest Plan.[64] Also in that year these two citizen initiatives, both strongly assertive in their ecological objectives, joined in producing a new publication, Wild Pennsylvania.

These were added to the almost solitary voice of the Sierra Club, which now took on some new life that focused on old-growth proposals for the state forests, with a special emphasis on the classification of all "wild areas" as "old-growth areas" and the adoption of a no-cut policy for them.[65] Network ties were fostered among these groups, which were enhanced when the Allegheny Group of the Sierra Club received a bequest to be distributed "on behalf of wildlife." Projects throughout the state were eligible for support, and this became an important project of the Club's Pennsylvania Chapter. Other organizations contributed to the growth of ecological activity in the state. A group of wildlife professionals with connections to the Hawk Mountain Sanctuary in northeast central Pennsylvania produced two studies of the state's wildlife and wild places, which were made available on the Web site of the Department of Conservation and Natural Resources.[66] The Pennsylvania Biodiversity Partnership (PBP), an informal organization of professional biologists, established an electronic networking list and produced the first of an anticipated sequence of reports, Biodiversity in Pennsylvania: Snapshot 2002.[67]

The Bureau of Forestry remained stubbornly resistant to this set of ecological initiatives in the final draft of its State Forest Management Plan, issued in 2003. Its major thoughts on such matters were included in two sections, "Ecological Considerations" and "Water Quality." On a wide range of subjects, such as natural areas and wild areas, plant sanctuaries, old growth, bioreserves, and species inventories, it offered affirmations of ecological objectives but few changes in past policies of limited action. One change suggested for the management of wild areas was a presumption of "no timber harvest," but with unspecified exceptions which the chief of the bureau would determine. And a goal was established that 20 percent of the state forest acreage would be managed as old growth, but with no stipulation of what this meant in terms of forest age or management policies.[68] Plant sanctuaries were reaffirmed and made "a formal part of the Forest Resource Plan," but with but no schedule adopted as to when and where they would be applied. While plant sanctuaries had been authorized by legislation in 1982, the Bureau of Forestry continued to describe action as "proposed" rather than "completed." The bioreserve system, long talked about, continued to be described in terms limiting human use but with no ecological management provisions. And the Pennsylvania Natural Diversity Index (PNDI) continued to be confined to an "inventory of rare, endangered and unique" species rather than an across-the-board program pertaining to "sensitive" species. Affirmation of the state's Gap Analysis Program held some promise for action of broader scope, but there were no site-specific land protection programs to implement it. And while considerable publicity had been given earlier to the Important Bird Area program sponsored by the state Audubon Society, it was not a part of the 2003 State Forest Plan's "ecological considerations."

The gap between state citizen initiatives in ecological forestry and the Bureau of Forestry was also emphasized by the disarray that had developed in the organization of biodiversity activities within the Department of Conservation and Natural Resources. The recommendations of the outgoing coordinator, Bob Hill, that the position be a "science advisor" in the office of the secretary of the DCNR rather than be relegated to a subordinate position within the Bureau of Forestry, had been adopted early in 2001, and in October it was announced that Steve Balzano had been appointed as the department's first director of biodiversity, a position that was described more as one of "coordination" rather than "direction" of department biodiversity affairs. Yet eight months later, in late June 2002, it was announced that Balzano had resigned.[69]

The advisory council to the Department of Conservation and Natural Resources deplored this situation and kept pressing for vigorous direction of the department's biodiversity affairs. The election in 2002 of a new gubernatorial administration and a new secretary for the DCNR, Michael DiBerardinis, provided another opportunity to include biodiversity programs in the Bureau of Forestry and the DCNR. In December 2002 it was announced that an Office of Biodiversity Conservation had been established in the Office of the Secretary of the DCNR, and that the Pennsylvania Natural Diversity Inventory and the Office of Wild Resource Conservation would be integral parts of that office. In June 2003 Sally Just, long associated with the department, was announced as the new director of the Office of Biodiversity Conservation, but the announcement provided little information about what new direction the office would pursue and how it would affect the Bureau of Forestry. DiBerardinis appointed several task forces to develop white papers to set department policies, and one dealt with "Conservation Science and Biodiversity." However, the task force was composed overwhelmingly of representatives from the Bureau of Forestry; its statements about biodiversity were highly generalized, and specific biodiversity issues were hardly mentioned.

While the two most useful earlier papers, one by the Ecosystem Management Advisory Committee concerning the distinctive opportunities provided by public forests in Pennsylvania, and the other by Bob Hill concerning the department biodiversity program had provided many suggestions as to the future course of such affairs in the department, these did not appear in the new white paper. It appeared that it was "business as usual" in Pennsylvania biodiversity programs.

The continued uncertainty about biodiversity programs in the Bureau of Forestry seemed to reflect disarray that stemmed from rivalry between resource agencies, relationships between the DCNR and the Bureau of Forestry, and lack of cooperation between the department and the legislature. The biodiversity program continued to display a gap between pretense and practice and served to thwart the interest in biodiversity expressed by citizens and scientists within the state.[70]

During these thirty years during which I participated in Pennsylvania forest affairs, several events or publications stand out as having significant potential to advance ecological forestry amid the overlying influence of commodity forest institutions. These include the "Special Roles" document drawn up by the Ecosystem Management Advisory Committee; the role of Bob Hill as ecosystem advisor to the Department of Conservation and Natural Resources, and his paper to the department assessing its biodiversity program; the initial response of Jim Finley and Steve Jones to the survey of forest attitudes in Pennsylvania, which soon evaporated; the brief tenure of

Steve Thorne as Goddard Professor in the School of Forestry; the "conditions" attached to the certification report about the state forests; the acid rain conference at Penn State organized by William Sharpe; and the varied contributions of ecological forestry advocates to the state's forest affairs. But these attempts at promoting ecological forestry made little headway amid the firm commitments of the state's "forest establishment" to commodity forestry.

While Pennsylvania, as well as most states, displayed in its policies a firm resistance to influences from ecological forestry as expressed by either citizen groups or scientists, a sharply different stance was developing in the federal government. Here, a vigorous movement to undermine ecological forestry was taking shape. Fed by a continued defense of commodity forestry from the industry, the professionals, and the agencies, it now evolved into a partisan attack mode through organization of anti-environmental strategies sharpened by the Gingrich revolution of 1994, and led by the private-enterprise ideology brought into the White House with the presidential victory of George W. Bush in 2000. With this new vigor in the attack on environmental forestry, the war in the woods entered a new phase.

 CHAPTER 6

The Skirmishes Become
a Full-Scale War

As the twentieth century turned into the twenty-first, the interplay between ecological and commodity forestry reached a new level of intensity. The context of issues which continued to play themselves out at the level of individual forest management became more generalized and manifest in a contest over the regulations to implement the 1976 act, a process of revision and counter-revision of regulations in place since 1982. This process now was shaped by the accumulated tendency over the preceding years to organize debate and action around partisan politics.

In the late 1970s the forest industry began to establish closer ties with the Republican Party. This was first evident in the Reagan administration's appointment of John Crowell, former general counsel of the Louisiana-Pacific Lumber Company, to the post of assistant secretary of agriculture in charge of the Forest Service. This connection between the industry and the Republicans grew over the years so that after the 1994 Republican congressional victory and the new leadership of Newt Gingrich in the Congress, Republican legislators with a strong anti-environmental record were placed in charge of the congressional legislative machinery. With the victory of George W. Bush in the election of 2000, industry and the Republican Party were primed to make an all-out onslaught on the influence of ecological objectives in national forest management. The most visible elements of this attack were the attempts to reverse the policies of the Clinton administration, but these only obscured an even more comprehensive attack on three decades of slow but steady environmental and ecological progress.

The Clinton Initiatives

At the advent of the administration of Bill Clinton in 1993, the time seemed ripe for an attempt to work ecological objectives more fully and formally into the context of national forest affairs, and the first evidence of that commitment appeared in the administration's attempt to bring new blood into the leadership of the U.S. Forest Service. The first effort was the appointment of a new chief whose experience and credentials would broaden the agency's perspective beyond its traditional commodity forestry objectives. This was Jack Ward Thomas, a wildlife specialist who had long been an employee of the agency but was not a member of the inner circle of the Senior Executive Service from which chiefs formerly had been selected. The appointment made manifest fissures within the agency, as those sympathetic to ecological forestry cheered the presence of a leader with a biological rather than a forestry bent, and the commodity forest advocates objected not only to a leader with broader views but to the fact that the appointment had drawn from an unconventional range of candidates.[1]

From the very start of his tenure, Thomas made clear that in his view the public had lost confidence in the Forest Service, and that his primary task was to restore public confidence. Yet Thomas was not at all clear as to what this meant in terms of substantive policy. On the one hand, he periodically affirmed the idea that, given the varied legislative mandates under which the Forest Service was required to work, "biodiversity" was now its main mission and that this should guide its direction. But on the other hand, he seemed to avoid the translation of those objectives into on-the-ground programs—he failed even to identify them in his diaries—and accepted the continuing dominant influence of wood production in the agency's mission.

Thomas soon became embroiled among contending national forest forces and their varied objectives and seemed to become stalemated amid the press of public demands on the one hand, and the Congress with its overwhelming commodity forestry bent on the other. He was increasingly frustrated by the welter of influences within the administration and the Congress, which restricted the freedom of the agency to make decisions based on its own professional judgments and direction. While the ecological forestry community had heralded his appointment because of his professional ties and his role in the Northwest Forest Plan, they soon became critical of his limited ability to forge substantive ecological objectives and he, in turn, came to blame their activities as a major source of demoralization within the agency. They were simply another influence, among many, that thwarted the independence and "professionalism" of the agency. In 1996, after only three years on the job, he decided to resign and to take up a career in the West among the wildlife scientists with whom he felt far more comfortable than with the politicians and bureaucrats in Washington. Thomas took up the post of Boone and Crockett Professor of Wildlife Management at the University of Montana.[2]

For its second attempt to move national forest affairs forward, the Clinton administration chose Michael Dombeck, head of the Bureau of Land Management and a water quality and fisheries specialist. His background enabled him to bring a perspective beyond commodity forestry to the agency's affairs. He formulated an approach to natural resource affairs quite similar to that of Aldo Leopold, with an emphasis on "land health" and a "land ethic." In contrast with Thomas, Dombeck was a member of the Senior Executive Service and hence not vulnerable on that score. Under Dombeck's leadership the administration fashioned a set of policies called the National Resource Agenda, which emphasized four topics: watershed health and restoration, ecologically sustainable forest and grasslands management, recreation, and roads. One could readily understand this combination of ideas as an effort to resolve long-standing issues with a new agency direction. It entailed a number of controversial objectives such as the protection of remaining roadless areas on the national forests, species viability, and old growth. The larger historical significance of this venture was an attempt to bring together into a coherent direction the varied statutory responsibilities under which the agency labored, ranging from the Multiple-Use Act of 1960, the National Environmental Policy Act of 1969, the Endangered Species Act of 1973, through the National Forest Management Act of 1976.[3]

The most all-encompassing of these issues were the regulations under which the 1976 National Forest Management Act was implemented. Ever since that act had been adopted, those regulations had been a major bone of contention, and although they had been approved in 1982 and were in force in subsequent years, almost all sides found them unacceptable and longed for major revision. During the first Bush administration the promulgation of the revised regulations had been postponed to avoid their involvement in the 1992 election, and when Thomas spearheaded their progress toward completion they were postponed once again for the same reason during the 1996 election. Dombeck and the Clinton administration took steps to revise the regulations and make them more responsive to the continuing changes in the social, scientific, and legislative climate within which the agency made its decisions.[4]

To facilitate this revision Dombeck appointed a new Committee of Scientists, much as was done by Congress in shaping implementation of the 1976 act. In its composition this committee differed markedly from the first Committee of Scientists, drawing from a wider range of professional disciplines and reflecting far more fully the enormous changes that had taken place in the public context of forest affairs. The committee identified many of these changes, sought to develop an approach to the most controversial issues, and hoped to establish a new general course for thinking about national forest policy.[5]

Two specific issues were the most far reaching, the issue of species viability and the role of science in the formation of forest plans. Attention to species viability had grown out of an attempt to apply the diversity provision of the 1976 act. In this provision, the Forest Service mandated that it would manage forest species so as to prevent their population decline, and thereby avoid their becoming eligible for consideration as threatened or endangered under the Endangered Species Act. This was known as a guarantee of species viability, and the species in question were referred to as "sensitive" species.[6] Forest management had to develop strategies for inventory, protection, and restoration; monitor outcomes; and budgets and professional skills had to be reordered to manage a much wider range of resources than was customary. Especially significant was the requirement now being imposed by the courts that the agency had to "survey" before "managing," that is, to obtain extensive knowledge about species on proposed sale areas before harvest would take place, so that negative effects could be avoided.[7]

These responsibilities for biodiversity resources, in the face of limited ecological skills among agency personnel, required that the forest supervisors draw upon scientists from many and diverse sources outside the agency to provide technical knowledge about species, their population trends, their viability, and their required habitats. Hence, the new regulations now called for the use of scientific peer review to provide scientific advice in drawing up forest plans and especially to make decisions about biological diversity. Seeking external advice was a standard procedure in managing threatened and endangered species, and in these cases a biological opinion from the Fish and Wildlife Service was required. The viability requirement, however, was mandated only for the Forest Service, growing out of the 1976 National Forest Management Act rather than the Endangered Species Act. It was therefore subject to agency regulations alone. Thus the new proposal would bring to the agency a similar degree of external scientific review for species management as had long been the case for threatened and endangered species.

The Committee of Scientists provided overall guidance to its specific proposals by establishing ecological sustainability as the objective of forest management. The forest was seen as an ecological system, within which wood production would be an important but subordinate use. This reflected the broader shift in public and scientific sentiment which had taken place, even though rather subtly, from the user focus of the Multiple-Use Act of 1960 to attention to the qualitative condition of forest resources, as was implicit in the mandates of such laws as the National Environmental Policy Act and the Endangered Species Act. The intent was to establish a firm "resource condition" as the ultimate goal of forest management to which the satisfaction of user interests and objectives would be adjusted, much as in the general objective of resource management that had been formulated by Aldo Leopold.

This reformulation of the objectives of national forest management became controversial as soon as the drafts of the committee's report became known. The chair of the committee, Professor Norman Johnson of Oregon State University, submitted his resignation, complaining that the committee's draft had too strong an "ecological" tone, but he was soon persuaded to return to the committee. However, another member of the committee, Roger Sedjo of Resources for the Future, submitted a dissenting view, criticizing the "ecological sustainability" objective, the "viability" provision, and the committee's statement that the national forests were in a severely degraded condition and badly needed restoration. These internal disagreements were readily available to the public as they were publicized on a committee Web site that encouraged public discussion; the Sedjo statement received several replies.[8]

The new forest regulations were finalized in the waning days of the Clinton administration, but by that time they had been fully publicized, extensively debated, and served to polarize the debate over forest policy along harder lines. In particular they aroused the more traditional sectors of forest affairs into a high-alert combative role with the argument that, instead of serving to bring together the diverse impulses which had arisen following the 1960 Multiple-Use Act, the proposal was in fact a major revision of that act and hence an unacceptable attempt to legislate administratively. By the time George W. Bush took office, the lines were set for a massive confrontation between the old and the new in national forest management.

The Bush Anti-environmental Revolution

The new administration of George W. Bush took its narrow and contested victory in the election of 2000 to be a mandate for sweeping changes in many fields of public policy. Some of the most extensive changes involved the public lands and especially the national forests. The administration set out to reverse three decades of environmental forest policy, including the practices inaugurated by the National Environmental Policy Act and the Endangered Species Act as well as the National Forest Management Act of 1976.[9]

In charting its objectives in forest policy, the administration took the course mapped out by the advocates of a greater role for wood production on the national forests: the wood products industry and the Society of American Foresters (SAF). The society called for "comprehensive legislative changes," while the industry was more inclined to avoid public debate and urged the administration to create changes by quieter and less publicized administrative action. Since massive changes did not seem possible in the legislative arena, the administration took the latter course, where it could act unilaterally. These recommendations emphasized changes in administrative procedures, such as the intra-agency Forest Service appeals process, the requirement that the agency rely on the Fish and Wildlife Service for biological opinions in threatened and endangered species cases, and regulations in the application of the National Environmental Policy Act. But the SAF also made clear that its major substantive concern was with the agency's viability program. In its statement of objectives it emphasized: "A key issue is the priority that should be given to maintaining a 'natural' diversity of plant and animal species." So far as the wood products community was concerned, the Forest Service was making the wrong decisions about such matters. While ideally the Congress should change the prevailing policy, absent that, the administration should require the agency to take a different tack.[10]

In pursuing these objectives the administration attempted to avoid high-profile confrontation; instead it took up quiet actions that were less likely to create widespread and sustained media attention and would avoid unpredictable and complicating court decisions.[11] The administration appointed low-profile administrators who were adept at unobtrusively engineering important changes in agency action while presenting a media image which emphasized "clarification" and "administrative efficiency" rather than revision of regulations, of which most represented directly the objectives of the wood products industry. Their purposes were clear: the forest industry and commodity forestry would play a far greater and even dominant role in the Forest Service. The initial appointments, of Ann Venneman as secretary of agriculture and Mark Rey as undersecretary, both of whom were closely associated with the extractive industries, set the tone.[12] They would be responsible for selecting a new chief of the Forest Service, which did not take place until a year later, in 2002.

The new leadership created significant openings for anti-environmental action. They defended mandates in environmental statutes only weakly. They challenged or ignored scientific knowledge relevant to environmental and ecological management decisions in favor of that advanced by commodity forest advocates. They undertook revisions of rules and regulations which had been drawn up to implement statutes with environmental and ecological objectives. For the analyst of administrative politics these diverse initiatives of the Bush administration constitute a gold mine of imaginative legal action that abundantly illustrates the enormous possibilities of quiet executive initiatives to change the course of policy.

These changes were made at many points in the agency's decision-making process. In some cases major decisions made by the previous administration were now reconsidered and plans revised; in other cases decisions in the pipeline but still not finalized were pulled back for revision; and in still other cases plans under formulation were drawn up to reflect the agency's preference for traditional wood production objectives and its attempt to reverse trends toward ecological forestry. Dombeck's directives to the supervisors to develop old-growth policies and plans were simply ignored in the face of the fact that harvest of old-growth areas was now an acceptable element in national forest plans and projects.

A significant reversal in policy was reflected in the public statements made by the previous chief forester, Mike Dombeck, and the new one, Dale Bosworth. Dombeck's "Natural Resource Agenda" emphasized four topics: watershed health and restoration, ecologically sustainable forest and grassland management, recreation, and roads.[13] In the summer of 2003 Bosworth announced quite a different agenda, framed in terms of "threats" rather than objectives, which he enumerated as invasive species, unmanaged off-road-vehicle use, loss of open space, and wildfire.[14] Bosworth simply ignored the context of "resource protection" that had been emerging since 1960, and sidestepped debates over the significance of ecological forestry objectives that Dombeck had sought as one of the main elements of his approach. Both Thomas and Dombeck emphasized that one of their major objectives was to restore the confidence of the public in the Forest Service, which had declined sharply in recent years. Bosworth did not mention this, and in this way conveyed his lack of concern for agency relationships with the public. Close observers of national forest issues could not fail to identify the sharply different directions in which the two chiefs sought to take the agency. The first four years of the George W. Bush administration specified these differences in a host of actions.[15]

Species Protection

The most persistent and far-reaching substantive issue in the contest between ecological and commodity forest management involved wildlife, and especially the expansion of the role of forest wildlife from game to nongame and biodiversity wildlife resources, invertebrates, plants, and fish. A number of laws and policies were involved, and the Bush administration developed a wide-ranging approach in its search for ways to modify earlier practices and interpretations to restrict benefits to wild resources and enhance wood production. Some tactics involved wildlife-related initiatives from outside the U.S. Forest Service, which posed restraints on the agency; modification of regulations and practices within the agency itself to favor wood production was another tactic.

The Endangered Species Act of 1973 posed the most severe restraints. That act applied to all federal land management agencies and required them to request the Fish and Wildlife Service (FWS) to provide a biological opinion as to the population status on the agency's lands of potential candidates as threatened or endangered species. Agencies were required by law to follow the FWS opinion and institute protective measures. The Bush administration made two significant changes in past practice. The most far reaching was to give the land management agency the discretion as to whether or not it would request a biological opinion, which meant that henceforth the crucial initiating decisions leading to protective action would be made by the Forest Service and not by FWS.[16] The second action, dealing with aquatic resources administered by the National Oceanic and Atmospheric Administration (NOAA), rejected the need to examine the effects of individual timber harvests on the water quality of its immediate watershed. The Bush administration appointed Mark Rutzick as senior advisor to the general counsel of NOAA, with responsibility for Pacific salmon protected under the ESA. Rutzick had been the lead attorney for the forest industry in the Northwest, which had requested major modifications in protective actions for wild salmon.

Still another strategy requested by the Northwest forest industry was taken up by the Bush administration, in this case a more direct challenge to the scientific information pertaining to the most celebrated of the North-

west forest wild resources, the spotted owl.[17] In 1994, as part of a program
for dealing with Pacific Northwest forest issues, an interagency monitoring
program had been established, one part of which would gather scientific
data on the population levels and distribution of the spotted owl. By the
time of the advent of the Bush administration this program had been under
way for six years. The forest industry, however, challenged the work of the
population biologists who were charting the owl's fate and argued that the
reported continued decline of the owl was greatly exaggerated. In fact, it
argued, the owl was never endangered, because the northern spotted owl
was only part of a larger group of spotted owls, including the California owl
and the Mexican owl; for purposes of the ESA all three should be considered as one species, and if that were done none were "threatened or endangered." The industry argued that an independent analysis of the northern
spotted owl should be undertaken to review the work of the interagency
committee. The administration did so by contracting out the task to a firm
of private consultants that received considerable financial support from the
timber industry. However, the consulting firm, under wide public scrutiny,
appointed a review committee of highly respected scientists independent
of the industry, rejected the industry claims that the three species of the
spotted owl were, in fact, one, and concluded that the owl was, indeed, still
declining in population.

While the role of wild resources protected by the ESA was the most
visible wildlife issue, the Bush administration also sought to change policy
around the issues of diversity and viability. A provision in the Forest Service
Manual read, "There must be no impacts to sensitive species without an
analysis of the significance of adverse effects on the populations, its habitat,
and on the viability of the species as a whole." This requirement from the
regulations of 1982 that the Forest Service inventory and account for "sensitive species" in order to prevent their further decline soon became a major
bone of contention between ecological forestry advocates and the agency.
The ecologists focused on the inventory requirement in order to chart the
ecological impacts of forest disturbances such as timber harvest and pressed
forward with its application. Under the pressure of such requirements, on
the other hand, the agency soon pulled back on the grounds that the task was
far beyond the agency's resources. For several years there was a continual set
of demands by the citizen groups that the agency conduct the required surveys, the agency hesitated to comply, the issue went to the courts, and the
courts sided with the citizen groups on the grounds that the regulations and
the manual clearly demonstrated a legal obligation to inventory.

A primary location of this drama was in the Southern Appalachians, where the issue had proceeded through two lawsuits.[18] In the first, the court affirmed the requirement, but the agency did not comply. In the second, in which the plaintiffs requested compliance, the agency responded by merely withdrawing eighty timber sales which were affected by the issue. At that point the agency's response was to modify each of the forest plans so that the inventory requirement was dropped. Finally in 2001, citizen groups acting through the Southern Environmental Law Center brought a third action focusing specifically on the plan revisions in which no environmental impact analysis had been made (the agency simply made a more perfunctory environmental assessment and declared that the decision involved "no significant impact") and the action had been taken with no public participation.

In its proposal to replace the Clinton regulations, the subsequent Bush administration "solved" the problem by eliminating the requirement to maintain viable populations of native wildlife species. At the same time it eliminated the requirement that supervisors monitor project impacts, leaving that up to the discretion of each national forest supervisor. Also dropped was the Clinton proposal that forest supervisors draw on external peer review of scientific decisions. This freed the supervisors from influence from ecological scientists outside the agency in general and the opinions of species specialists in particular. Thus, in implementing both the Endangered Species Act (ESA) and the National Forest Management Act, individual forest supervisors would now have much more authority to act independently from both the agency's own regulations and the requirements of the ESA.[19]

Modifying Forest Plans: The Pacific Northwest Plan

A more concrete and substantive reading of the administration's commodity objectives could be followed in actions on the various forest plans and programs either already in place or in the making. Significant changes appeared in plans for a number of western forests, such as the Tongass in Alaska, the Sierra Nevada forests in California, the Bitterroot National Forest in western Montana, and Pacific Northwest forests. The administration declined to include in its plan for the Southern Appalachians the most important provisions of the citizens' proposal, which had received widespread publicity and support in the region. These changes were made through agency initiatives with far less public involvement than had been the case in previous years. And they had greater impact in light of the new agency-wide regulations that environmental impact statements would no longer be conducted at the forest plan level. That new rule gave the supervisors far more freedom to make their own choices in formulating forest plans; the results of this soon

appeared, when the new forest administration withdrew and revised existing plans and formulated new ones.

The greatest controversy over forest plans came with the Bush effort to
modify the Northwest Forest Plan approved by the Clinton administration
in 1993. The issue focused on three aspects of that settlement: the requirement that the managing agencies survey certain forest lands for the presence
of species before they would be allocated for logging; the Aquatic Conservation Strategy that was devised to protect salmon; and the protection of
specific endangered species, namely the spotted owl and the marbled mur-
relet. All of these would lead to removing forest lands from timber harvest.
The forest management agencies themselves, both the Forest Service and the
Bureau of Land Management, with jurisdiction over 2.4 million acres of forest land in western Oregon, chafed under these responsibilities and wished
to reduce them, but the immediate and most influential driving force in
the Bush administration's approach to them was the timber industry in the
Pacific Northwest.

In April 2003 the Earthjustice office in Seattle, Washington, through
a Freedom of Information Act lawsuit, obtained documents that demonstrated the role of the industry in modifying the 1993 Pacific Northwest
Program.[20] In its initial proposal to the administration in April 2002, "A
Global Framework for Settlement of Litigation Challenging Federal Agency
Actions Relating to the Northwest Forest Plan," the industry set forth its
demands for settling the issues in four industry-initiated lawsuits. It also
recommended that administrative action—what it called "administrative
tools," rather than action in the courts—be taken in order to avoid embar-
rassing legal decisions that might result.[21] The administration complied with
most of the industry proposals and the resulting action followed closely the
industry recommendations. Given their deep misgivings about responsibilities under the Northwest Plan, the federal agencies involved, both the U.S.
Forest Service and the Bureau of Land Management, were more than willing
to follow the industry's lead.

In fact, almost as soon as the plan had been approved in 1994, the agencies made clear that they would limit the application of the "survey and
manage" requirements by modifying both the stipulated date of their implementation and by reducing the number of species to which they applied.
The zeal with which they procrastinated in carrying out the provisions of
the plan indicated that they had neither knowledge nor interest in managing
on behalf of old-growth-dependent species and harked back to the forestry
profession's long-standing and profound aversion to the idea that ancient
forests were of any value. They seemed to share the contempt expressed by

industry representatives in belittling the importance of invertebrates and plants and to ignore the significant approach of the plan in its attempt to manage so as to prevent sensitive species from becoming threatened or endangered. Working in tandem, the agency and the industry willingly joined with the administration in undermining the objectives of the scientists who had brought the subject of biodiversity into the plan.[22] Much in contrast, ecological scientists argued that over the years new research had demonstrated the need to pursue the protection of many species more vigorously.[23]

The changes in the Pacific Northwest Plan were significant beyond that region, as they served as a dramatic instance of many of the larger issues in which the Bush administration sought to advance commodity objectives and reduce ecological objectives in forest management. In its approach to the nationwide task of "survey and manage" that had evolved over the years, it installed a substitute that emphasized a focus on area-wide habitat rather than protection of individual species. If there was adequate habitat then there would be adequate species protection. This reversed the customary relationship between species and habitat that had emphasized the need to conduct population studies to focus on the population condition or "viability" of species and the need to provide habitat to reverse declines and guarantee "viability." A habitat analysis provided opportunities simply to affirm the opinion that a species was in satisfactory condition if the habitat was available, an opinion that would be expressed not by species specialists but by forest supervisors who decided for themselves the adequacy of habitat.

The controversy over "survey and manage" reflected a more fundamental difference between ecological and commodity forestry—the degree to which forest managers should include in their program activities the full range of forest plants and animals. The ancient forests of the Pacific Northwest presented this problem quite sharply, since they were heavily populated by a wide range of species, including bryophytes, lichens, fungi, microinvertebrates, and other lesser-known species that were usually ignored in debates over endangered species. A wide range of scientists specializing in these species had been instrumental in bringing them into the Northwest Plan, and the plan required that the agencies identify their presence, via field inventory, as the first step in protective management.

However, almost as soon as the plan was adopted it was rather clear that most parties involved in implementation were none too enthusiastic about provisions for this wide range of "lesser" species, and that their lethargy was a result of their lack of conviction that those species were important enough to spend management resources on them. The forest industry felt that they were a waste of time, spoke of those species in derogatory terms,

and equally belittled the scientists and field biologists who were their advocates. As one of its strategies the industry toyed with the legal argument that
lichens, fungi, and mosses were not subject to endangered species protection
because the law dealt only with plants and animals and those species were
technically neither. Moreover, the media, while they were eager to give the
spotted owl the status of a signature species worth public attention, thought
of the allocation of management time and effort to inventory and protect
these lesser species as a waste of resources. It remained for ecological scientists to defend their importance in letters to agency management and for
citizen reform groups to do the same in litigation. The issue pinpointed the
vast gulf between the two worlds of ecological and commodity forestry.

The Pacific Northwest plan involved watersheds and the role of their
condition on salmon populations as well as terrestrial wildlife.[24] There was
general agreement that the reduction of forest cover through wood harvest
was a crucial factor in the population decline of wild salmon, and causal relationships had been established between the two. Moreover, in the Aquatic
Conservation Strategy the case was made that overall watershed conditions
were the aggregate and cumulative results of many smaller harvest projects. Hence the improvement of watersheds depended on the control of the
cumulative aquatic effects of each harvest. But those who objected to the
idea that timber harvesting should be curtailed to protect salmon habitat
argued that site-specific watershed relationships were misleading. The detrimental effects of site-specific timber harvesting were readily overcome,
so they argued, because the beneficial effects of the wider area maintained
by extant forest areas could readily outweigh the detrimental effects of individual harvests. Considering the watershed as a whole would enable forest
managers to argue, as they often did with many ecological resources, that a
site-specific harm was acceptable because of its limited impact on the wider
watershed. The administration took up this argument, advanced by the forest industry, and in litigation proceedings rejected the arguments of fisheries
and watershed protection advocates.[25]

The Tongass National Forest

The Bush reversal of previous forest policies in the Pacific Northwest Plan
was only the most comprehensive of its efforts to use the planning process
to enhance wood production and limit ecological forest objectives. The Tongass National Forest administration, for example, had identified 123 areas as
qualifying for proposed wilderness classification, and was in the process of
selecting candidates from that group.[26] The Southeast Alaska Conservation
Council had identified 23 for designation. But in drawing up the revised

Tongass plan the Bush administration accepted none of them, exempted both Alaskan national forests from the "roadless rule," and called for no further wilderness designations for the Tongass. At the same time the Alaska congressional delegation took parallel action to make this decision stick by obtaining a legislative rider that prohibited any legal appeals from that decision, thereby insulating the administration from further citizen action.[27]

The Tongass was the site of extensive karst formations; arguments over their protection were instructive of the clash between ecological and commodity forest objectives. When karst formations were becoming prominent in forest management there, the Tongass administration hired a cave expert, Steve Lewis, to identify the significance of the karst resource. As he discovered its extent he also found that the Forest Service carried out only a limited degree of protection for the caves. Soon he resigned his post to become co-director of the Tongass Cave Project under the direction of Timothy H. Heaton of South Dakota State University, financed by the National Science Foundation. The issue became how much land was needed to protect the caves, and what extent of protection was desired. Lewis became one of the numerous scientists independent of the agency who served as an external critic of its protection policies. The new Bush regulations enabled the Tongass administration more readily to reject the advice of the Tongass Cave Project leaders.[28]

The Bitterroot Forest Rehabilitation Program

In the year 2000 some 300,000 acres of the Bitterroot National Forest in western Montana were burned and the subsequent "rehabilitation" program confronted the new Bush administration with one of its first forest-specific controversies. The supervisor, Rodd Richardson, proposed a salvage sale of some 176 million board feet on a 46,000-acre timber sale. Mark Rey, the new undersecretary of Agriculture, whose close ties to the timber industry inevitably marked him as a vigorous spokesman for increased commodity wood production on the national forests, approved the plan but with a significant proviso that it could not be subject to an administrative appeal and that potential objectors would have to go directly to the federal courts.

Among the opponents, several groups jointly proposed a different approach to the burned-over area in the form of a Conservation and Local Economy Alternative (known as Alternative G), in which a significant area would have been off limits to "salvage" harvest; a model burned-area recovery plan would be adopted to protect homes; forest replanting, road rehabilitation, and protection of fish and wildlife and streams would be instituted. This formed the basis of an appeal to Supervisor Richardson's proposal, the appeal which Rey rejected. It was well known that in response to the Rey decision, the conservationists would go to the courts. When this happened, U.S. District Court judge Donald Malloy ruled that Rey's decision to rule out an administrative appeal was contrary to the law and ordered the parties to Missoula, Montana, to participate in two days of mediation under the direction of yet another federal judge, Michael Hogan of Oregon. As a result the parties forged an agreement in which 27,000 acres of roadless old-growth forest and sensitive fish habitat were removed from the initial proposal to log 46,000 acres. The Bitterroot salvage proposal provided one of the first opportunities to identify the approach of the Bush administration to national forest planning and management: direction from Washington to resolve disputes instead of insisting on resolution at the local level, supervision of a more local process by the federal courts, and preference by the administration for a commodity wood production program rather than a balance between commodity and ecological objectives.

Despite this agreement, however, the Bitterroot administration forged ahead with a vigorous salvage program and was slow to institute the "replanting and rehabilitation" part of the agreement. Jennifer Ferenstein, one of the leaders of the environmental group that participated in the dispute resolution process described the results, "What we haven't seen is the restoration work being accomplished. What we have seen is the logging going forward." In the early days of the dispute Richardson had proposed to his superiors in Washington that several small 5,000-acre salvage cuts be instituted prior to a larger project, in order to provide an opportunity to build working relationships at the forest level, but Rey rejected this. The same problem of actions that build confidence among contending parties versus actions that threaten it and create mistrust appeared in the implementation of the agreement which the federal judge had fostered.[29]

The Sierra Nevada Plan

The Sierra Nevada Forest Framework, encompassing the seven national forests of the Sierra Nevada Mountains in California, became the most far-reaching and at the same time the most contentious of national forest plans. It incorporated ecological objectives more fully than did other plans and became a model as to the direction that ecological forestry advocates thought the agency should take. It was developed with considerable input from ecological scientists interested in forestry and hence represented an intensive parallel collaboration between citizen groups and scientists in forest affairs.[30]

The forest reform community, represented by the Sierra Nevada Forest Protection Campaign, gave strong support to the framework, which had been approved by regional forester Brad Powell in January 2001. According to Craig Thomas, conservation director of the campaign, "The Sierra Nevada Framework represents a major step forward. . . . The plan begins the process of protecting and restoring the Sierra Nevada's ecosystems, which have been degraded by decades of logging and road building sanctioned by the U.S. Forest Service." While forest reformers filed no administrative appeals to the framework, 234 appeals were filed largely by industry and "wise use" groups protesting the increased restrictions on logging medium-sized and old-growth trees. The appeals were filed with the new Bush administration and hence faced new administrators who were friendly to the pleas of commodity forestry advocates. The new secretary of agriculture, Ann Venneman, had recently represented the coalition Sierra Nevada Access, Multiple-Use and Stewardship (SAMS), composed of eighty-five local groups, including timber firms, snowmobilers, chambers of commerce, and off-road-vehicle enthusiasts, a coalition that led a vigorous fight against the plan. Mark Rey, who would review the appeals as undersecretary, had long been a lobbyist for the forest industry.

The agency soon positioned itself to make major changes in the framework. In October 2001, Brad Powell, the regional forester who had steered through the framework, was transferred to another region and replaced by Jack Blackwell, who was instructed to review the framework decision. In November 2002, Forest Service chief Dale Bosworth affirmed the Sierra Nevada Framework Record of Decision, denied all issues in each of the 234 appeals, but instructed the new regional forester to review key aspects of Powell's decision, including those pertaining to old growth and wildlife, and emphasis on fire protection measures to protect homes and communities; at the same time Blackwell chose to review the impact of the framework on grazing and recreation interests. This range of review subjects, as the agency affirmed, were intended to respond to the administrative appeals even though they had been formally denied.[31]

The agency review of the framework involved reversals of the process by which it had been developed. That process had involved the creation of two major scientific reviews of the condition of the Sierra Nevada forests. One, a $7-million undertaking funded by the U.S. Congress, the Sierra Nevada Ecosystem Project (SNEP), had been carried out by the Wildland Resources Center at the University of California and had detailed four problems: the impaired aquatic/riparian systems of the region; the degree to which timber harvest had increased fire severity; the adverse impact of loss of riparian and forest habitat on wildlife; and the damage done to riparian areas by mining, dams, diversions, road, logging, residential development, and recreational activities. Neither those making the appeals nor the Forest Service sought to bring a similar degree of scientific analysis and investigation to the review, but simply emphasized the complaints of the various timber, grazing, and recreational interests.

By the end of 2001, fire policy had taken center stage in national forest affairs and played an important part in the Sierra Nevada Framework debate. The framework considered fire issues and emphasized the protection of communities and homes through thinning smaller trees and prescribed burning to reduce fuel loads. But the wood production community insisted that larger trees away from communities also be harvested as a fire protection policy. This debate soon encompassed not only the problem of thinning as a desirable method of fire protection, but also the problem of acquiring funds to pay for the thinning. Forest managers had long faced the fact that while thinning was desirable for both silvicultural and fire protection objectives, buyers of thinned products were scarce. The Forest Service had sought to attract buyers by including larger, older, and hence more valuable trees in the timber contracts. Thus, instead of obtaining appropriations to finance thinning, the agency would cover the cost through selling larger and older trees.

The initial proposals drawn up by Blackwell's review team were issued in February 2003. On the whole they drew back from the ecological proposals of the Powell proposal and moved the framework toward greater accommodation of wood production.[32] The maximum diameter for timber harvest was increased, with considerable emphasis on the need to cut larger trees to pay for the costs of thinning. Wildlife habitat for the spotted owl on the forests was reduced by recalculating owl populations to support a rosier picture as to their size, and by arguing that less habitat on public forests was needed because habitat on private lands should be taken into account. It rejected prescribed burns emphasized in the Powell plan on the grounds that they would be too dangerous and too limited. And it gave special emphasis to the difficulties of implementing the original plan in on-the-ground management. The reaction of the two contending groups was predictable. While the forest reform community argued that the second proposal involved considerable backsliding from ecological objectives, the California Forestry Association lauded it as "good for the environment."[33]

Individual and Regional Forest Plans

The most significant revisions of on-the-ground policy took place in the far quieter actions involved in changing old individual forest plans and drawing up new ones. In one of the earliest cases before the appointment of the new chief forester, agriculture secretary Ann Venneman reversed an action of the previous chief, Mike Dombeck. Dombeck had returned three plans on Colorado national forests—the Arapaho-Roosevelt, the Routt, and the Rio Grande—for revision on the ground that they had failed to adequately address responsibility for species viability. Venneman reversed Dombeck's decision and announced that she would soon announce new viability standards and offer "general guidance" concerning the basic principle of viability.[34]

One of the first plans to be revised was that for the Southern Appalachian Region. The new proposed management for five of the area's forests reflected only minimal influence from the agency's extensive survey of public attitudes in the region or the citizen plan for the region's forests. The Southern Appalachian Forest Coalition reported that the proposals "drop key water, wildlife and forest protection, allow increased timber production, and leave some of our favorite places open to road building, logging and unchecked disturbance." More specifically the plan was deficient, so the coalition argued, in its proposals for wilderness, roadless areas, riparian protection, old-growth protection and monitoring, its proposal to increase the level of logging, and its "inappropriate" use of fire.[35]

Debate over the revision of the plan for the five national forests in this region was accompanied by a sensational incident, marked in the forest reform community but little noticed elsewhere. A scientist with twenty years of service with the Cherokee National Forest, Quentin Bass, had undertaken research as to the conditions of the forests of the Southern Appalachians before extensive timber cutting and before the establishment of the national forests there. The Forest Service had long concluded that these forests had gone through a succession from early to middle to late stages of growth, which had followed earlier disturbance by fire. On the contrary, Bass concluded, the forests had been for many years mixed-aged forests that were relatively stable. The information countered the long-standing statement by the Forest Service that the forests required large-scale logging and prescribed burns to mimic natural conditions that would create the "early successional" forest required to produce older merchantable timber. The Bass analysis and recommendations were given to the agency administrators, who rejected them and continued to base their arguments for scheduling increased harvests on older views. Bass argued to the U.S. Forest Service that failure to incorporate the new knowledge violated the agency's planning requirements. His case was taken up by a group of southeastern regional organizations including the Southern Environmental Law Center and the Forest Service Employees for Environmental Ethics.[36]

A major reversal of policy for the Southern Appalachians involved changes in the proposed forest plans that were made quietly and without public notice or involvement. The earlier proposal, which had been discussed in public meetings, emphasized environmental restoration in which logging would be permitted only as a by-product of managing for other values such as wildlife habitat and recreation. This seemed to follow the agency's own analysis of the results of its survey of public opinion and its stated goals of watershed health, recreation, ecosystem sustainability, wildlife habitat, recovery of threatened and endangered species, old-growth forests, and remote recreation opportunities. But a few months later the Forest Service regional leadership team decided to allow individual forests to designate lands where the primary emphasis would be "the purposeful growing, tending, harvesting, and regeneration of regulated crops of trees." This effort to establish areas on the national forests devoted predominantly to wood production had long been an objective of the wood products industry. They continued to deplore the lack of such a provision in the Multiple-Use Act of 1960. While that act spelled out the authorized uses of the national forests, it did not specify the relative balance that should be maintained among them and this, so the industry argued, was a deficiency which should be corrected.[37]

Roadless Areas

The national forest issue that aroused the most extensive media attention and the widest public interest during the second Bush administration was the Clinton administration proposal to protect 58.5 million acres of roadless national forest land from further road building or development. The proposal was drawn up over a period of three years and involved the most extensive public participation ever for a national forest issue—six hundred public meetings throughout the country and 1.6 million written and oral comments. The proposal, announced early in 2001 at the end of the Clinton administration, immediately met the vigorous opposition of the wood products industry and was high on the schedule of Clinton proposals that the Bush administration set about to reverse. The state of Idaho, at the instigation of the Boise Cascade Lumber Company, sued to rescind the action (it was joined by Utah and Alaska), and while the Bush administration only postponed rather than rescinded it, it gave only minimal support to the action in the courts. The federal judge ruled in favor of Idaho, on the grounds that the public process was far too limited; his decision was later overruled in an appeal to the Ninth Circuit Court of Appeals in San Francisco. When a Wyoming federal judge then ruled against the roadless rule, the Bush administration selected that decision as more definitive.[38]

The Bush administration made clear its opposition to the Clinton proposal on the grounds that certain groups in the West, which it identified as· "states, tribes and local communities," had not been fully consulted, and that it would reopen the process to allow changes. The administration treaded rather warily around the issue, realizing full well the popularity of the roadless area proposal. Of the written and oral comments in the initial review, some 95 percent supported the idea, and a later nationwide survey indicated that 67 percent supported it, with support from 76 percent of Democrats, 66 percent of independents, and 58 percent of Republicans. Two weeks after the appointment of Dale Bosworth as the new chief forester, the administration announced that it would retain, rather than rescind the rule, and would solicit comment on keeping or changing it. This time there were 726,440 replies, among which 97 percent said that the rule should stand. The agency then proceeded to undermine this conclusion by the argument that only 52,432 of the replies were "original responses," and the remainder were form cards, letters, or e-mails, which would not be counted. An analysis of the 726,440 responses made clear the division within the country over the issue. On the one side were many members of Congress, scientists, religious leaders, recreationists, conservationists, environmentalists, and the public who favored protecting roadless areas from commercial logging and road building. On the other, the timber, mining, forest products, and helicopter industries, along with off-road-vehicle advocates and anti-environmental politicians, were opposed to protection of roadless areas. In the spring of 2003 the revised rule kept the framework of the original Clinton proposal, added a considerable number of exclusions and exceptions, and provided that governors, if they chose, could opt out of its provisions.[39] Later, in finalizing the proposal the administration changed the strategy to require that each governor would have to petition to opt into any protection for roadless areas in that state.

The Clinton roadless area proposal had two somewhat related but quite different components. One pertained to the areas still roadless, which were subject to protection. But another proposal accompanied it which called for a reduction of the current national forest road system, now consisting of

400,000 miles of roads and facing a maintenance backlog of $8 billion. Prohibition of roads on roadless areas was intended to head off a further increase of this looming cost, but maintenance costs for existing roads were to be reduced by the requirement that each national forest should examine its roads and identify those that could be eliminated or restricted so as to downsize the system. This proposal generated far less publicity than did that calling for protection of roadless areas, but led to a more quiet process, often with the cooperation of forest reformers who had long argued that the national forest road system was far too large and should be curtailed.[40]

The Bush administration's response to the Clinton roadless area initiative was an integral part of its more comprehensive anti-wilderness program. In many emerging forest plans, the supervisors had been giving support to at least some proposed additions to the national wilderness system. That now changed. The most dramatic cases were on the Tongass and Chugach national forests in Alaska, where the administration's negative attitude toward wilderness had the full support of the state's congressional delegation. The new chief forester, Dale Bosworth, made clear that he would not propose new designations on the grounds that the issue had already been dealt with by the supervisors at the forest level.

Forest Health

During the early years of the twenty-first century, public discussion of national forest issues adopted a new general language of "forest health," with a Forest Health Initiative from the administration and legislation approved by the Congress known as the "Healthy Forests Act."[41] The immediate focus for discussion of "forest health" was the spate of dramatic forest fires in the West, but underlying its rather fuzzy meaning were the persistent differences between ecological and commodity perspectives. On the surface, the debate over fire policy involved a choice as to where scarce funds would be spent—on protecting the homes of the forest-urban interface, the so-called "red zone," or on the wildland fires of the deeper forest. But on a less visible level that identified the deep chasm between the two perspectives was the objective of "forest health," the condition to which forests damaged by fire should be restored.

To commodity foresters, the phrase "forest health" merely expressed the long-established programs in which they sought to protect growing trees from insects, pests, and fire. The prominence of fire prevention and fire fighting was, in fact, nothing new. But as the cost of fighting western fires rose, the issue of fire prevention as a way of avoiding those costs did so as well. That so many people now built homes in forests near urban com-

munities as weekend or permanent homes gave this issue a high degree of
visibility. Attention converged on the red zone, as homes were destroyed by
fire. Homeowners were urged to protect their homes by building with fire-
resistant materials and clearing away flammable materials for a quarter-mile
or so around them. Local firefighters made clear that they would simply
bypass buildings that were vulnerable because of the failure to follow fire
prevention practices, and insurance companies began to require such preventive measures as a condition of renewing insurance policies.

Fire policies came to emphasize "ladder fuels," densely spaced small
trees that could quickly transmit ground fires to the canopy to become
"crown fires," which spread more quickly and were uncontrollable from
the ground. Hence measures to reduce these fuels became a major element
in fire prevention, in particular, either thinning and removing the smaller
trees or conducting "prescribed burns" in seasons when such burns were
readily controllable. It was widely agreed that "thinning" should be a major
element in forest fire prevention. But the cost of thinning quickly became
the most controversial issue. The market for thinned products was almost
nonexistent, and contracts drawn up to remove thinnings attracted few bid-
ders. National Forest personnel who drew up the timber contracts made
clear that the cost of including thinnings in contracts for larger trees was
much less—some argued a quarter of the cost—than the cost of paying for
removal in contracts confined to thinnings.[42] Hence the forest agencies were
prone to lump a thinning project with a proposal to harvest larger trees that
were marketable, so that the sale of larger trees would cover the unprofitable
disposal of smaller ones.

The issue soon pitted the forest industry against the environmental community. The industry argued that fire-prevention measures should include
larger trees deeper in the forest away from fire-endangered communities,
while the environmental community argued that it was precisely the larger
trees that were the least fire-prone, and that to cut them would only increase
fire danger. In this fashion the advocates of environmental and ecological
forestry became the champions of community action to protect the "red
zone," and the advocates of commodity forestry supported the proposition
that the way to protect forests from fire was to increase timber harvest in the
more remote areas.

As the debate over the allocation of limited resources to fire prevention
measures proceeded in the legislation known as the "Healthy Forests Initiative," citizen groups concerned with forest ecology became more intimately
involved with community fire preventive action. They not only advocated
that federal funds be directed toward community protection but also took

up measures to work with communities in fire protection, joining in community networks and fire protection work days, for example, on thinning and wood clearing projects. Some collaborative actions focused on raising funds to employ local workers on thinning and other fire protection activities. Such activities tended to create a connection between citizen groups' interest in wildlands and their newly forged interest in forest areas of human settlement.

The debate over forest health had implications beyond its immediate relevance for fire issues, for it sharpened the lines of division between commodity forestry, with its emphasis on trees, and ecological forestry, with its emphasis on forests. Does forest health pertain to trees that are protected from insects, pests, and fire, or does it pertain to the condition of the entire forest as an ecological system? Is the important damage in forests from natural causes or from human disruptions? Is action to repair damage and restore health a matter of harvesting and reproducing trees or one of ecological restoration? Commodity foresters had ready answers to these questions, for they had long emphasized the threats posed by insects, pests, and fires, but to ecological foresters these questions raised more recent ideas about ecological restoration.[43]

The two groups—advocates of commodity forestry on the one hand and ecological forestry on the other—argued on opposite sides of the issue when the first maintained that a healthy forest could be maintained only if logged and managed for wood product production, and the second that a healthy forest required limits on logging and human intrusion. To those in commodity forest institutions, what was called the "regulated" forest, from planting to harvest with the cycle repeated again, was the "healthy" forest, and only with logging at the harvest end of the cycle could "health" be assured. The old forest that the public had long prized was "unhealthy," and it was prized only because of public ignorance about such affairs.

Ecological forestry advocates, with their focus on the forest as a vast variety of species in ecological relationships, defined a healthy forest as a forest that was rich in species and managed in such a way as to promote the continued viability of those species. A forest was unhealthy in which competing vegetation was suppressed or destroyed in order to specialize on the increase in trees with merchantable wood fiber; even-aged monocultures that replaced varied species of varied ages with single species of the same age were equally unhealthy. Ecological foresters looked upon the national forests as a vast reservoir of species which had declined markedly in the course of development throughout the country and were now "on the brink." What they saw around them in the forests was something destroyed and about which their managerial custodians seemed to have less than serious interest. No wonder that they came to the issue of "forest health" with the overriding theme of the prime importance of "forest restoration," and this in the face of the continued assertion by the wood production advocates that the nation's forests were in very good shape.

The contrast between ecological and commodity views of forest health was sharpened by an exchange between two groups of professionals, one group from the forestry schools and the other a wide range of ecological scientists in other institutions, and President Bush early in 2003. On April 16 of that year a letter to the president signed by 220 ecological scientists questioned the wisdom of commercial timber harvest on the national forests. Describing themselves as "conservation-minded scientists with many years of experience in biological sciences and ecology," they stated that 13,000 plant and animal species were located in the national forests and argued that "it is now widely recognized that commercial logging has damaged ecosystem health, clean water, and recreational opportunities." Most of the signers were associated with a wide range of academic departments, not one of which was a forestry school.[44]

Two weeks later the president received another letter, signed not by scientists but by the presidents of the Society of American Foresters, the National Association of Professional Forestry Schools and Colleges, and the National Association of State Foresters. The second letter conveyed a markedly different view of a "healthy forest." It asserted the importance of timber harvest on the national forests, implying that the authors of the first letter were not representative of the scientific forest community, and asserting their own role as more valid speakers for that community. This exchange was stark evidence not only of the division within the scientific community over what scientific knowledge was important in forest affairs, but also over which scientists should be called upon to advise forest management policy. It was also a clear indicator of the distinctive kind of science represented not only in the forestry schools, but also upon which the Society of American Foresters and the National Association of State Foresters drew. A marked feature of the second letter, in contrast with the first, was the pointed attack on the ecological scientists by the leaders of the commodity forest organizations. Debates over forest affairs, they wrote, are "not well served by statements that lack scientific objectivity no matter how many scientists sign on to them." "It is objective science that accurately characterizes the issues at hand," so their letter read, and in an accompanying report on the episode by the Society of American Foresters, the president was advised to ignore the advice of the ecological scientists "in favor of forest management strategies supported by credible scientific evidence."[45]

The debate over the "healthy forests" legislation sharpened the division between commodity and ecological forestry by subordinating the entire issue of forest management to the fire crisis. Amid the tension of that debate, one heard little of the need to repair forest damage beyond that of rescuing burned trees as salvage or cutting them to prevent future burning. Emphasis on the damage done by harvesting timber, building roads, fostering even-aged monocultures, or simplifying habitat; the value of species such as birds and salamanders; the importance of wide-ranging viability management; the desirability of maintaining significant areas of older forests, all remained relatively hidden amid the overriding influence of the commodity forestry community in the professions, the administrative agencies, the Congress, and the executive office of the president.

Forest Restoration

Public debate on forest health gave impetus to a growing component of ecological forestry known as "ecological restoration," with an organization and journal all its own. Displaying a wide application to varied geological and biological circumstances, ecological restoration activities now led to a specialized emphasis on forest restoration involving closer ties between the forest reform movement and ecological science in general, and to on-the-ground forest practitioners in particular.

Ecological forest restoration arose out of local natural resource circumstances that varied depending on both resources and resource history. I have already described a case that arose in the Bitterroot National Forest as a response to a massive timber harvest project proposed by the Forest Service.[46] There, action to protect communities from fire included the protection of homes; replanting burned areas; road rehabilitation; and protection of fish, wildlife, and streams. A similar development on the Gifford Pinchot National Forest in Washington featured thinning projects for community fire protection, erosion control action, and efforts to begin replacing monoculture tree plantations with all-aged growth.[47] The Wildlands Recovery Project, originating in the New Mexico–Arizona area but spreading gradually throughout the country, emphasized the "healing" of "wounds" such as road building, clearing away excessive young thin trees, and replacing clear-cutting with selection cutting and all-age management.[48]

Debate over post-fire restoration was brought more fully to public attention in 2003 in the aftermath of the Biscuit fire, 500,000 acres in extent, which took place in 2000 on the Siskiyou and Six Rivers national forests in southwestern Oregon and northwestern California. Here the local salvage team recommended a cut of 100,000,000 board feet, which protected riparian and other sensitive areas. Local wood production leaders, including a member of the county commission, hired Professor John Sessions of the Oregon State University at Corvallis to formulate a larger cut. Sessions recommended a salvage cut of two billion board feet. The regional forester then overruled the local forester and proposed a plan for a one-billion-board-foot salvage program.

This led to a public controversy between commodity foresters and ecological foresters over the impacts of salvage cuts on forest restoration, with the former championing the benefits of heavy cuts and the latter the benefits of lighter ones. The debate was enlivened by a study carried out by Oregon State graduate students, peer-reviewed and published in *Science* magazine, which argued that heavy cuts retarded restoration. In turn, commodity foresters at Oregon State, with the support of the dean, attempted to persuade the editor of the magazine to withdraw publication, a proposal which was declined.

Controversy over the Biscuit salvage led to a bill in Congress that would speed up salvage cuts by reducing environmental analyses and citizen involvement. This, the so-called Baird-Walden bill, generated a dispute between commodity and ecological forest scientists. The commodity foresters, supported by the Society of American Foresters, cited scientific studies that advocated rapid salvage cutting to restore the forest as a source of wood production. Those with an interest in ecological forestry, however, presented to the House committee a letter signed by 169 scientists from a wide range of institutions who opposed the bill on the grounds that the salvage program it fostered was ecologically harmful. The differences between these two groups of scientists made clear once again that so-called disputes over forest science were actually disputes over two different conceptions of what a forest was all about."[49]

Such emphases on forest restoration, which began to emerge among citizen reform organizations throughout the country, led to a nationwide collaborative effort to develop a "Citizen's Call for Ecological Forest Restoration," which was issued in May 2003. While more extensively rooted than the immediate circumstances of the national "healthy forests" debate, it was moved ahead markedly by that debate. As the letter announcing the principles stated, "The Restoration Principles stand in stark contrast to the so-called Healthy Forests Restoration Act of 2003." The Bush administration's "Healthy Forest Initiative," so restoration advocates argued, "undermines key environmental laws in order to increase logging and road building on National Forests, thereby creating an even greater need for ecological restoration in the future."[50]

The statement of restoration principles was signed by 120 forest reform organizations throughout the country that were distinguished by their forest activities at the community and state level and that included none of the prominent national organizations active in national forest policy affairs. Many of these organizations had become involved in the affairs of their local national forests and they were knowledgeable about their circumstances, often focusing on specific actions to remediate ecological damage to forests. It was to date the most extensive cooperative venture of ecological forestry organizations that participated in forest affairs at the individual forest level.[51]

The statement identified the problem: "centuries of intensive resource extraction, development and short-sighted management activities, and invading exotic species have fundamentally altered most of America's forests. The results are loss of fish and wildlife habitat, reduced water quality, increased floods, the conversion of biologically rich old-growth and native forests to sterile tree plantations, failing ecosystems, and economic and social harm to the communities and workers who depend on forest resources." Therefore, "There is an urgent need to reverse these declines by preserving the remaining wild forests and repairing the damage from past mismanagement. We share a vision of ecological restoration that encompasses all natural ecological processes and native fish, wildlife and plant species while enhancing the human connection to the natural world."

The debate over the Healthy Forests Act of 2003 sponsored by the Bush administration generated a contrasting proposal called the Forestry and Community Assistance Act, which sought to protect residential communities and their water supplies from fire through thinning and prescribed burns; to protect old growth and roadless areas; to provide funds for forest and watershed restoration; and to establish a "healthy forest reserve" program on private lands to promote the protection and recovery of diverse species. The proposal included appropriations for restoration activities that would not be tied to timber contracts for cutting larger trees. The bill was an important attempt to bring a broadened perspective to forest restoration, but it made no headway in Congress.[52]

The Procedural Revolution

The massive changes that the Bush administration fostered in how national forest decisions were made were crucial in bringing about substantive changes in policy and practice. Over the preceding three or four decades, advocates of ecological forestry had used a variety of procedures to advance their objectives. They mobilized public input into regulatory proposals; they promoted involvement in formulating individual forest plans and in preparing alternative plans; they appealed plans through the agency's appeal procedures and some beyond that to the courts; they brought judgments from scientists outside the agency to bear on agency decisions and defended scientists within the agency when their opinions had been overruled by management superiors.

These procedural strategies became the target of attacks on ecological forestry by commodity forestry advocates; the substantive influence of ecological forestry could be reduced considerably by making changes as to how decisions were made. One could hardly avoid the conclusion that the administration had conducted a systematic review of the procedural landscape to identify ways in which changing decision-making procedures could be used to modify significantly the substance of decisions. The focus on procedural logjams came to be the common ground on which varied sectors of the commodity forestry community joined with the Bush administration in seeking to curtail ecological forestry.

The most obvious of these innovations was the refusal to reveal documents pertaining to administrative decisions.[53] More widely publicized was the attempt to reduce the degree to which the administration solicited public or independent scientific input into major regulatory changes. The most well known of these was the roadless rule, which the Clinton administration had worked out with six hundred public meetings across the country; the Bush administration held no such meetings in making its massive revisions. Or in a less-publicized case, the plan for the Southern Appalachian National Forests, fashioned with considerable public opinion surveys and involvement, now was drastically changed without any similar procedures or even any publicity. At the same time, the forest-wide regulations that had been formulated with input from a Committee of Scientists in 1979, 1982, and again in 2000, now were revised by the Bush administration without any such procedure at all.

One of the most important procedural changes involved the requirement by the National Environmental Policy Act of 1970 for environmental impact statements (EIS).[54] This requirement actually had little up front effect but far-reaching, more subtle effect on forest policies. The EIS required that administrative actions not be taken without a prior examination of their environmental consequences, and that alternative courses of action be laid out to allow the agency to make a reasoned choice. The EIS did not establish grounds for making choices in an environmental or ecological direction; the decision-making procedure, however, would bring the implications of the decision fully to light and force the agency to root that decision in a reasoned choice. The National Environmental Policy Act provided an opportunity for the Council for Environmental Quality, which administered the act, and the courts to apply a substantive standard for EIS decisions, but they did not, and relegated the EIS to a procedural test, exclusively, without substantive requirements. Hence an agency decision usually could not be questioned on substantive grounds.   .

However, the courts applied an extensive procedural test, requiring a "searching and inter-disciplinary" analysis of environmental implications, which often served as a challenge to agency actions on the grounds that its decisions were perfunctory and not well informed. If the agency made a decision without such an informed basis, it could readily be viewed as "arbitrary and capricious" and hence unacceptable. These requirements for full disclosure of the decision-making process put agencies under some pressure to add staff with environmental and ecological knowledge of forests simply in order to fulfill the knowledge requirements of the EIS. Through this narrow but significant procedural "crack," ecological forest perspectives began to enter into the agency's deliberations. Professional specialists with training in wildlife, ecology, and hydrology were added to the agency's personnel and hence constituted a significant sector within the agency staff which was far more friendly to ecological forestry thinking.

It was this crack which the commodity forestry advocates within the Bush administration now sought to close, and they did so in a variety of ways. One strategy was to reduce the use of the EIS. For many years forest supervisors had sought to limit the extent of EIS preparation by a more perfunctory "environmental assessment," which allowed the agency to simply say that there was a "finding of no significant environmental impact" after only cursory on-the-ground analysis. But there were also so-called "categorical exclusions" that exempted certain categories of activities from environmental analysis. This now was extended by the Bush administration to include a range of activities pertaining to "forest health" such as fire and disease prevention. An even more wide-ranging and significant limitation on the EIS was the new requirement that supervisors not undertake environmental impact analyses of forest plans, as had been the practice throughout the national forest system since the National Forest Management Act of 1976. Henceforth the EIS process would be applied only to specific projects and not to plans. This would reduce considerably the ability of forest reform groups to influence the direction of forest policy. Still another important modification of the forest plan process was the decision to give supervisors the freedom to limit the choice to two alternatives—the agency's chosen plan or the continuation of the present plan—rather than requiring presentation of a customary five alternatives.

Public land agencies had long chafed under the expression of public opinion on its proposed actions and sought to blunt the extensive support for ecological forest policies by developing their own rules for determining which expressions of opinion were legitimate and which were not. The use of such public input was often left to the individual forest administrators, who at times simply lumped together all expressions of opinion received on reply cards. Often the argument was made that such expression could readily be ignored, because the "public input" process was not intended to involve "counting votes" but only to serve as a source of ideas which the agency might take into account in formulating an action position. The Bush administration now developed a uniform policy for the entire agency that at first excluded replies that involved "yes" or "no" expressions of opinion and required that only those opinions in which the writer provided written reasons for their views would be considered. In the face of intense opposition it drew back. In some cases the administration solved this problem by simply avoiding public input for its revised forest policies and found ways to restrict recognized public opinion to a much smaller segment of the public responses.

The most significant Bush administration effort on this score was its attempt to modify the work of its Content Analysis Team, which functioned in the agency's Content Analysis Service Center.[55] The CAT team had earned a high reputation for quality performance in the analysis of public input into management proposals, including, for example, the roadless rule, but it had run into problems with the administration for taking public input too seriously. One of the issues involved the CAT team practice of counting postcard and Internet mail messages, to which the administration objected. Another was the directive from Undersecretary Mark Rey that in its reports the team was not to use the words "many," "most," "oppose," "support," "impacts," or "clear-cuts" and was to use the words "some," "state," "comment," "effects," and "even-aged management." The tension between the administration and the CAT team resulted in outsourcing content analysis to private contractors as part of the administration's comprehensive outsourcing program. This decision was made without determining if it would be cost effective, and despite the documented high quality of the CAT program. One surmises that

Rey was interested primarily in reducing information about public opposition to the agency's policy innovations, and thereby eliminated one of the
few sectors of the Forest Service which had strong public support.

As part of the new mandate to develop periodic agency-wide plans, the
Forest Service sought to gauge public opinion on forest matters by arranging for public opinion polls. This confirmed the persistent results of polls
conducted by regional branches of the agency and other organizations that
the public valued wildlife, watershed protection, and wilderness as the top
objectives of national forest management, and placed wood production and
motorized recreation at the bottom. The survey conducted in the year 2002,
however, added an unusual twist by developing a set of questions which
would screen the replies on the basis of respondents' "knowledge" about
national forest affairs. This would divide the survey replies between those
who were more "knowledgeable" and those who were less so, which could
provide the agency with the possibility of arguing that the more knowledgeable respondents were less committed to ecological forestry objectives.[56]

The appeal process offered significant opportunities for citizens—as
well as the extractive industries—to influence agency management decisions. This involved appeals within the agency's internal "judicial" system
as well as appeals to the federal courts. The administrative appeal system,
as was the case with many federal agencies, was intended to enable many
issues to be settled more rapidly and informally than was the case under the
more formal procedures of court litigation. Most appeals from the decisions
of forest supervisors were dealt with expeditiously within the administrative appeal system, and few were taken further to the courts. But to the
Forest Service and its extractive industry clientele, even that process gave too
many opportunities for ecological forestry objectives to be implemented,
and hence there was a continual effort to restrict the use of appeals.

The Bitterroot National Forest case involving competing forest plans,
cited earlier, presented the most extreme case, one in which Undersecretary
Rey not only denied the alternative plan proposed by citizens, but ruled that
the decision could not be appealed within the agency. The court rebuffed his
effort and ruled that the parties involved should undergo mediation under
the court's supervision. An even more extreme approach to the problem was
when the Alaska delegation obtained a rider on an appropriations bill that
prohibited the wilderness decisions on the Tongass National Forest from
being taken to the courts at all, a case of legislative preemption of judicial
decision making. The more usual case, however, was to develop legislative
jurisdiction over the manner in which appeals could be made—who could
bring them, the length of time following a decision within which an appeal

could be made, the length of time within which the court was required to make a decision, and the factors which the court had to take into account. Both the Forest Service and the extractive industries were continually attempting to obtain this kind of restrictive legislation, and several substantive issues were encumbered with it.

The most dramatic case of this kind came in the Bush administration's attempt to secure its "Healthy Forests" legislation in 2003. The charge was advanced by both the administration and the wood production industry that environmental organizations were hampering fire prevention efforts by appealing projects that the agency argued were needed to reduce fire potential. The issue usually involved the choice in allocating funds between protection for communities by thinning and prescribed burns, or removing larger trees in the more remote forestlands. When the agency attempted to link the two in a single contract in order to obtain revenue from the sale of larger trees to fund removal of smaller ones, citizen organizations often questioned the wisdom of using funds for this purpose when they should be concentrated, so they argued, on smaller trees. When commodity forest advocates argued that citizen groups by their appeals were responsible for enhancing fire danger, others, including the Congressional Budget Office and the Ecological Restoration Institute at Northern Arizona University, argued that appeals presented no such problem because they were dealt with expeditiously within the agency appeal system. Nevertheless, the appeals issue continued to be an integral part of the Bush "Healthy Forests" Initiative and encumbered the main problem of allocating funds to enhance community fire protection.

These ventures in modifying substantive policy by modifying procedures were bold efforts on the part of the Bush administration primarily because they ran counter to one of the main concerns of the federal courts, namely that executive branch agencies should be closely supervised by the courts in order to make sure that they were "fair" and not "arbitrary and capricious." All sides should have an equal opportunity to participate in decision making, and decisions should be well informed. But that was precisely the nub of the procedural controversies; the administration was attempting to limit public participation and was quite willing to substitute personal opinion for informed decision making. The Bush procedural initiatives challenged so many customary procedures that their outcome was unpredictable. The least that could be said was that, much as was the outcome of the Bitterroot case, they would generate much more extensive litigation than had been the case in the past.

However, the Bush administration had already devised a procedure to deal with court cases, by declining to defend federal environmental laws that were the substance of industry challenges, favoring the anti-environmental decisions in cases in which different courts had rendered different decisions, and arranging out-of-court settlements that would preempt court action.[57] The industry challenge of the Northwest Forest Plan, which involved four court cases, was the best-documented case. Here a settlement was proposed by the industry attorney as a way of ending the litigation, a settlement accepted by the Bush administration that, as the industry attorney argued, could be carried out by administrative action alone and would avoid the unpredictable results of litigation. But this was only typical of a great number of such cases argued during the years 2001–2003, in which the administration declined to defend laws against challenges to them by industry, a strategy documented by a study completed by attorneys for the citizen organization, Defenders of Wildlife.[58]

The Fate of Ecological Forestry Initiatives within the Forest Service

As the twentieth century turned into the twenty-first, the advent of ecological forestry began to affect the political cohesiveness of the U.S. Forest Service. Dissent from within and attacks from without increased, and new strategic vantage points developed from which those foresters with an ecological bent could voice their views. An early dissident to play a role on the larger scene of forest affairs was Leon Minckler, who after leaving the agency developed close relationships with the citizen forest reform movement, as I have described earlier. Minckler had a firm base from which to express his views as a member of the forestry faculty of Syracuse University.

Prior to the Bush initiatives in the early twenty-first century several agency personnel had followed in Minckler's footsteps. One was Gloria Flora, who had been supervisor of the Lewis and Clark National Forest in Montana and who had become known for her independent views when she approved the sharp restriction of oil and gas drilling in the Rocky Mountain Front on grounds of protecting the area's unique environmental quality.[59] Flora was transferred to the Humboldt-Toiyabe National Forest in Nevada, which was one of the "hot spots" of anti-agency antagonism. Amid a climate of local intimidation of agency staff, she resigned when she felt that she did not receive sufficient support from her superiors in coping with the public attacks. After leaving the agency she became director of Sustainable Obtainable Solutions, located in Missoula, Montana, an organization founded to assist communities "dependent on public lands" to work out environmentally acceptable solutions to public lands problems. She worked closely with the citizens' group Coalition to Protect the Rocky Mountain Front, with particular emphasis on defending the Front from the increasing pressures of the Bush administration to expand oil and gas production in the West. The group was particularly energized to action when secretary of agriculture Ann Venneman, in a speech at Missoula, asserted that the area would not be "off the table" in the search for oil and gas. As another step in this drama, the Senate rejected an amendment to the energy bill in 2003 offered by Senator Baucus of Montana to make the Rocky Mountain Front off-limits to oil and gas drilling. However, the issue became so intense in Montana during the 2004 presidential campaign that the Bush administration announced that it would withdraw the Front from consideration for drilling.

A more far-reaching independent perspective on agency affairs came from the Forest Service Employees for Environmental Ethics, which drew in a core membership of current and retired agency employees and attracted considerable citizen membership as well. Its eight-member board of directors in 2003 consisted of four retired or former agency employees (an archeologist, a wildlife biologist, a district ranger, and an information specialist) and four current employees (an economist, a fisheries biologist, a journalist, and a botanist). The organization became a major source of independent observation and criticism of agency policies. FSEEE was especially active in defending agency specialists whose professional opinions were challenged by their forest supervisors, and it sponsored the quarterly *Forest Magazine*, with the subtitle *Conserving Our Natural Heritage*, beginning in 1999. Affirming that it was "neither a part of, nor is it affiliated with, the U.S. Forest Service," FSEEE became the first ongoing source for an "inside view" of agency affairs and played a unique role in modifying the hitherto impenetrable wall surrounding the agency.[60]

The actions of the Bush administration added top-level agency representatives to the growing body of former agency employees whose experience was now brought to bear on examining policies from the outside. Three of these who left with the Bush revolution took up posts with academic institutions: Jim Lyons, former undersecretary of agriculture who steered many of the Clinton era reforms to fruition, at the School of Forestry and Environmental Studies at Yale University; Jack Ward Thomas to a chair in Wildlife Management at the University of Montana at Missoula; and Mike Dombeck to a chair at his alma mater, the University of Wisconsin at Stevens Point. Such posts enabled these top-level former employees, all of whom formerly had considerable responsibility for agency affairs, to interpret for the public the massive innovations in forest policy which the Bush administration now was engineering.

In the summer of 2003, for example, Thomas and Dombeck coauthored a public statement in which they advocated that all old-growth forests be protected from harvest on the grounds that this would be the most important single step that the Bush administration could take to defuse the intensity of public debate which now enveloped forest issues in the Pacific Northwest.[61] The proposal was supported also by Jerry Franklin, one of the most well-known forest leaders of the region, in a conference at Seattle in October 2003. At the same time, Dombeck coauthored a history of the nation's public lands incorporating ecological/environmental approaches, speaking from his experience in heading both the Bureau of Land Management and the U.S. Forest Service. With firm roots in an academic institution, Dombeck was now free to make his own independent contribution to the nation's forestry debate.[62]

Three of those who departed the agency soon after the advent of the George W. Bush administration, Jim Furnish, Rob Mrowka, and Christopher Wood, had been brought to Washington by Mike Dombeck as partners in his new team. Furnish, former supervisor of the Siuslaw National Forest in Oregon, had been known as one of the leaders more receptive to the "new winds"; Mrowka had been supervisor of the Fishlake National Forest in Utah; and Chris Wood had been employed by the Forest Service, the Bureau of Land Management, and American Rivers. Furnish became deputy chief of the Forest Service; Mrowka became one of the major architects of the two overriding documents of the new team, the Natural Resource Agenda, and new regulations to replace the 1982 implementation of the 1976 Forest Management Act; and Wood became the senior policy and communications advisor to the Forest Service chief for four years. All three now left the agency as the new Bush policies took shape.

But they did not go quietly. Furnish became a forestry consultant and from that position became a vocal opponent of the Bush forestry program; he assisted those who drew up and publicized the "Forestry and Community Assistance Act," which was prepared as an alternative to the Bush Healthy Forests Restoration Act of 2003.[63] The Forestry and Community Assistance Act would have provided funding for community fire and watershed protection projects independent of the sale of larger trees, and would protect larger and older, fire-resistant trees by establishing a "healthy forest reserve program" on private lands. Mrowka, on the other hand, resigned from the Forest Service and prepared a lengthy statement recounting the history of attempts to reform the agency and emphasizing the resistance to change on the part of the "old guard," who were now given enhanced influence in the agency by the Bush administration policies.[64] Chris Wood became vice president for Conservation Programs for Trout Unlimited in September 2001. In this capacity he helped to organize Alaskan hunters, and through them hunting groups throughout the nation, to oppose the Bush administration's decision to increase logging in the Tongass National Forest. At the same time, he rallied hunters from the Rocky Mountain states to oppose Bush's energy policies there because of the damage to game habitat which they threatened.[65]

A variety of circumstances, many of them connected with the still quite limited ecological perspective within the Forest Service, now interacted to puncture the long-standing professional cohesion of the agency, which had been based on a common commitment to forestry with a central focus on wood production. The close relationships between professional training, public forest management, and forest science focused on wood production had been the major elements in the long-recognized uniqueness of the internal esprit de corps of the service.[66] Now, however, the agency became marked by internal divisions between old and new rather than cohesiveness, as it was influenced by the entry into the ranks of forest management of professionals from a number of other natural resource disciplines, each one of which had its own organizational commitments that were separate from the Society of American Foresters; by the social and cultural division within the agency between line and staff personnel; and by the broader public and scientific pressures on the agency to move in an ecological direction. Successive agency leadership, from Dale Robertson through Jack Ward Thomas and Michael Dombeck, well recognized the new circumstances that challenged the agency to mend its relationships with the public and also to repair its internal fissures. But the resistance of the old to the new within the agency remained a powerful force, and the old became far more influential in the administration of George W. Bush. Whether or not the new would survive the counterrevolution remained to be seen.

CHAPTER 7

In Search of the Future Forest

The rise of ecological forestry and its engagement with more traditional commodity forestry created intense debates over public forest policy in the last third of the twentieth century. This continuing debate will undoubtedly shape public forest affairs for much of the foreseeable future.

The ecological forestry drive involved two sets of forces, one from ecological science and the other from the citizen reform movement, both of which sprang from the same large-scale cultural changes that are described variously as environmental and ecological. The scientists and the reformers rarely worked in formal association but took parallel courses of action and thereby reinforced each other in the world of public affairs. The reform side of this parallel activity received most attention from the media and policy analysts, but the role of ecological science was highly influential. At times the scientists were the leading actors and the reformers the followers. In the Northwest Forest Plan, for example, it was the scientists, not the reformers, who brought some 400-odd species, in addition to the northern spotted owl, into the debate and thereby broadened the scope of forest-based wild resources that were at stake in protecting old growth. The reformers simply followed the scientists' lead. One could repeat this observation for a variety of new forest resource perspectives that were associated less with the reformers, and more with the expanding scientific horizons generated by the workings of traditional scientific inquiry now applied to the world of ecology.

The role of the citizen-based forest reformers grew as the limited perspectives of the earlier nationally organized environmental groups were augmented by a wide range of regional, state, and local organizations. These groups mobilized individuals closer to their local forests, and through involvement in outdoor recreation or through field experiences, citizens found both personal scientific interest and aesthetic pleasure in the ecological world that the evolving environmental and ecological culture was bringing into view. The 1976 National Forest Management Act, which focused on planning for individual national forests, stimulated citizen engagement both with the specific ecological circumstances of the forests in their own backyards and with more formal ecological knowledge.

The ecological initiatives of the reform groups and scientists were met with stubborn resistance by the advocates of more traditional commodity forestry, who drew back to defend themselves. The influence of the wood products industry waxed and waned over the years. The industry looked upon the wilderness and recreation legislation and the failure of the timber supply act of 1969 as major defeats, while it enjoyed considerable influence in the Forest Management Act of 1976 and during the subsequent years of the Reagan administration. While the Clinton years involved a number of setbacks for the industry, the second Bush administration and the Republican control of Congress presented the opportunity to work commodity objectives into both legislation and administration more fully than had been the case in the previous third of a century.

Professional and governmental organizations were integral participants in the resistance of commodity forestry to ecological thinking. Professional forestry has been marked by intense professional specialization on wood production rather than the larger realm of the forest ecosystem, and has become increasingly insular over the years, as it rejected initiatives to broaden its perspective and share forest management with those who sought to emphasize the wide range of ecological resources other than wood fiber. Here I have taken only a first step in elaborating the peculiar role of forestry amid the broader history of biology and ecology, but I give it special emphasis because for the most part it has remained hidden behind the façade of the profession's marked self-confidence. The forest issues of the last several decades simply cannot be understood outside this history of a profession that has become immobilized by its own self-created public isolation.

Ecological and commodity forestry arose from and were sustained by quite different strata of American public life. Ecological forestry had a more popular and mass-based origin, while commodity forestry was more associated with the nation's institutional leadership. This difference was examined systematically for the first time in the 1977 opinion survey sponsored by the American Forest Institute. At that time the prevailing popular sentiment was more environmental than ecological, more focused on outdoor recreation and wilderness preservation. The survey was initiated largely to advise the forest industry as to where to focus its public relations and political strategy, and the authors cautioned the industry that because of the very strong environmental opinions held by members of the public it would not be feasible to conduct a media campaign to counteract forest environmental objectives. However, since institutional leaders, especially governmental leaders, were friendlier to commodity forestry, they should be the targets of the industry's media campaign; they were more receptive to the wood production industry's interests.

This advice was an excellent predictor of the future political course of the contest between ecological and commodity forestry. Public opinion surveys in the ensuing years, some conducted from nationwide and some from statewide samples and increasingly focused on ecological issues, continued to emphasize the very high level of public interest in the forests as sources of wildlife and water quality and the very low level of support for wood production. At the same time, the development of ecological values in the public arena was closely associated with strategies to open decision making to public scrutiny, and with the wide availability of environmental analyses and the availability of the courts to those advocating environmental and ecological objectives—the entire range of ingredients of what came to be called "transparency" in public decision making, all supplemented in recent years by the rapid availability of information on the Internet. The wood products establishment tried to limit these avenues for public information and influence and continually emphasized the time and effort that they required rather than the substantive issues at stake. The George W. Bush administration cooperated with the wood production industry in this effort to constrain ecological influence both from the public and from scientists.

In the preceding chapters, I have described a range of ecological forestry objectives and their fate in federal and state forest policy. In general these include such issues as biodiversity; habitat; structural forest diversity; the promotion of mixed-age tree stands; the use of native forest benchmarks; watershed management; old growth; long-term natural forest evolution; human disturbances such as roads, motorized vehicles, and clear-cutting; soil quality retention and enhancement; and protection and restoration measures. If the reader wishes to track these issues in the future in order to observe "which way the wind is blowing," I suggest asking the following questions:

Biodiversity: To what degree are resources, for example, budgets and staff, devoted to species inventory and monitoring, and especially to monitoring of "sensitive" as well as "threatened and endangered" species?

Habitat: Are forest areas classified in terms of types of habitat, and is "critical habitat" identified and devoted to the improvement of species populations?

Native forest benchmarks: Are significant efforts being made to identify forest characteristics at the time of European settlement and to outline in historical fashion their evolution toward the contemporary forest?

Watersheds: Are watersheds measured systematically, including the additive effects of many watershed activities and their cumulative effect over time?

Stand management: Does silvicultural practice promote all-aged instead of even-aged stands?

Old growth: Is forest age described in terms of old forest species such as fungi and lichens as well as trees over three hundred years old, and managed not in terms of the wood fiber value of older trees but the value of the entire forest ecosystem?

Human impact: Are major disturbances such as roads, power lines, harvest techniques, and motorized vehicles, including recreational vehicles, controlled so as to minimize disruption and fragmentation of ecosystems?

Sustainability: Are ecological resources zoned for protection, and are financial resources devoted to restoration of disturbed areas such as roads and monocultures?

Soils: To what degree do human and natural influences destroy soil microorganisms and impair their nutritional quality?

This range of ecological objectives can be followed through the forest plans that are now standard practice for national forests and the larger state forests. Since the National Forest Management Act of 1976, the forest plans mandated by that act have been the focal point of debate and choice in forest matters. Forest reformers have sought to influence those plans directly and indirectly by shaping and gathering support for alternative plans. Their opponents, however, have sought to restrict what goes into a forest plan, for example, the Bush administration's decisions to prohibit supervisors from conducting environmental impact analyses of plans and to encourage supervisors to make their own choices and not seek external advice about their scientific underpinnings. The Sierra Nevada Framework provided an excellent opportunity to observe the interplay of ecological and commodity forest initiatives, as it was approved during the Clinton administration and then revised by the succeeding Bush administration.

Two forest plans that were completed in late 2003 had contrasting outcomes for groups advocating ecological forestry; both reflect the varied roles of regional groups actively involved in their forest areas. One that was unsuccessful in implementing ecological objectives involved the Medicine Bow National Forest in Wyoming. In this case, the Biodiversity Conservation Alliance, located in Laramie and representing some twenty-one regional groups in Colorado, Wyoming, and Montana, drew up their own 185-page plan for the Medicine Bow as one of the alternative plans among the final choices considered by the Forest Service.[1] It incorporated a considerable number of ecological analyses and objectives. However, the alternative chosen by the Forest Service contained few of these and was more oriented toward commodity production than the previous plan. It contained proposed wilderness area of only 28,000 acres, about half as much as the agency proposed in a December 2002 draft plan. It also limited protection for wildlife and left even limited protection to the discretion of the supervisor; changed specific road densities in the earlier plan to none in the new one; and gave the supervisor much leeway for plan implementation. On the whole, the plan moved backward rather than forward in fostering ecological objectives.[2]

In contrast, one of the few plans with an ecological orientation that remains relatively unscathed as of this writing is that for the Hells Canyon National Recreation Area managed by the Wallowa-Whitman National Forest in eastern Oregon. In this case, the ecological objectives incorporated into the 1975 Hells Canyon National Recreation Area Act remained unrealized in the 1982 plan, and its aftermath even advanced the degradation of the area's natural values, but a new plan issued in the spring of 2003 under the leadership of the Wallowa-Whitman National Forest supervisor Karyn Wood turned out quite differently. The area would be managed as a "healthy ecosystem that is an integral component of a larger biological region . . . an area of high biological diversity and endemism"; over 245,000 acres of currently vacant livestock allotments would be closed to livestock grazing and instead managed for biodiversity and native plant values; road density would be reduced to 1.25 miles per square mile, requiring the closing of about 200 miles of road; and forests would to be allowed "to function in a nearly natural manner" with wildfire resuming "a more natural role."

Much lay behind this change. Continual efforts by the citizen group the Hells Canyon Preservation Council to bring ecological objectives to bear on the area's management were an important influence; another was the pronouncement by a team of federal biologists working on the Interior Columbia Basin Ecosystem Management Project that the region was the only area of "high ecological integrity" in eastern Oregon and Washington; still another was the establishment by the citizen council of a Hells Canyon monitoring group composed of twelve professionals representing varied interests and specialties including hunting, forestry, botany, geology, wildlife biology, wilderness, and tribal interests. But perhaps even more crucial was the council's organization of the Chief Joseph National Preserve Project, which would establish the entire Hells Canyon–Wallowa ecosystem as an ecological preserve and transfer it to the National Parks System for management. The proposal gathered formal endorsement from a wide range of regional groups as well as a few national ones and hence could be presented as having community support well beyond the Hells Canyon Council itself. If the preserve project survives, it might well identify the ingredients that could lead to success for ecological land management elsewhere. And it is those ingredients that the close observer might track in order to judge future ecological progress in forest management.[3]

It would be equally important to pursue the more difficult task of tracking the course of the forestry profession and the U.S. Forest Service, the more subtle and slowly changing patterns of innovation and response in the rich institutional context of professional training in forestry, the recruitment of agency personnel from those schools at one point or another in the spectrum of institutional change, and the course of influence on the agency itself arising from its gadfly critics in the Forest Service Employees for Environmental Ethics. Especially intriguing are the new patterns of professional commitments within the Forest Service resulting from the slow but steady invasion of the agency by ecological ideas, as it comes under pressure to consider a wider range of ecological resources.

The fate of the publication titled *Lingua Botanica: A Journal for FS Botanists and Plant Ecologists* may be a bellwether of the future. Its first issue declared: "These pages are the fruit of efforts put forth by a group of people who are passionately dedicated to the grand botanical heritage of this nation's public lands." The function of the publication, as it stated, was to communicate among botanists and plant ecologists within the Forest Service, to convey the interests of botanists and plant ecologists to others both within and outside the agency, and to serve as an educational tool. The issues produced over the first four years, 2000–2004, reflected a wide range of subjects both strictly scientific and policy-related, and its announcements of job openings for botanists included notices for positions in federal land management agencies beyond the Forest Service. Early in 2005, *Lingua Botanica* was discontinued.[4]

Finally, indicators of partisan politics might well tell the tale as to the changing fate of ecological or commodity forest objectives. The rapidly evolving partisan role of the Republican Party in advancing commodity forestry and limiting ecological forestry has been and will continue to be a decisive factor in the evolution of this contest. The Democratic Party has included a significant and often majority environmental contingent, so one can well take more than a passing interest in the Republican Party platforms, policy proposals, decisions made by Republican administrations, and the balance of party power in Congress.[5] Especially significant is the fate of that moderate contingent of Republicans who look to the party's conservation past for inspiration, as represented in Republicans for Environmental Protection. Throughout its young history this organization has given support to ecological forest objectives and has encouraged those few environmentally oriented Republicans in Congress to take stands contrary to the dominant party leadership. The activities of Republicans for Environmental Protection might well serve to identify steps toward a more ecological perspective on forests for the Republican Party and for the nation.[6]

NOTES

NOTE: Many documents cited here from periodicals and all from the Internet are photocopied and deposited in the files of the Forest List section, Lists 1 and 2, in the Samuel P. and Barbara D. Hays Environmental Collection, the Environmental Archives, the Archives of Industrial Society, Archives Service Center, University of Pittsburgh (cited as EA).

Preface

1. A number of excellent books deal with the more dramatic issues such as the spotted owl case. See, for example, Steven Lewis Yaffee, *The Wisdom of the Spotted Owl: Policy Lessons for a New Century* (Washington, D.C.: Island Press, 1994); William Dietrich, *The Final Forest: The Battle for the Last Great Trees of the Pacific Northwest* (New York: Penguin Books, 1993); Kathie Durbin, *Tree Huggers: Victory, Defeat and Renewal in the Northwest Ancient Forest Campaign* (Seattle: The Mountaineers, 1996). These books, however, do not extend the reader's attention to the geographically larger, and usually less dramatic, forest scene that is the subject of this book.

Books with a longer time span, for the most part, cover earlier periods of time and do not interpret events since the National Forest Management Act of 1976. These include Harold K. Steen, *The U.S. Forest Service: A History* (Seattle: University of Washington Press, 1976); David A. Clary, *Timber and the Forest Service* (Lawrence: University Press of Kansas, 1986); Paul W. Hirt, *A Conspiracy of Optimism: Management of the National Forests since World War Two* (Lincoln: University of Nebraska Press, 1994).

2. See Opinion Research Corporation, *The Public's Participation in Outdoor Activities and Attitudes toward Wilderness Areas* (1977). For example, in response to the question: "Do you think the U.S. Forest Service should try to increase the yield and sale of tim-

ber from the national forests, or should it continue to preserve these trees in their natural state," 28 percent agreed with the "increase yield" option and 62 percent with the "preserve these trees" option.

3. Steve Jones and Jim Finley, "Policy and Management Implications: The General Public and Forestry Issues," reprint of survey report; Myron R. Schwartz, "The Follow-up Survey for the Analysis of Attitudes and Knowledge of the Stewardship Program in Pennsylvania: Summary Statistics," copies of both in Samuel P. Hays, *Forest Papers* (Boulder, Colo.: privately printed, 2003), a collection of forest-related papers pertaining primarily to Pennsylvania, in Forest List 2, EA.

4. Public Survey Report, Southern Appalachian National Forest, "A Survey of Residents of the Greater Southern Appalachian Region to Describe Public Use and Preferred Objectives for Southern Appalachian National Forests" (Southern Region of National Forest Systems, FS; Southern Research Station, FS; University of Tennessee, July 2002). A copy is posted on the Web site: http://www.srs.fs.fed.us/trends/sanfrpt.html. For the Forest Service survey of national attitudes on forest issues see Deborah J. Shields, Ingred M. Martin, Wade E. Martin, and Michelle A. Haefele, *Survey Results of the American Public's Values, Objectives, Beliefs, and Attitudes Regarding Forests and Grasslands: A Technical Document Supporting the 2000 USDA Forest Service RPA Assessment*, Gen Tech. Rep. RMRS-GTR-95 (Ft. Collins, Colo.: U.S. Department of Agriculture, Forest Service, Rocky Mountain Research Station, 2002).

5. The first use of which I am aware of the term "ecological forestry" to describe a distinctive approach to forestry questions was by Leon Minckler, critic of the Forest Service, whose activities in the Society of American Foresters are described in chapter 3. His initial statement in a series of four pamphlets published by the National Parks and Conservation Association used the term "environmental forestry," but the next three in the series used the term "ecological forestry." For citations see chapter 3, note 17.

Chapter 1: New and Old Forestry

1. The best treatment of wilderness affairs combining both policy issues and the role of citizen activity is Doug Scott, *The Enduring Wilderness* (Golden, Colo.: Fulcrum Publishing, 2004).

2. Scott, *The Enduring Wilderness*, has a good, brief account of de facto wilderness. An article outlining details in the move to create the first citizen-initiated proposal, the Lincoln-Scapegoat area in Montana, is Tom Price, "From Hardware to Software: How the Wilderness Movement Got Its Start," *High Country News* (Paonia, Colo.), January 29, 2001, 20.

3. The eastern wilderness movement does not yet have its historian. Scott, *The Enduring Wilderness*, has a brief but very good account. A considerable number of documents pertaining to it, including the development of proposals for the Allegheny National Forest in which I participated, are in Forest List, EA.

4. For a more elaborate statement of the development of ecological perspectives

within the previous wilderness perspective see Samuel P. Hays, "From Wilderness to Wildlands: Stages in the Evolution of the Wilderness Movement," unpublished paper in Hays, *Forest Papers*, 131–40, copy in Forest List 2, EA. The publication which most fully captures this link between wilderness and the broader realm of ecological forestry is *Wild Earth*, a quarterly published first in 1990 in Richmond, Vermont, and discontinued in 2004. State and regional organizations usually dealing with the issues of particular national forests have generated several dozen publications that provide more concrete information about the specifics of ecological forestry. Some also deal with state forest issues. Many of these publications are in the files in EA.

5. For details about the Timber Supply Act see Dennis C. Le Master, *Decade of Change: The Remaking of Forest Service Statutory Authority during the 1970s* (Westport, Conn.: Greenwood Press, 1984), 21–26.

6. The first well-known critique of clear-cutting was produced at the request of Montana senator Lee Metcalf in 1970 by Arnold Bolle, dean of the School of Forestry at the University of Montana. Entitled "A University View of the Forest Service" and billed as "a scientific investigation of clearcutting," it was published as a U.S. Senate document.

7. See "Clear-cutting Practices on National Timberlands: Hearings before the Subcommittee on Public Lands of the Senate Committee on Interior and Insular Affairs," 92nd Congress, 1st Session, 930 (1971).

8. For a brief account of the Nixon clear-cutting executive order see Charles F. Wilkinson and H. Michael Anderson, *Land and Resource Planning in the National Forests* (Washington, D.C.: Island Press, 1987), 144–46.

9. Various writers about NEPA have remarked on the failure to implement the policy section of the act. See, for example, Matthew J. Lindstrom and Zachary A. Smith, *The National Environmental Policy Act: Judicial Misconstruction, Legislative Indifference and Executive Neglect* (College Station: Texas A&M University Press, 2001).

10. A statement about the implications of ecological science for the national forests is John Aber et al., "Applying Ecological Principles to the Management of the U.S. National Forests," *Issues in Ecology* (Washington. D.C.: Ecological Society of America), Spring 2000. Various alternative forest plans, described in more detail in chapter 2, include many references to forest ecological science.

11. Application of the ESA to land management, including the national forests, has given rise to many general analyses. Few, however, go beyond the details of controversies over specific species, such as the spotted owl in the Pacific Northwest, to trace the impact of the law on the incorporation of ecological management into the programs of the national forests. A useful overview of the act and its subsequent history is Bonnie B. Burgess, *Fate of the Wild: The Endangered Species Act and the Future of Biodiversity* (Athens: University of Georgia Press, 2001). It should be emphasized that the National Environmental Policy Act (NEPA) and the Endangered Species Act (ESA) played quite different roles in forest affairs. The ESA was limited to rare and endangered species in its resource objectives, but carried mandatory management

requirements which all federal agencies were legally bound to carry out. NEPA had no such mandatory policy requirements but was limited to considering environmental effects; yet these effects were broadly conceived, required "comprehensive and inter-disciplinary" analysis prior to action, and thus provided opportunities to elaborate a more comprehensive and ecological resource management.

12. A focal point for extensive cooperative action on endangered species was the Center for Biological Diversity, located in Tucson, Arizona; its activities can be followed on its Web site: http://www.sw-center.org/.

13. The first edition of the initial text on dendrology in the McGraw-Hill American Forestry Series, William M. Harlow and Ellwood S. Harrar, *Textbook of Dendrology Covering the Important Forest Trees of the United States and Canada* (New York: McGraw-Hill, 1937), noted that existing books were unsatisfactory. Sargent's *Silva of North America* was too extensive in species coverage, and other books were too local.

14. The most extensive account of this relationship between agency timber policy and the market through gearing harvest to local mill capacity is by David Clary, *Timber and the Forest Service* (Lawrence: University Press of Kansas, 1986). Two of the most celebrated cases in which the agency made special decisions to link timber sales and a sustainable, long-term community industry were the fifty-year contracts for the Tongass National Forest, dealt with in chapter 4, and the attempt to link private and public supplies that Congress authorized in the Cooperative Sustained Yield Act of 1944 but that was applied in only one case, the Shelton Working Circle on the Olympic Peninsula, which brought together national forest land and land of the Simpson Logging Company. For a brief account of this case see Gordon Robinson, *The Forest and the Trees: A Guide to Excellent Forestry* (Washington, D.C.: Island Press, 1988), 44. An excellent account of wood production as the primary preoccupation of the Forest Service is Hirt, *A Conspiracy of Optimism*.

15. A good account of the way in which the U.S. Forest Service sought to replace old "unproductive" forests with "productive" planted forests with a harvest rotation of eighty to one hundred years is Nancy Langston, *Forest Dreams, Forest Nightmares: The Paradox of Old Growth in the Inland West* (Seattle: University of Washington Press, 1995).

16. The "silvicultural imagination" that dominated thinking about wood production involved the elimination of the "natural forest" and its replacement with the "well-regulated" forest, which involved, at least in theory, carefully controlled forest growth from seedling to harvest. The Forest Stewards Guild, a vigorous critic of the dominant brand of thinking in the forestry profession, described this "modern industrial forestry" view as one in which "foresters must remove all trees and start over again to make the forest productive . . . which justifies the familiar clearcut, burn and plant regime." To the guild, natural forces rather than human manipulation were the fundamental basis of sound forest management. See the brief treatment of the guild in chapter 4.

The importance of silviculture in forest affairs is reflected in its dominant role in forest research. Several publications reflect this emphasis: Harold K. Steen, *Forest Service Research: Finding Answers to Conservation's Questions* (Durham, N.C.: Forest History Society, 1998); R. Keith Arnold, M. B. Dickerman, and Robert Buckman, *View from the Top: Forest Service Research* (Durham, N.C.: Forest History Society, 1994); Harold K. Steen, *An Interview with Carl E. Ostrom* (Durham, N.C.: Forest History Society, 1994).

17. The Forest Stewards Guild, a group of professional foresters not associated with the Society of American Foresters, looked upon high-grading as contrary to the ethics of their profession. A study of the choices made by those who won logging contracts on the Tongass National Forest indicated that, when allowed to choose, the contractors usually chose the larger trees and avoided the smaller ones. When the agency allowed contractor selection on the Biscuit salvage cut in the Siskiyou National Forest in 2004, the court, in response to a citizen complaint, ruled that the agency personnel had to mark the individual trees for cutting.

18. The role of the General Federation of Women's Clubs as the most significant citizen support for the forest reserves in the early twentieth century is briefly described in Samuel P. Hays, *Conservation and the Gospel of Efficiency: The Progressive Conservation Movement, 1890–1920* (Cambridge: Harvard University Press, 1958). The role of the Federation of Women's Clubs has yet to receive its serious historian.

19: Enos Mills's role in forest affairs of the early twentieth century has been described in Alexander Drummond, *Enos Mills: Citizen of Nature* (Boulder, Colo.: University Press of Colorado, 1995).

20. When bills to establish national parks were introduced in Congress, the Forest Service modified them to permit timber cutting, and when bills appeared to expand national parks by adding national forest acreage to them, the agency made the same suggestions. Pinchot's views on this were rarely stated publicly but appeared in letters and reports. See Hays, *Conservation and the Gospel of Efficiency*, 195–98.

21. Exploration of the divergence between commodity and aesthetic features of the forest reserves has been stymied for many years by the almost exclusive emphasis on the Pinchot-Muir debate and the Hetch Hetchy controversy. A fuller account would stress that the issues were much more extensive and include many policy pronouncements that Pinchot made, and the individuals and groups that, in opposition to Pinchot, championed the separate administration of national parks, including J. Horace McFarland and the American Civic Association, the General Federation of Women's Clubs, Secretary of the Interior Richard Ballinger, and U.S. Representative John Lacey. It would also elaborate on the significance of the 1908 Governor's Conference as a turning point in the relationships between Pinchot and his most important previous support, the Women's Clubs. The problem receives good attention in Drummond, *Enos Mills*, 197–202.

22. The prime mover in the drive to establish a National Park Service was McFarland. His role is well covered in Ernest Morrison: *J. Horace McFarland: A Thorn for Beauty* (Harrisburg: Pennsylvania Historical and Museum Commission, 1995).

23. There is considerable literature about these developments. See, for example,

the personal experience of Horace M. Albright in Horace M. Albright, as told to Robert Cahn, *The Birth of the National Park Service: The Founding Years, 1913–33* (Salt Lake City: Howe Brothers, 1985).

24. The ecological presence in the national parks is covered in Richard West Sellers, *Preserving Nature in the National Parks* (New Haven: Yale University Press, 1997).

25. See Hays, *Conservation and the Gospel of Efficiency*, 22–26, for the very close connection between forestry and watershed protection during the early years of the forest reserves. A study which detailed this relationship further is Ronald F. Lockmann, *Guarding the Forests of Southern California: Evolving Attitudes toward Conservation of Watershed, Woodlands and Wilderness* (Glendale, Calif.: A. H. Clark, 1981). The federal agency on which the watershed protection advocates relied most heavily in the 1890s was the U.S. Geological Survey, which advocated ideas about the way in which forests protected water sources. This agency seemed to drop out of national forest affairs after the Forest Service was established.

26. Inventories of forested watersheds to determine the relationship of watershed protection and watershed condition were hardly mentioned in National Forest affairs. One of the first and most adequate was prepared by the Inter-Agency Monitoring Program established under the Pacific Northwest Forest Plan adopted by the Clinton Administration in 1993. See Gordon H. Reeves et al., "Aquatic/Riparian Effectiveness Monitoring Plan" (AREMP), which outlines a watershed-wide monitoring program for the plan and is one of the most comprehensive such monitoring systems devised for assessing the condition of forest watersheds. The plan is available on the Internet: http://www.reo.gov/monitoring/watershed/cover-aremp-report.htm.

27. The problem of the aesthetic effects of clear-cutting arose within the Forest Service as early as 1908. Its implications for agency policy unfolded only gradually. At first it was worked out only within the agency with little objection from the wood products industry, because of the industry's relative indifference to such policies at the time. But after World War II, the industry was much more aware of the decline in acreage available for wood production and became quite vocal as to the amount of land that the visual corridor policy withdrew from potential wood harvest. The issue increased in intensity in the 1960s, when the industry opposed the wild and scenic rivers and hiking trails programs on the grounds that their corridor policies would withdraw too much forest land from the timber harvest base. Wilkinson and Anderson, *Land and Resource Planning*, describe this as part of the Forest Service timberland "availability" issue.

28. An extensive treatment of forests and wildlife is a collection of articles edited by Harold K. Steen, *Forest and Wildlife Science in America: A History* (Durham, N.C.: Forest History Society, 1999). While this book contains a good account of wildlife science in a variety of agencies, it provides little insight as to the gradual emergence of the use of the national forests for hunting and fishing.

29. For a history of the National Wildlife Federation, see Thomas B. Allen,

Guardian of the Wild: The Story of the National Wildlife Federation, 1936–1986 (Bloomington: Indiana University Press, 1987).

30. While forest professionals thought of wildlife habitat as derived from the forest conditions accompanying the forester's preferred harvest and regeneration methods, the wildlife specialists thought of habitat in more independent terms associated with the needs of wildlife. This prompted the Wildlife Society, for example, to become associated with habitat-based ecological forest groups, whereas the professional foresters did not. The activities of the Wildlife Society can be followed on its Web site.

31. The difficulties displayed by commodity forest advocates in absorbing wildlife into their management strategies are described in two reports by committees sponsored by the Society of American Foresters to consider the role of wildlife in forests: "Report of the Committee on Game Management with Reference to Forestry," *Journal of Forestry* 37 (1939): 130; and "Second Report of Game Policy Committee," *Journal of Forestry* 35 (1937): 228. The 1939 report described the difficulty in integrating the two: "The difficulty is in large measure due to the lack of appreciation of the real meaning of wildlife management. In cases where those in charge of a forest think that the information incidentally picked up while fishing or marking timber in a watershed is all that is needed for the management of its wildlife, we cannot hope for much progress." This response by foresters is dealt with briefly by Wilkinson and Anderson, *Land and Resource Planning*, 283–84.

32. In 1936 the Forest Service established a Division of Wildlife with eighty-three specialists, emphasizing game. But this was curtailed during World War II, and after the war a return to the prewar policies occurred only slowly. See Wilkinson and Anderson, *Land and Resource Planning*, 184–85.

33. See Wilkinson and Anderson, *Land and Resource Planning*, 172.

34. By the 1990s the adverse effect of deer on tree seedling reproduction had become a major concern of every segment of the forestry establishment in Pennsylvania, as well as those few environmental groups interested in forest affairs. When the team that assessed the state's forests for certification produced its report, it cited excessive deer population as the most important threat to the state's forests, and stated that the solution of this problem was essential to continued certification under the Forest Stewardship Council. See chapter 5, and Wilkinson and Anderson, *Land and Resource Planning*, 233–34, for a more extensive statement of this problem.

35. Expansion of the field of wild resources from game to an extensive range of wildlife was marked by the growth of nongame wildlife programs at the state level. These were known also as "non-consumptive" wildlife uses and often were defined as "wildlife not legally hunted." These programs grew along with state natural area programs and were financed through voter-approved funds from the sale of wildlife auto license plates and refunds on state income taxes. They resulted in a variety of activities such as inventory of nongame wildlife resources, or special protective and restoration programs, distinctive to each state, such as for loons in

many northern states, Kirtland's warbler in Michigan, or the whooping crane in Wisconsin. See "The Spotting Scope Newsletter" published by the Michigan Department of Natural Resources, which describes state nongame wildlife activities. An organization called Watchable Wildlife, Inc., has published guidebooks on the wildlife species of most states and maintains a Web site. These nongame wildlife programs and public interest in them could well be viewed as a bridge between the earlier interest in hunted wildlife and more recent interest in biodiversity.

36. The Wildlife Society illustrates the vast increase in interest in wildlife over the traditional wildlife-as-game policies of earlier years. See its Web site to explore this broader range of wildlife interests.

37. An influential statement about the value of hunted wildlife, the North American Game Policy, of which Aldo Leopold was a major inspiration and author, was changed in 1973 to the North American Wildlife Policy to reflect the broadening interest in wildlife. This emphasis posed major problems for those committed to federal and state game programs established earlier and who now resisted sharing their resources with programs fostering wildlife other than game. The problem was illustrated by the debate over changing the name of state "game" agencies to state "wildlife" agencies. The shift took place in most states, if for nothing more than the more attractive public image it conveyed, but some states held out, for example Pennsylvania, where the terminology "game commission" and state "game lands" continued unchanged.

38. The standard accounts of the 1976 act are Le Master, *Decade of Change*, and Wilkinson and Anderson, *Land and Resource Planning*. Both of these accounts focus primarily on legislative and administrative history with limited treatment of the broader social context of forest policy. An account of the legislative maneuvering that accompanied the passage of the act by a leader of the environmental initiative is Brock Evans, "Shaping the National Forest Management Act of 1976: A Participant's View," reprinted in Samuel P. Hays, *Forest Papers*, vol. 1, pp. 83–95 (EA).

39. For the Monongahela decision see Le Master, *Decade of Change*, 55–58, and Wilkinson and Anderson, *Land and Resource Planning*, 41–42, 73–74, 154–55.

40. For the extent of industry organization in the controversy see Evans, "Shaping the National Forest Management Act," note 38, above.

41. The planning context for national forest affairs had two quite different components. One, formulated by the Resources Planning Act of 1974, set up a top-down planning process in which national goals were set by the Forest Service in Washington, D.C., and then transmitted down through the regions and the individual national forests. At the same time, however, a more bottom-up process had been evolving over the years in which each national forest responded to its specific resource and constituency circumstances. The top-down process seemed to be shaped by the national needs of the agency in its budget negotiations in the nation's capital. But the bottom-up process responded to local circumstances. It was this process which the National Forest Management Act of 1976 fostered, which had been influenced heavily by locally based proposals for de facto wilderness and

which the NFMA spread further to the entire range of forest issues. A good discussion of the tenuous relationship between top-down and bottom-up planning and their quite different national and local contexts is in Wilkinson and Anderson, *Land and Resource Planning*, 76–90.

42. Le Master's account of NFMA in *Decade of Change* includes a brief review of the Randolph bill, but gives the reader no inkling of the emerging role of ecological forestry either as a scientific development or as a step in the development of forest-related environmental/ecological thinking or action by citizens. Documents pertaining to the effort to advance the Randolph bill are in Box 22, The Forest Reform Movement 1, in Forest List, EA.

43. The forest reform groups placed high importance on a "marginal lands" provision included in the Randolph bill, discussed in committee deliberations but finally deleted. It was intended to identify lands of low timber productivity ("marginal" lands) and argue that they should be devoted to noncommodity uses. In forest agency language this was known as the "suitability" issue, i.e., criteria for determining that certain lands were not suitable for wood production. The legislation did not include such a provision. For an extended discussion of the issue see Wilkinson and Anderson, *Land and Resource Planning*, 162–70.

44. An excellent source in which to track forest reform reaction to national forest policy during the Reagan administration is *Forest Watch*, edited by Randall O'Toole in Eugene, Oregon (file in EA).

45. See the Wilderness Society et al., *National Forest Planning: A Conservationist's Guide* (n.p., 1983). After the act was passed, the Wilderness Society took up leadership to implement its environmental and ecological provisions. This role was much in contrast with that of the American Forestry Association, which was more aligned with wood production objectives and which through its executive vice president, William E. Towell, had sought to work out a middle ground in the debate through an "Areas of Agreement" group. These different roles were related, arguably, to changes in the organizations' membership. In 1976 both organizations were roughly equal in membership at approximately 75,000. A decade later the American Forestry Association had declined to 20,000 while the Wilderness Society had grown to over 250,000. Towell's role in the proceedings is described in Le Master, *Decade of Change*.

46. By the end of the 1980s, citizens were involved in the case of almost every national forest. There are few individual case studies with details about the degree and strategies of citizen involvement. One of these, focused on a specific national forest, reflects the gradual incorporation of ecological objectives into a wilderness perspective. It is Suzanne Marshall, *"Lord, We're Just Trying to Save Your Water": Environmental Activism and Dissent in the Appalachian South* (Gainesville: University Press of Florida, 2003), in which chapters 4–6, pp. 111–218, are devoted to citizen attempts to influence management on the Chattahoochee-Oconee National Forest in north Georgia.

47. The context for wilderness action can be followed in the periodic reports

of wilderness activity issues by the Wilderness Society under various formats. The most recent is entitled *Wilderness Report*, with the first issue in 1998; it is available on the society's Web site.

48. Events in the early years of evolving action under the National Forest Management Act of 1976 are covered in Samuel P. Hays, "The New Environmental Forest," *University of Colorado Law Review* 59 (1988): 517; reprinted in Hays, *Explorations in Environmental History* (Pittsburgh: University of Pittsburgh Press, 1998), 131–55; see especially pp. 136–53.

Chapter 2: Shaping an Ecological Forestry Program

1. A more elaborate statement of the objectives in ecological forestry is contained in two series of papers written and distributed by Samuel P. Hays in the 1990s: "Pennsylvania Forest Briefs" and "Pennsylvania Forest White Papers, 1–24," both in Hays, *Forest Papers*, bound copies of which are deposited in Forest Papers 2, EA.

2. A wide range of different types of citizen forest organizations arose, most of which were obscured by the media emphasis on the more visible national organizations in Washington, D.C. State organizations grew at about the same pace as did national ones and gradually developed larger budgets and staffs than did the state branches of national organizations. Specialized groups formed around an interest in particular species. The planning requirements of the National Forest Management Act of 1976 stimulated the formation of citizen groups around individual national forests, which sought to shape that forest and stimulated significant citizen knowledge about the forest through personal field observation and documentary research.

3. For a more elaborate statement of the development of ecological perspectives within the wilderness perspective see Hays, "From Wilderness to Wildlands."

4. The development of regional organization was significant in the history of citizen groups and grew out of both the state and national environmental organizations that took shape in the late 1960s. State groups found that their objectives often coincided with organizations of nearby states focusing on a region-wide ecosystem or problem, and state activities evolved into regional activities, while national organizations centered in Washington, D.C., began to decentralize many of their activities into regions, with regional offices, in the 1980s. These two trends came together to shape regional environmental organizations.

5. For the Wildlands Center for Preventing Roads see http://www.wildland scpr.org/ and especially its quarterly publication, the *Road RIPorter*, some issues of which are in Wildlands Center for Preventing Roads folder, Forest List 2, EA. The Wildlands Center distributed a useful document concerning the economic benefits of road removal, "Investing in Communities, Investing in the Land," Summary Report by Wildland Center for the Prevention of Roads, adapted from "Reinvestment in Jobs, Communities and Forests; the Benefits and Costs of a National Program

for Road Removal on U.S. Forest Service Lands, A Preliminary Analysis," a study by the Center for Environmental Economic Development (CEED), 2003. Activities of the following organizations can be followed on their Web sites: the Center for Biological Diversity, the Northwest Old Growth Campaign, the Wilderness Society, Forest Service Employees for Environmental Ethics, and the Wildlands Project. Each of these organizations frequently produced well-researched papers that were readily available on the Internet and were used by organizations throughout the country.

6. For more information, see the Web sites of Earthjustice, Western Resource Advocates, the Western Environmental Law Center, and the Southern Environmental Law Center.

7. There are many conservation organizations devoted to research and protection for individual species. Some examples of organizations and Web sites (the dates indicate year of establishment) are: the Organization for Bat Conservation, http://www.batconservation.org/; the Wolf Conservation Center located at South Salem, N.Y., http://www.nywolf.org/about/html; the International Wolf Center at Ely, Minnesota (1985), http://www.wolf.org; the Great Bear Foundation, Missoula, Montana, http://www.greatbear.org; the North American Loon Fund, Gilford, New Hampshire; the National Bighorn Sheep Interpretive Center at Dubois, Wyoming (1990), http://www.bighorn.org; the Peregrine Fund (1970) of the World Center for Birds of Prey at Boise, Idaho (1984), http://www.peregrinefund.org; the North American Bird Conservation Initiative (1998), http://www.bsc-eoc.org/; the Wildflower Center, Austin, Texas, http://www.wildflower.org/; the North American Native Plant Society, Etobicoke, Ontario, Canada (1984), http://www.nanps.org/; the Butterfly Web site, http://www.butterflywebsite.com/; the Hummingbird Web site, http://hummingbirdwebsite.com/; Frog and Toad Web site; http://www.thefrogsite.com/; the Dragonfly Web site, http://www.dragonflywebsite.com/.

8. Strategies of citizen groups in using the various governmental opportunities to advance their objectives can be grasped through the handbook produced by the Wilderness Society, the Sierra Club, the National Audubon Society, the Natural Resources Defense Council, and the National Wildlife Federation: National Forest Planning: A Conservationist's Guide (Washington, D.C., 1983).

9. The Forest Service Employees for Environmental Ethics, established in 1988, grew out of the initiative of Jeff DeBonis, a timber planner for the Willamette National Forest in western Oregon. He became concerned with the way in which management bypassed the technical advice of its staff in favor of preferred policy choices that advanced commodity rather than ecological objectives, and he looked upon this as an issue of environmental ethics. He gathered a core of Forest Service employees, who formed the board of directors, and solicited support in the form of memberships from the public. FSEEE publications, initially a newsletter, Inner Voice, which later became a section of Forest Magazine, serve as important sources of information about Forest Service activities.

10. For a general introduction to forest issues in the Northeast see Christopher McGrory Klyza and Stephen C. Trumbulak, *The Future of the Northern Forest* (Hanover, N.H.: University Press of New England, 1994); Christopher McGrory Klyza, *Wilderness Comes Home: Rewilding the Northeast* (Hanover, N.H.: University Press of New England, 2001). Sources following northeast forest issues include Northern Forest Forum (1991–), files in Box 25, Forest List 1, EA; see also *Maine Environmental News*, http://www.meepi.org/, a news service for Maine environmental issues, and especially the feature stories on Maine forests by Phyllis Austin, writer for the former newspaper, *Maine Times*.

11. See publications of the Northern Forest Alliance: "Forestry for the Future"; "Northern Forest Wildlands: Landscape Conservation for the 21st Century"; "Shaping the Northern Forest Economy: Strategies for a Sustainable Future"; "The Northern Forest: Investing in the Future." See also http://www.northernforestalliance. org; and Northern Forest Alliance folder, Northeast section, Forest List 2, EA.

12. Nulhegan and Victory Basin Wildlands; "The Benefits of Roadless Areas for Biodiversity, Wildlife Management, Forest Health and Watershed Integrity," prepared by the Northern Forest Alliance (Montpelier, Vt., n.d.).

13. Society for the Protection of New Hampshire Forests; "New Hampshire's Vanishing Forests: Conversion, Fragmentation and Parcellization of Forests in the Granite State." To follow the role of the society in New England forest affairs see its periodical publication, *Forest Notes*, published in Concord, New Hampshire, copies of which are in EA, filed under "List of State Material." See also http://www. spnhf.org.

14. See RESTORE: The North Woods folder, Northeast section, Forest List 2, EA. The organization's Web site is http://www.restore.org.

15. See "The Sierra Club Finds 'Green' Certification of the Irving Allagash Woodlands Unacceptable," an announcement of the publication of a report by Mitch Lansky, "Grade Inflation? SCS Certification of Irving's Allagash Timberlands; A Report for the Sierra Club in May 2002." See also: "A Critical Analysis of the Forest Stewardship Council," prepared for the Sierra Club of Canada by Charles Restino and reprinted in *Northern Forest Forum* 8, no. 2 (Spring 2000); "Welcoming a Green Giant to Maine," an article from the *Northern Forest Forum* 8, no. 3 (Spring 2001); Phyllis Austin, "Hard Times in Irving's Woods," *Maine Times*, May 25–31, 2001.

16. A general background to southeastern forest issues is Chris Bolgiano, *The Appalachian Forest: A Search for Roots and Renewal* (Mechanicsburg, Pa.: Stackpole Books, 1998).

17. Public Survey Report; Southern Appalachian National Forest; A Survey of Residents of the Greater Southern Appalachian Region to Describe Public Use and Preferred Objectives for Southern Appalachian National Forest (Southern Region of National Forest Systems, FS; Southern Research Station, FS; University of Tennessee, July 2002). A copy can be obtained at http://www.srs.fs.fed.us/trends/sanfrpt .html.

18. A brief account of the impact of the chip mill industry on the forests of the

Cumberland Plateau, with a focus on Tennessee, is Alex Shoumatoff, "The Tennessee Tree Massacre," *On Earth* (publication of the Natural Resources Defense Council) 25, no. 4 (Winter 2004): 15–25. For an extensive analysis of changes in a section of the Cumberland Plateau see Jonathan Evans and David Haskell, "An Assessment of Forest Change on the Cumberland Plateau in Southern Tennessee," issued by the Landscape Analysis Laboratory, University of the South, Sewanee, Tennessee (2003). For the activities of the Dogwood Alliance, as reflected in e-mail messages and newspaper and other accounts, see Dogwood Alliance folder, Southern States section, Forest List 2, EA; see also http://www.dogwoodalliance.org.

19. See "Southern Forest Resource Assessment," Executive Summary, and various related material in Southern Forest Resource Assessment folder, Southern States section, Forest List 2, EA; also environmental analysis of the assessment in the same folder.

20. For material on the Southern Appalachian Forest Coalition see folder under that heading in Southern States section, Forest List 2, EA; see also http://www.safc.org/.

21. "Return the Great Forest: A Conservation Vision for the Southern Appalachian Region," copy in Southern States section, Forest List 2, EA.

22. David John Zaber, "Southern Lessons: Saving Species through the National Forest Management Act" (Washington, D.C.: Defenders of Wildlife, February 1998), copy in folder under that title in Southern States section, Forest List 2, EA.

23. Information about Heartwood, including a list of its constituent members and a record of its litigation activities, "Heartwood Forest Watch: A Success," can be found on its Web site: http://www.heartwood.org. Documents pertaining to the earlier more local citizen groups from which Heartwood developed are in Box 23, Environmental Organizations: The East, Forest List 1, EA. Further documents such as Heartwood's "Citizens Guide to Protecting Your National Forests," are in the Heartwood folder, Midwest section, Forest List 2, EA.

24. See Appalachian Restoration Campaign, "Proceedings from the 1996 Central Appalachian Ecological Integrity Conference" (Massanutten Springs, Va. 1996).

25. Material about Indiana events, including the Indiana Forest Alliance and "A Conservationist's Alternative Plan for Management of the Hoosier National Forest," is in the Indiana folder of Forest List 2, EA. This material was obtained from the Indiana Forest Alliance Web site.

26. Earlier issues of the publication of the Allegheny Defense Project, the *Hellbender* (named for the Hellbender salamander), can be found in Box 28, Citizens' Organizations: The East, Forest List, and later issues in the Allegheny Defense Project folder, Pennsylvania section, Forest List 2. The ADP Web site is http://www.alleghenydefense.org. The ADP files also include copies of several court cases and other miscellaneous material about its activities. The ADP plan for the Allegheny National Forest is "Allegheny Wild! A Citizen's Vision for the Allegheny National Forest," Clarion, Pa., May 2003; a copy can be downloaded from http://www.alleghenywild.org.

27. An introduction to the Rocky Mountain West is Jill S. Barron, ed., *Rocky Mountain Futures: An Ecological Perspective* (Washington, D.C.: Island Press, 2002).

28. For details about the Southwest Forest Alliance see Southwest Forest Alliance folder, Mountain States section, Forest List 2, EA. See also the Web site of the Alliance: http://www.swfa.org/.

29. See the Southwest Forest Alliance papers: "Disappearing Legacy, Destruction of the Ponderosa Pine Ecosystem," and "Natural Process Restoration Principles," available on the alliance's Web site.

30. See details about the Sky Island Alliance and the Sky Islands Conservation Network in the Sky Island Alliance folder, Mountain States section, Forest List 2, EA; see also http://www.skyislandalliance.org/.

31. For the content and scope of the Sky Island project see the Sky Islands Wildlands Network Conservation Plan, described briefly on the Network, ibid.

32. The Sky Island Alliance volunteer program, including its wildlife monitoring, wilderness mapping, riparian inventory and monitoring, and road closure programs are described on its Web site.

33. For details about the Southern Rockies Forest Network, see under that title in the Mountain States section, Forest List 2, EA. Of particular interest is the Southern Rockies Ecosystem Project, available on the Web site of the Southern Rockies Ecosystem Project. See also http://www.southernrockies.org/.

34. *The Southern Rockies Wildlands Network Vision* (Golden, Colo.: The Colorado Mountain Club, 2003).

35. For material about the Greater Yellowstone Coalition, see its publications and reports under Box 2, The Greater Yellowstone Region, in the Regional Environmental Records section of EA. This includes several reports drawn up by the coalition as well as its publication "Greater Yellowstone Report," 1985–1997. Publications and copies of the report in subsequent years are in the Mountain States section of Forest List 2, EA. The coalition's Web site is http://www.greateryellowstone.org/. The Web site includes the membership of the coalition's Science Council. An account of the Craighead grizzly research which initiated the basis for the concept of the greater Yellowstone ecosystem is John J. Craighead, Jerry S. Summers, and John A. Mitchell, *The Grizzly Bears of Yellowstone: Their Ecology in the Yellowstone Ecosystem, 1959–1992* (Washington, D.C.: Island Press, 1995).

36. During the summer of 1990 I directed the public land policy section of an environmental seminar for college students managed under the auspices of the Honors College at the University of Pittsburgh, which used Yellowstone National Park as a laboratory and was located on a ranch just east of the Park. Since the seminar was held during the midst of the intense debate over the Yellowstone "vision document," I drew upon leading figures in the debate as seminar speakers and gathered relevant documents for the students. The files contain these documents; they also contain copies of several articles and a bibliography pertaining to the Greater Yellowstone Ecosystem as well as publications opposing the Yellowstone

Ecosystem concept by the Wyoming Heritage Society, the de facto state Chamber of Commerce of Wyoming. The relevant documents are in Box 3, The Greater Yellowstone Region, Regional Environmental Records section, EA.

37. For details about the Alliance for the Wild Rockies see under that title in Mountain States section, Forest List 2, EA. See also http://www.wildrockiesalliance .org/.

38. From the Alliance for the Wild Rockies statement of objectives, Alliance for the Wild Rockies folder, Forest List 1, EA.

39. A general introduction to the issues on the Sierra Nevada forests is Timothy P. Duane, *Shaping the Sierra: Nature, Culture, and Conflict in the Changing West* (Berkeley: University of California Press, 1998); for more specifics see Sierra Nevada Forest Protection Campaign. For an ecological perspective on the Sierra Nevada see Forest Service Employees for Environmental Ethics, *Blueprint for Sierra Nevada National Forests* (Eugene, Ore., 1999). See the reports of the Sierra Nevada Ecosystem Project (SNEP) and folders in EA.

40. See Oregon Natural Resources Council folder under "Oregon" in lists, "States" and "Organizations" in EA, and Pacific Coast States section, Forest List 2, EA. The council's Web site is http://www.onrc.org/. The "Oregon Wild Atlas," one of the council's main projects, is at http://www.oregonwild.org/atlas/.

41. See material in Forest List 2, EA, under "Washington," and the Northwest Ecosystem Alliance folder. The alliance's activities can be followed in its magazine, "Northwest Ecosystem News," available on its Web site and copies in the folder in EA, and its e-mail letter, "ecosystem—e-news," current and some recent issues available on the alliance's Web site at: http://www.conservationnw.org/.

Material about Washington State activities is located in several places in EA: List of State Material, Washington, Box 1, contains documents pertaining to issues involving the Washington state forests; Forest List 2, under the category Pacific States, Washington, contains folders pertaining to the Timber, Fish and Wildlife program and its subsequent transformation into the Forest and Fish program. Certification material is in the folder Washington State DNR Certification Proposal. Forestry activities of the Washington Environmental Council can be followed in its publication *Voices*, issues since 2000 located in Washington Environmental Council folder, Pacific States section, Washington, Forest List 2, EA. See also the council's Web site: http://www.wecprotects.org.

42. A general introduction to issues on the Tongass National Forest is Carolyn Servid and Donald Snow, eds., *The Book of the Tongass* (Minneapolis, Minn.: Milkweed Editions, 1999). For an argument vigorously anti-ecological see K. A. Soderberg and Jackie DuRette, *People of the Tongass: Alaska Forestry under Attack* (Bellevue, Wash.: The Free Enterprise Press, 1988).

43. Events in the evolution of issues on the Tongass National Forest can be followed in the publications of the Southeast Alaska Conservation Council under the folder Alaska, Forest List 2, EA. See especially the organization's publication the *Ra-*

ven Call and a variety of papers, e.g., "Defending the Promise of Tongass Reform," a report on the Forest Service's failure to implement the Tongass Timber Reform Act (March 1992). See also documents in List of State Material, Alaska, EA.

44. A wide variety of materials produced by citizen groups convey the "biodiversity message." See, as examples, Maine Natural Resources Council, "Maine's Natural Heritage . . . Life Depends On It! Protecting Maine's Plant and Animal Legacy," a statement supporting the establishment of an Ecological Reserve System for Maine (Augusta: Maine Natural Resources Council, January 2000); Forest Service Employees for Environmental Ethics, "The Secret Forest Experience" project, a curriculum for students with special emphasis on biodiversity, terrestrial forest arthropods, fire ecology, and forest soil microorganisms (Eugene, Ore.: Forest Service Employees for Environmental Ethics, 2001); issues of *Chicago Wilderness*, published by Chicago Wilderness (1996–), "an unprecedented alliance of 169 public and private organizations working together to study and restore, protect and manage the precious natural ecosystems of the Chicago region for the benefit of the public"; the *Illinois Steward* (Urbana, Ill.: University of Illinois, 1991–), a publication aimed "to increase awareness and respect for the natural world." Southern Rockies Forest Network, "Biodiversity Conservation," under the Southern Rockies Forest Network folder, Mountain States section, Forest List 2, EA. For a focus on biodiversity specifically on the national forests see "Getting on Message: Eastern Forests and Biodiversity," http://www.biodiversityproject.org/publications.htm. For a study of the attitudes of Americans toward biodiversity see *Americans and Biodiversity*, a survey conducted by Belden Russonello and Stewart for the Biodiversity Project (Washington, D.C.: The Biodiversity Project, April 2002).

45. The basic strategies of inventory, management (protection and restoration), and monitoring now being applied to biodiversity resources are precisely the same as those long applied to wood fiber resources. One way of describing the challenge of ecological forestry is the pressure to shift the balance of standard management practices from the earlier overwhelming concentration of budgets and skills on commodity management objectives to a more equal balance with ecological management objectives.

46. Emphasis on a lack of knowledge of most forest species was a major theme of a 2003 report on the decline of wildlife and wildlife habitat in Pennsylvania, "Birds Are the Only of Vertebrates in Our State Whose Population Trends Have Been Carefully Investigated," Ben Moyer, *Pennsylvania's Wildlife and Wild Places: Our Outdoor Heritage in Peril* (Harrisburg: Pennsylvania Department of Conservation and Natural Resources, 2003), 11.

47. Using the stand as the main unit for forest analysis and management inhibits the development of categories, such as habitats, for other forest resources. Silviculturists tend to think that all forest resources can be accessed through stand classifications, a practice which relegates resources other than plants that produce wood fiber to a derivative and second-class status. My first encounter with this problem came in the first meeting of the Ecosystem Management Advisory Committee of

the Pennsylvania Bureau of Forestry on February 6, 1997, when the bureau's chief forest planner, Dan Devlin, argued that no categories of habitat for classification purposes was needed because habitat just "came along" as the measurements of stands were made. See my notes for that meeting in my files pertaining to meetings of the Committee, dated February 6, 1997, a copy of which is included in Hays, *Forest Papers*. See also George D. Davis, "Biological Diversity: Saving All the Pieces," vol. 1, *Fulfilling the Promise of the Adirondack Park* (Elizabethtown, N.Y.: The Adirondack Council, 1988). This has led to competition between a system based upon groupings of plants known as plant communities and groupings of types of habitat which are based upon the relationships between plants and animals on the one hand and their physical and biological environments on the other. Stand vs. habitat classifications provide a sharply defined context for tracking the resistance of an older way of thinking in terms of commodity forest objectives to a newer way of thinking arising from ecological objectives.

48. One reflection of the interest in habitats is the development of field guides to habitats on an order similar to the field guides to species. See two books by Janine M. Benyus, formerly with the North Central Experiment Station of the U.S. Forest Service: *Northwoods Wildlife: A Watcher's Guide to Habitats* (Minocqua, Wis.: North-Word Press, 1989); and *The Field Guide to Wildlife Habitats of the Eastern United States* (New York: Simon and Shuster, 1989).

49. Citizen reformers were especially critical of clear-cutting because of its role in transforming a mixed-age forest into an even-aged one with resulting habitat implications. See, for example, Edward C. Fritz, *Sterile Forest: The Case against Clearcutting* (Austin, Tex.: Eakin Press, 1983). Objections to the conversion of diverse hardwood forests to pine monoculture in the Southern Appalachians, fostered by the southern wood products industry, played a major role in shaping the diversity provision in the 1976 National Forest Management Act. This was one of the first statements of diversity in a rather simplified and limited form, which became far more extensive and complex in later years.

50. For thinking on native forests among forest reform groups see the activities of the Native Forest Network (Missoula, Mont.), http://www.nativeforest.org/. The native forest issue was especially active in the Great Lakes area, with an emphasis on restoring segments of the earlier pre-aspen white pine forest of the region. Especially striking was the extensive attempt by the Ouachita National Forest to reconstruct the composition of the native forest in its region.

51. Activities by citizens in support of old-growth forests developed quite separately in the Pacific Northwest and the East. Activities of the Northwest Old Growth Campaign can be followed on http://www.nwoldgrowth.org/. Old-growth promotional activities arose in the East toward the end of the twentieth century. See a review of these activities in Samuel P. Hays, "Eastern Old Growth" and an extensive review of the Williamstown conference by Hays, "Northeastern Old Growth Conference, Report, Williamstown, Mass., Oct. 28–30, 1994," both in Hays, *Forest Papers*, 337–42 and 343–62. For a general review of eastern old growth see Mary

Byrd Davis, *Eastern Old Growth Forests: Prospects for Rediscovery and Recovery* (Washington, D.C.: Island Press, 1996).

52. A brief but succinct statement of the importance of headwater streams is Winsor H. Lowe and Gene E. Likens, "Moving Headwater Streams to the Head of the Class," *BioScience* 55, no. 3 (March 2005): 196–97. Ecological objectives in watersheds took many forms, usually depending on the ecological circumstances and the state of policy development and debate in different regions. In Maine, for example, the ecological viewpoint found expression in Mitch Lansky's "Comments on Proposed State Riparian Standards," a critique of the draft of proposed harmonized statewide standards, produced by the Maine Forest Service; the comments emphasized the importance of including smaller streams in the standards. A copy of the comments is in the Maine folder, The Northeast section, Forest List 2, EA. For an example of riparian issues see the Oregon case in *Oregon Insider: A Biweekly Digest of Environmental News*, nos. 12, 18, and 26/27, in Oregon folder, States section, EA.

53. A citizen-initiated case that is intended to move management from inventory to protection is the Important Bird Areas project instituted by the Audubon Society. In this project citizen and scientist teams identify areas with high numbers of species or populations of individual species which then hopefully will lead to protection. The Pennsylvania Audubon Society, said to be the first to institute this program, identified seventy-six critical bird breeding, migratory stopover, feeding, and overwintering areas in the state and reports ten protective actions involving both public agencies and a private corporation. See http://pa.audubon.org/iba/.

54. In 2003 citizens' reform organizations issued a set of forest restoration principles titled, "Citizens' Call for Ecological Forest Restoration: Forest Restoration Principles and Criteria," signed by 120 forest reform organizations throughout the country. See http://www.nativeforest.org/campaigns/public_lands/cc_5_30_02.htm. A copy of the report is also in Forest List 2, EA.

55. Citizen-inspired litigation involving Forest Service policies and practices provides extended examples of these ecological forest objectives advocated by both citizen groups and ecological scientists. Some involve challenges as to the adequacy of ecological analysis under the Environmental Impact Statement (EIS) process required by the National Environmental Policy Act; others often involve the failure to "survey and manage" either for endangered species or for Management Indicator Species (MIS). One example is a case involving appeal of a proposed timber harvest on the Cherokee National Forest, *Cherokee Forest Voices et al. v. USDA Forest Service*, Watauga Ranger District, Cherokee National Forest, January 26, 2004. The suit was brought by the Southern Environmental Law Center; a copy is in the Center's folder in Forest List 2, EA.

56. Ecological forest science is scattered in a wide range of professional journals, most of them highly specialized and geared toward a small professional clientele. Several sources that are readable for a more general audience are *BioScience* (1950–), published by the American Institute of Biological Sciences; *Natural Areas Journal* (1980–), published by the Natural Areas Association; *Frontiers in Ecology and the*

Environment (2003–), published by the Ecological Society of America; and Conservation Biology (1987–), published by the Society for Conservation Biology. An excellent window into ecological forest research is provided by the reports of the five forest-related research sites in the twenty-four-site group called the Long-Term Ecological Research Network, financed by the National Science Foundation. These are located at the H. J. Andrews Experimental Forest at Blue River, near Eugene, Oregon; the Harvard Forest in Petersham, Massachusetts; the Hubbard Brook Research Forest in Hubbard Brook, New Hampshire; the Coweeta Hydrologic Laboratory at Otto, North Carolina; and the Cedar Creek Natural History Area in Minnesota. Each has its own Web site and as a group they can be accessed through the LTER Web site: http://lternet.edu/. Ecological research carried out under the auspices of the National Park Service is included in issues of Park Science.

A comprehensive statement about the implications of ecological science for management of the National Forests is John Aber et al., "Applying Ecological Principles to the Management of the U.S. National Forests" Issues in Ecology (Washington, D.C., Ecological Society of America), Spring 2000. For a statement from an ecological scientist about biodiversity on the national forests see E. Norse et al., Conserving Biodiversity in Our National Forests (Washington, D.C.: Wilderness Society, 1986).

57. A classic statement about biodiversity is R. F. Noss and A. Y. Cooperrider, Saving Nature's Legacy: Protecting and Restoring Biodiversity (Washington, D.C.: Island Press, 1994). Birds and bird habitat, and more recently neo-tropical migratory songbirds, comprise one of the more well-established subjects in specialized ecological science; see John Terborgh, Where Have All the Birds Gone? Essays on the Biology and Conservation of Birds that Migrate to the American Tropics (Princeton, N.J.: Princeton University Press, 1989). Extensive biodiversity monitoring programs are under way in a wide range of sites and under the auspices of different management agencies. One of the most extensive for a single area is the All-Taxa Biodiversity Inventory for the Great Smokies National Park. A far more extensive but less intensive project is the International Biodiversity Observation Year: http://www.nrel.colostate.edu/projects/iboy/.

For statements of the value of biodiversity and the lesser species see the Web site of the All Species Foundation, an organization "dedicated to the complete inventory of all species of life on Earth within the next 25 years—a human generation." And the Xerces Society, "Why Are Invertebrates Important? Panel on Biodiversity and Ecosystems, President's Committee of Advisers on Science and Technology (PCAST)"; "Teaming with Life: Investing in Science to Understand and Use America's Living Capital, with a Brief Description and Statement of the Importance of Bryophytes, Lichens, Epiphytes, Fungi, Vascular Plants, Arthropods, Mollusks, Amphibians and Mammals." See also Bruce Marcot, "Classification of Key Ecological Functions (KEFs) as Used to Describe Ecological Roles of Fungi, Lichens, Bryophytes, Nonvascular Plants, Vascular Plants, Invertebrates, and Vertebrates, in the Inland West U.S.," http://www.spiritone.com/~brucem/crbkefs.htm. Christine G. Niwa, Roger E. Sandquist, and Rod Crawford, "Invertebrates of the Columbia River Assessment Area," PNW—GTR-512, http://www.fs.fed.us/pnw/pubs/gtr512.pdf.

The Xerces Society, which specializes in invertebrates, put it succinctly, "To protect our natural capital, our Nation's biodiversity and the ecosystems within which it thrives, we need to have an extensive and frequently updated environmental knowledge base. This knowledge base is required to evaluate alternative plans for managing biodiversity and ecosystems as we work to optimize the union between the environment and the economy."

Ornithology had long been a subject of scientific interest and in the environmental era became a major topic of ecological interest, expanded greatly by new techniques of inventory and monitoring fostered by radio telemetry, and with renewed support from a variety of new organizations and institutions. Of special interest are forest habitat for birds and especially neo-tropical migratory songbirds, which became an active funding interest of the National Fish and Wildlife Foundation. See the series of articles in Box 70, Songbirds, Subject File section, EA.

58. A successful combination of concern for the decline in a single group of species, amphibians, is reflected in both inventory and protective measures for frogs. The work of scientists seeking to chart and understand the decline of amphibians is recorded in the publication *Froglog*, newsletter of the Declining Amphibian Populations Task Force, a bimonthly which was first issued in 1989, edited by John W. Wilkinson, Department of Biological Sciences, The Open University, Walton Hall, Milton Keynes, MK7 6AA, U.K., an international body with U.S. ties at the University of Arizona. A Nature Conservancy project at its Kankakee Sands property in the Grand Kankakee Marsh in northern Indiana reported success in restoring frog populations at fragmented marsh properties when linked through corridors. See Bob Broadman (biologist at Saint Joseph's College, Rensselaer, Indiana), "Amphibian Biodiversity Recovery in a Large-Scale Ecosystem Restoration," *Froglog* 59 (October 2003). This project was closely tied to efforts by the citizen group Friends of the Kankakee to create the Kankakee Marsh National Wildlife Refuge.

59. Varied types of disturbance have led to the analysis of the ecological consequences of each. See, for example, on the effect of roads, S. Trombulak and C. A. Frissell, "Review of Ecological Effects of Roads on Terrestrial and Aquatic Communities," *Conservation Biology* 14 (2000): 18–30; G. Hermann, M. J. Furniss, R. R. Ziemer, and M. H. Brookes, *Forest Roads: A Synthesis of Scientific Information* (Portland, Ore.: USDA, Forest Service, 2001). Or see a brief list of studies on the effect of timber harvest on forest nutrient budgets, herbaceous understories, soil compaction, invertebrates and avian species, hydrology, forest lepidoptera, salamanders, and soil chemistry, in Pennsylvania Wildlands Recovery Project, *The Pennsylvania State Forest Resource Management Plan: A Wildlands Perspective* (n.p., Sept. 2003). Acid deposition as a major forest disturbance is a concern especially in Pennsylvania, which bears the brunt of deposition originating in the Ohio Valley region. See William E. Sharpe and Joy R. Cronon, eds., *The Effects of Acid Deposition on Pennsylvania's Forests: Volume I, Proceedings of the 1998 Pennsylvania Acidic Deposition Conference* (University Park, Pa.: Environmental Resources Research Institute, 1999). For the role of acid rain in creating long-term changes in soil nutrients see University of Maine Forum for

Science, Industry and Business, "Acid Rain Study Reaches Milestone, Confirms Soil Nutrient Depletion," *Innovations Report*, March 29, 2004; this project can be explored on the Internet under the title, "The Bear Brook Watershed Manipulation Project." On noise see Autumn Lyn Radle, "The Effect of Noise on Wildlife: A Literature Review" (University of Oregon, World Forum for Acoustic Ecology), http://interact.uoregon.edu/MediaLit/WFAE/readings/radle.html.

60. A summary of ecological research on the impacts of urbanization on species diversity and especially native species is Michael L. McKinney, "Urbanization, Biodiversity, and Conservation," *BioScience* 52, no. 10 (2002): 883–90. Professor John M. Marzloff at the University of Washington, Seattle, developed the idea that in the face of urbanization, which reduced avian diversity markedly, the national forests were a major reservoir from which urban populations could be replenished.

61. A study of the soils that are "dynamic components of terrestrial ecosystems" and their classification in terms of the degree to which they are undisturbed or are "in danger" is Ronald Amundson, Y. Guo, and P. Gong, "Soil Diversity and Land Use in the United States," *Ecosystems* 6, no. 5 (October 2003): 470–82.

62. Lawson, "Economic and Ecological Benefits of a Diverse Forest Stand," *Forest Planning* 4, no. 2 (May 1983): 12. In September 1987, the House Subcommittee on Natural Resources, Agricultural Research and Environment considered a bill on biological diversity and asked groups to testify on the advantages and disadvantages of a legislated standard of biological diversity in the United States. Forest Service chief Dale Robertson did not supply a national standard or definition, but he did support the importance of maintaining biological diversity. Yet he defined diversity in the then-current Forest Service terms of varieties of specialized management zones rather than biological diversity within a "mosaic of age classes," as ecologists were prone to emphasize. See Lawson, "Chief Propounds New Emphasis on Diversity," *Forest Watch* 8, no. 5 (November 1987): 5.

63. The classic scientific statement about forest fragmentation is Larry D. Harris, *The Fragmented Forest: Island Biogeography Theory and the Preservation of Biodiversity* (Chicago: University of Chicago Press, 1984).

64. Ecological corridors are closely connected with the problem of fragmentation, for it is through such corridors that fragments can be connected to form ecological pathways for species. For the interest of citizen organizations in scientific studies of corridors, see "New Studies Show Corridors Work," *Wild Pennsylvania* (publication of the Pennsylvania Wildlands Recovery Project), Winter 2003.

65. The Andrews work on "old forests," led by Jerry Franklin, began much earlier than did the network of twenty-four Long Term Ecological Research centers but became one of them. See http://www.fsl.orst.edu/lter/.

66. For a project by ecological scientists under the leadership of Prof. David Stehle of the University of Arkansas called The Ancient Cross Timbers Consortium for Research, Education and Conservation, comprising institutions in Oklahoma, Texas, Missouri, and Arkansas to study old growth in the Midwest, see "Consortium to Study, Preserve Ancient Forest," news report from the University of Arkan-

sas, Fayetteville, as reported in *Science Daily*, October 27, 2003. Stehle was a frequent speaker at the Eastern Old Growth conferences.

67. One of the ten "conditions" attached to the certification of the Pennsylvania State Forests was the requirement that it move its almost exclusive emphasis on even-aged management toward an all-aged forest. This recommendation of the review team appointed under the Forest Stewardship Council program was fully supported by one of the peer review members, Jerry Franklin.

68. Kathryn A. Kohm and Jerry F. Franklin, eds., *Creating a Forestry for the 21st Century: The Science of Ecosystem Management* (Washington, D.C.: Island Press, 1997). Several essays in this compilation elaborate on the practice of exempting forest elements from harvest cuts in order to create bridges from the existing to the future forest.

69. Several items outline the range of watershed issues. One, Gordon H. Reeves et al., "Aquatic and Riparian Effectiveness Monitoring Plan for the Northwest Forest Plan" (AREMP), outlines a watershed-wide monitoring program for the Pacific Northwest Forest Plan, and is one of the most comprehensive such monitoring systems devised for assessing the condition of forest watersheds. The plan is available on http://www.fs.fed.us/pnw/pubs/gtr577.pdf .

Another which outlines the limited significance of the Best Management Practice (BMP) programs in many states is Steve Kahl, "A Review of the Effects of Forest Practice on Water Quality in Maine," a report to the Maine Department of Environmental Protection, Bureau of Land and Water Quality Control, Augusta, Maine, October 1996, in Box 32, State Forest Affairs, Forest List, EA. This study reviews BMP programs in many states.

70. For a statement about the differences in terminology between the ecological and the commodity outlook in forestry see Samuel P. Hays, "A Challenge to the Profession of Forestry," in James C. Finley and Stephen B. Jones, eds., *Practicing Stewardship and Living a Land Ethic*, Proceedings of the 1991 Penn State Forest Resource Issues Conference, Harrisburg, Pa., March 26–27, 1991 (Pennsylvania State University, 1992).

71. Controversy over the role of these "lesser species" in the ancient forests of the Pacific Northwest gave rise to a number of attempts on the part of citizen and scientific groups to elaborate their role in forest ecological relationships. Some of these are in the Survey and Manage folder, Pacific Northwest Forest Plan section, Forest List 2, EA. One is a compilation of sections of the Northwest Forest Plan, "All Creatures Great and Small," drawn up by the Oregon Natural Resources Council. Another is a document, "Why Are Invertebrates Important?" produced by the Xerces Society, one of the ecological organizations to advance interest in invertebrates. Still another is the document "Teaming with Life: Investing in Science to Understand and Use America's Living Capital," drawn up by the President's Committee of Advisers on Science and Technology (PCAST), Panel on Biodiversity and Ecosystems, March 1998, http://www.ostp.gov/Environment/html/teaming cover.html.

Chapter 3: The National Response to Ecological Forestry

1. Michael Coffman's Web site, which includes biographical information and the text of his article, "International Domination of U.S. Environmental Law and Private Property," is http://www.discerningtoday.org.

2. Robert G. Lee, *Broken Trust, Broken Land: Freeing Ourselves from the War over the Environment* (Wilsonville, Ore.: Book Partners, 1944).

3. Patrick Moore, *Green Spirit: Trees Are the Answer* (privately printed and obtainable from Moore's Web site, http://www.greenspirit.com/).

4. Alston Chase, *In a Dark Wood: The Fight over Forests and the Rising Tyranny of Ecology* (New York: Houghton Mifflin, 1995).

5. For Harry V. Wiant's paper, "Stand Up for Forestry," see http://www.ever greenmagazine.com/news/speeches/WiantSpeech.html.

6. The reaction of industry to the legislative proposals of the 1960s can be followed in the pages of *American Forests*, publication of the American Forestry Association, between 1959 and 1964. See especially the writings and testimonies of Kenneth Pomeroy, forester for the association.

7. Craig W. Allin, *The Politics of Wilderness Preservation* (Westport, Conn.: Greenwood Press, 1982).

8. The 2003 statement of policy by the AF&PA, called "New Federal Forestry; Managing Federal Forests in the 21st Century," emphasizes primarily the role of federal agencies in dealing with threats to wood fiber production in the form of insects, pests, and fire. Much of the statement of policy is a series of attacks on environmental organizations for their use of the courts in achieving their objectives. Other than that generalized series of attacks, the statement contains no recognition of ecological forestry or its objectives, either in terms of policy or practices. Ecological/ environmental action by citizens is attributed only to the desire of organizations to fuel public emotions so as to increase organizational membership, with no recognition of ecological objectives or of the role of ecological scientists in forest affairs. The views and activities of the AF&PA can be found on its Web site: http://www .afandpa.org/.

9. For an account of the Timber Supply Act from the vantage point of a congressional staffer see Le Master, *Decade of Change*, 19–32 (see chap. 1, n. 5). The significance of the issue to the emerging environmental community is related in "Timber Supply Act: Anatomy of a Battle," *Sierra Club Bulletin* 55 (March 1970): 8–11.

10. Samuel P. Hays, "The New Environmental Forest," *University of Colorado Law Review* 59 (1988): 517. The industry's proposal to modify the multiple objectives of the Multiple-Use Act of 1960 in favor of dominant wood production zoning continued into the twenty-first century. See material pertaining to the proposed USFS plan for the five Southern Appalachian forests, in which planners rejected their earlier proposal that "timber production would be a 'byproduct' of managing for other resource values and objectives" and proposed instead, without public comment, that the plan give forests the option to allocate lands to a "timber pro-

duction" emphasis. See publicity for the proposal, "Forest Service secretly targeting southern mountains for major logging," issued jointly by Public Employees for Environmental Responsibility, the Southern Appalachian Forest Coalition and the Southern Environmental Law Center, August 28, 2003. These items are in the Southern Appalachian Forest Plan folder, section Southern Appalachians section, Forest List 2, EA.

11. For a perceptive account of the politics of the 1976 act from the vantage point of a participant from the environmental community, see an account by Brock Evans, "Shaping the National Forest Management Act of 1976: A Participant's View," in Hays, *Forest Papers*, 83–95, copy in Forest List 2, EA. For the viewpoint of Society of American Foresters, see its running comment during the debate in the *Journal of Forestry*.

12. An excellent running account of national forest events under John Crowell during the Reagan administration is continued in the publication, *Forest Planning* (later *Forest Watch*) (1980), published by Cascade Holistic Economic Consultants, directed by Randall O'Toole, of Eugene, Oregon. See, for example, "Crowell and the Shadow of Louisiana Pacific," *Forest Planning* (April 1981). For the "revolt of the supervisors" see a brief account in Hirt, *A Conspiracy of Optimism*, 272–74, especially, "Forest Supervisors in the Northern Region were among the most prominent in the reformist faction, and they developed extensive explanations of why their Reagan era forest plan timber targets could not be implemented."

13. Further elaboration of the industry "backlash" in the second Bush administration is in chapter 6.

14. *Evergreen Magazine*, which describes itself as "the world's most widely read forestry magazine," was founded in 1986, with initial funding from a "small group of southern Oregon lumber companies interested in promoting wider citizen involvement in the federal government's congressionally mandated forest planning process. In the years since its founding, the magazine has assumed a much wider role, providing forums for scientists, policy makers, landowners and community leaders across North America." Details about the publication can be obtained from http://www.evergreenmagazine.com.

15. The Web site of the National Council for Air and Stream Improvement contains information about its history and its research schedule; it provides a comprehensive picture of the range of research which the evolving ecological objectives in forest management generated as a defensive strategy on the part of the forest industry.

16. The publication of the Society of American Foresters, the *Journal of Forestry*, in 2003 in its 101st year, is issued from 5400 Grosvenor Lane, Bethesda, Md., 20814–2198; its Web site, accessed under the society's title, contains a running account of the organization's policy positions. See, for example, "National Forest Reform in the Second Session of the 107th Congress: Viewpoints of the Society of American Foresters." Especially relevant is the section of the *Journal* each month which reports items on forest scientific research; this is heavily oriented toward commodity for-

est research (silviculture, technology, and economics) with very little about ecological forest research, for which the reader has to go to publications in the fields
of biology and ecology.

A considerable amount of information about the activities of the society is
available on its Web site. See several categories of information under titles: "About
Forestry," "Policy and Press," and its periodical, the Forestry Source. While the SAF
usually remained relatively diplomatic with its opposition to ecological forestry,
it took an uncharacteristic stance amid the Roadless Area program fostered by the
chief forester, Mike Dombeck, during the latter years of the Clinton administration. As reported by Dombeck, "The Society of American Foresters went so far as
to inform the chief that his continued membership in their organization would
depend on the outcome of their 'ethics investigation' into his involvement in the
roadless area issue." See Michael Dombeck, Christopher A. Wood, and Jack Edward
Williams, From Conquest to Conservation: Our Public Lands Legacy (Washington, D.C.: Island
Press, 2003), 108.

17. The documents pertaining to Leon Minckler's activities are in the "Leon
Minckler file," Box 22, Forest List 1, EA. They include the proposal, the relevant
correspondence concerning it, his description of the entire SAF episode in "A Report to the Forest Ecology Working Group," SAF, September 17, 1974, his later
"Proposal for an Environmental Quality Subgroup," also rejected, and copies of his
reports published by the National Parks and Conservation Association. A copy of
his "Report" is in Hays, Forest Papers, 73–76.

18. The list of organizations associated with the American Institute of Biological
Sciences is printed in the early pages of each edition of BioScience. These included
the American Ornithological Union, the American Society of Ichthyologists and
Herpetologists, the American Society of Naturalists, the American Society of Plant
Biologists, the Association of Tropical Biology, the Association of Ecosystem Re-
search Centers, the Association of Southeastern Biologists, the Biological Sciences
Curriculum Study, the Botanical Society of America, the Cooper Ornithological
Society, the Ecological Society of America, the Entomological Society of America,
the Herpetologists' League, the International Society for Ecological Modeling, the
International Society for Ecosystem Health, the National Association of Biology
Teachers, the National Museum of Natural History, the Natural Areas Association,
the Nature Conservancy, the Organization for Tropical Studies, the Organization
of Biological Field Stations, the Society for Conservation Biology, the Society for
Ecological Restoration, the Society for the Study of Amphibians and Reptiles, the
Society of Wetland Scientists, the Soil Science Society of America, the Southern Appalachian Botanical Society, the Torrey Botanical Society, and the Western Society
of Naturalists.

19. The Web site of the National Association of State Foresters contains copies of
its newsletter, "Washington Update," which began publication in 1984. It includes
records of its annual meetings and resolutions approved and a running account of
its policy positions on pending legislation.

20. Although the NASF was interested in a variety of ecological forestry issues, for example, the potential listing of the lynx as an endangered species, its most continual interest was in the impact of forest practices on water quality, the development of EPA nonpoint source water policy, and efforts to establish federal and state regulation of forest practices to reduce nonpoint source pollution. The limited significance of best management practices in the effect of forest practices on water quality is reflected in the continual debate over the results of such practices, that for the most part they represent voluntary standards and that the state agencies have no usable data with which to measure those results. The quiet recognition of this problem is reflected in the proposal that a federal water monitoring program for BMPs be established called "Watershed Forestry Assistance" as a line item in the Forest Service budget for 2004, and the support of such a measure by the American Forest and Paper Association. See testimony submitted to the Senate Appropriations Subcommittee on Interior and Related Agencies by John Hesselbuttel, vice president, Forest and Wood Products Division, American Forest and Paper Association, April 18, 2003, 2.

21. See the National Association of Professional Forestry Schools and Colleges, representing sixty-nine organizations, http://www.napfsc.org/. Here information is provided about each of its member schools and colleges. Information as to the particular position of each school and college on the commodity-ecological spectrum has to be gleaned from information of the Web site of each school or college (the descriptions here are drawn from those sites), and especially its curriculum, the commodity or ecological character of the research of its faculty, and what is indicated by the content of its annual and biennial reports. Some sense of the direction in which each institution is moving can be obtained from the presence of student groups with distinctive ecological or commodity tendencies, such as a student branch of the Society for Conservation Biology or the student branch of TAPPI, a well-known production forestry body. Useful also are the periodic reports issued by each institution.

22. For details about the Goddard Chair, see http://goddard.cas.psu.edu/. The statement of the roles of professional forestry described there draws heavily on the thinking of Daniel Kemmis of the University of Montana and his book *Community and the Politics of Place* (Norman: University of Oklahoma Press, 1990).

23. Some sense as to the personnel pattern within the Forest Service can be obtained from an agency recruiting document, "Make a Difference—Challenge Yourself with a Forest Service Career" (U.S. Dept. of Agriculture, 1990). While the occupational categories listed as potential career positions and their total number (in all grades) within the agency are instructive, they do not necessarily provide precise categories. The largest categories are Forestry technician (7,457) and Forester (5,287). The list includes Wildlife Biologist (686); Hydrologist (254); Fisheries Biologist (237); Botanist (44); Ecologist (80); and Microbiologist (14).

24. A useful sociological study of Forest Service personnel is James J. Kennedy

and Thomas M. Quigley, "How Entry-level Employees, Forest Supervisors, Regional Foresters and Chiefs View Forest Service Values and the Reward System," a 1989 survey done for the Sunbird Conference, second meeting of forest supervisors and chiefs (Tucson, Ariz., November 13–16, 1989).

25. An equally useful set of follow-up studies were done by Paul Mohai. See two articles in *Policy Studies Journal* 23, no. 2 (June 1995), one by Mohai, "The Forest Service and the National Forest Management Act: Assessing Bureaucratic Response to External and Internal Forces for Change," 247–52; and Jennifer C. Thomas and Paul Mohai, "Racial, Gender and Professional Diversification in the Forest Service from 1983 to 1992," 296–309. By the 1990s a terminology had arisen within the Forest Service in which the resource specialist newcomers were known as "ologists."

A good brief account of the resulting internal tensions within the Forest Service is Paul Hirt, *A Conspiracy of Optimism*, 281–92.

26. The divisions between old and new within the Forest Service are often described as a difference in outlook between the "line" officers at the level of individual national forests who manage the forests on the ground, and the staff in regional offices and the Washington office who provide the expertise required by new forest obligations. For a lucid account of the relationship between the agency line and staff personnel and the impact of environmental and ecological factors in that relationship, see Jack Ward Thomas, "Appropriate Roles of Line Officers and Technical Staff" in "Northwest Forest Plan Review," which Thomas conducted at the request of Jack Blackwell, regional forester in the Pacific Southwest (California) region, dated June 26, 2003, in Northwest Forest Plan Review folder, Forestry section 2, EA.

27. Material pertaining to the Seventh American Forest Congress and the role of the schools of forestry in it is in Box 30, Forest List, EA.

28. In 1994 Perry Hagenstein, a forest consultant in Boston, Massachusetts, who was attempting to obtain support for the Duluth Manifesto, asked me to review it. My analysis, sent to Hagenstein, along with relevant documents is in Box 30, Forest List, EA.

29. Steps leading to the organization of the Congress are in Forest List 1, EA. The files include details of the roundtable process in Indiana, facilitated by the School of Forestry at Purdue University. While the roundtable process was described publicly as an extensive attempt to bring all parties to forestry issues together in each state to formulate ideas, the process was probably far more varied and less effective. The headquarters of the Seventh Congress planning at the Forestry School at Yale University, for example, reported to me that no such process was under way in Pennsylvania because no sponsor had agreed to conduct the desired meetings. However, the Goddard Professor of Forestry at Pennsylvania State University reported to the Seventh Congress staff that the informal planning advisory sessions sponsored by the Bureau of Forestry were the acceptable equivalent and, on her own initiative, reported that the group had approved of the Seventh Congress "principles." See her letter in Box 30, Forest List 1, EA.

30. The mythology of the Seventh Congress is well represented by various re-ports and publicity releases in Box 30, Forest List 1, EA.

31. Documents pertaining to citizen involvement in the Congress are in Box 30, Forest List 1, EA.

32. See the "communities newsletter," publicity from the communities com-mittee, in Box 30, Forest List 1, EA.

33. For the forestry context in New England, from which the concern for "tra-ditional uses" and the role of conservation easements arose in response, see the folders under the New England section, Forest List 2, EA.

34. The most exhaustive analysis of the ecological and legal implications of conservation easements come from Maine. See copies of the following in the folder "Conservation Easements" in Forest List 2, EA: Mitch Lansky, "An Analysis of the West Branch Easement Language," August 10, 2001; Karen Woodsom, "Easements v. Wilderness"; e-mail message from Carole Haas, with excerpts from comments by Maine's attorney general on the West Branch easement language; "Conservation Easements in the Northern Forest: Principles and Recommendations for the Devel-opment of Large-Scale Conservation Easements in the Northern Forest," produced by the Northern Forest Alliance, May 2001, http://www.northernforestalliance .org/newspubs/1easements/NFAeasements.htm.

35. The development of the West Branch (of the Penobscot) easement (some 270,000 acres) bought the various controversial facets of large-scale easements into the public debate more forcefully than previous cases. Because the owner of the lands was unknown for some time (it was Yale University), and because some pro-visions of the easement required that the wood production activities that the ease-ment would protect should remain secret, the question came to the fore that it was not appropriate that public funds be used to finance a private business operation. Because it took a number of years to develop the details of the wood production operation that would be protected by the easement, many of its details came to be publicized only later; they were compared (unfavorably) with easement require-ments of the state conservation department. The proceedings led to a change in the holder of the easement from the state to the Forest Society of Maine (a private wood production organization) and thereby reduced the potential of public over-sight of the easement program. The issue also helped to launch a review of the For-est Legacy Program by the U.S. Congress, which led to the recommendation that the Forest Service needed to have better oversight of projects using funds from the program. It also resulted in the creation of the working forest easement guidelines adopted by the board of Land for Maine's Future.

The West Branch easement is covered in some detail in a series of articles by Phyllis Austin in *Maine Environmental News*, May 8, 2002, June 26, 2002, August 2, 2002, September 25, 2002. See also David Lewis, "Easements and the West Branch Project," *Maine Woods* (a publication of the Forest Ecology Network) 5, no. 1 (Late Winter 2001). See also Meredith Goad, "Deal Rewrites Book on Conservation," *Portland Press Herald*, January 11, 2004. Goad wrote, "The lesson learned from the project and the influence it had on state policy will likely reverberate for years to come." Document in Maine folder, Forest List 2, EA.

36. A great number of documents about certification are in Box 31, "Certification," Forest List, EA. These include reports from the Forest Stewardship Council and two papers by the author, "Forest Certification in Pennsylvania: An Evaluation of the Report Concerning Pennsylvania State Forests by Scientific Certification Systems," March 20, 1998; and "Certification Reviewed—1998," January 1, 1999; both are in Hays, *Forest Papers*. Copies of several regional standard-setting documents are in folders in the Certification section, Forest List 2, EA; see especially the sections in the standardized format of the reports titled, "Principle #5: Benefits From the Forest" and "Principle #6: Environmental Impact," from which one can conclude that ecological forestry was thought of in terms not of goals but of impacts of wood production objectives. The activities of FSC and especially the work of its twelve regional committees in developing standards for their regions can be obtained from the FSC Web site, http://www.fscus.org/.

37. The most serious problem faced by FSC, with its early ties to environmental organizations, was to respond positively to the environmental/ecological standards espoused by those groups and, at the same time, make certification based on those standards acceptable to forest landowners. Thus some agreement as to the standards required for "ecological forestry" was imperative, and here I am concerned with the degree to which those standards are consistent with the ecological forestry objectives outlined in this book. A statement drawn up by a reform forest leader and submitted to FSC as a contribution to its development of standards is Mitch Lansky, "Comments to FSC-US Standards Committee on Draft FSC-US National Indicators, Nov. 28, 2000," a copy of which is in the Certification, Main Articles folder, Certification section, Forest List 2, EA.

38. The certification program of the Forest Stewardship Council was supported by several environmental organizations in the United States, and in particular the World Wildlife Fund, the National Wildlife Federation, and the Sierra Club. These grew out of their interest in the international dimensions of forestry affairs. For the most part, however, their activities in certification were carried out somewhat separately from the activities of their own members in domestic forest affairs, and hence the crucial issues of standards and enforcement were not "on their radar screen." During the late 1990s, for example, I had several telephone and e-mail conversations with the Sierra Club representative, who was based in Washington, D.C., on certification matters, and found that he was neither aware of nor informed about the citizen forest reform movement in the United States.

39. Documents relating to the competition between the FSC and the SFI are in Box 31, Certification, in Forest List 1, EA. See also the ads in the *Journal of Forestry* in several issues during 2001 and 2002. The competition led to several attempts to compare the programs of the two. One, "Comparative Analysis of the Forest Stewardship Council and Sustainable Forestry Initiative: Consensus Statement on Salient Similarities and Differences between the Two Programs" prepared by the Merid-

ian Institute (October 2001), and another, "Behind the Logo: An Environmental and Social Assessment of Forest Certification Schemes," produced by FERN (May 2001), are in the Comparative Analysis of Different Systems folder, Certification section, Forest List 2, EA.

40. The forest reform movement, in general, was skeptical about if not hostile toward certification on the grounds that its standards were inadequate and vague and were not enforced. A few reform organizations were caught up in the competition between the FSC and SFI, strongly supporting the former and opposing the latter, and seemed to pay little attention to the problems of standards and enforcement. See Forest Reform and Certification folders in Box 31, Certification, in Forest List 1, EA, and comments by forest reform organizations on regional standards. See, for example, the comments of the Dogwood Alliance and the Southern Environmental Law Center on the Southeastern regional standards, in correspondence to the Southeastern FSC Working Group, September 20, 2001; also opposition to the application of the FSC standards to the state forest lands of Wisconsin by the John Muir Chapter of the Sierra Club, October 2, 2001; both in Certification, Regional Standards folder, Certification section, Forest List 2, EA.

The Sierra Club of Maine formally appealed to the FSC the "green" certification of J. D. Irving Company's Allagash woodland, but then dropped it and instead made public the results of its own report on Irving's forestry practices, conducted by Mitch Lansky, a longtime authority on forest practices in Maine. Irving's lands had been certified by FSC as a "well-managed natural forest," but according to Lansky, FSC standards had not been met and the "high marks [assigned to Irving's forest management] appear to be based more on promises or process than on actual activities on the ground." See report, "The Sierra Club Finds 'Green' Certification of the Irving Allagash Woodlands Unacceptable," Maine Sierra Club, November 22, 2002, *Maine Environmental News*, Maine Environmental Policy Institute, http://www.meepi.org/files02/irvintro.htm.

Development by the Forest Stewardship Council of the "Standards for Best Forestry Practices" for the Maritime region of eastern Canada (New Brunswick, Nova Scotia, and Prince Edward Island) by the Maritime Region Standards Committee (MRC) became intensely controversial and was widely known among FSC circles in the United States. One timber company, the J. D. Irving Company, for which its 188,000-acre Black Brook District in New Brunswick had already been certified by FSC, participated in the development of the standards, but immediately on their approval by the regional committee, the Irving representative, Irving's chief forester, Blake Brunsdon, lobbied to have them rejected. In response, Hank Cauley, executive director of the FSC U.S. Board requested the board to ask the MRC to modify the standards in accordance with Irving's demands. The Irving lobbying pressure with FSC was remarkably successful, with the FSC making one concession after another over a period of eighteen months in a futile effort to encourage Irving to accept compromises over key standards, none of which Irving accepted.

The entire episode affirmed the weakness of FSC in advancing ecological objectives in forest management in the face of persistent and determined pressure from the timber industry. At the same time the FSC forwent an opportunity to make definitive interpretations of a number of its principles, including natural forest conversion, ecological reserves, and the use of biocides, by dismissing a formal appeal on these issues by the Sierra Club of Canada on the technical grounds that the club was seven hours late in filing its appeal documents. This episode, the only case I have run across in which the inner workings of the FSC certification process is described in detail, is elaborated in Charles Restino, "A Critical Analysis of the Forest Stewardship Council" prepared for the Sierra Club of Canada, and printed in the *Northern Forest Forum* 8, no. 2 (Spring 2000). A copy is included in the Maine section of Forest List 2, EA.

41. In 2002 the organization which gave rise to certification, The Rainforest Alliance, issued a report by Simon Counsell and Kim Terje Loraas that criticized the Forest Stewardship Council's program as having "serious flaws," including a flawed forest audit system. The report stated, "In particular the FSC's authorized auditors have a vested commercial interest in certifying timber companies regardless of whether or not they actually comply with FSC's strict requirements."

42. There was little noticeable public awareness of or interest in certification and far more interest in the boycotts of the retail outlets for wood products, such as Home Depot. See the Home Depot Boycotts folder, Certification section, Forest List 2, EA.

43. By 2004 it appeared that the FSC had reached a peak in its achievement, one in which it remained far behind, in acreage certified, compared to the Sustainable Forestry Initiative of the American Forest and Paper Association. Moreover, the ten years of experience with certified industries led to considerable misgivings on the part of industries that had undergone certification on the grounds that the implementation and audits of their practices were too expensive, and fears that the environmental/ecological standards that they felt were too high would soon in the future go even higher as a result of the completion of the FSC regional standard-setting processes. As a result, Robert Hrubes, the head of Scientific Certification Systems, one of the two certification agencies in the United States working under the FSC, reported in 2002 that due to considerable opposition to the FSC program on the part of landowners, SCS would sponsor still another certification program, to be called Cross and Gold, with less strict standards as a way of attracting these forest landowners. See Certification, Main Articles folder, Certification section, Forest List 2, EA, and especially two articles by Seth Zuckerman, "Forest Certifier Steps Out on His Own: Scientific Certification Systems to Offer Private Green Label" and "Fight Over the Soul of the Green Seal: Independent Eco-Label Highlights Challenges Facing Forest Certification."

44. To track the smaller forest owner and their objectives in owning woodland, the U.S. Forest Service inaugurated a National Woodland Owner Survey, beginning in 2002. The results of the survey's first two years are the subject of Brett J.

Butler and Earl C. Leatherberry, "America's Family Forest Owners," *Journal of Forestry* 102, no. 7 (October/November 2004): 4–14. The authors pose the question, "Will aesthetic enjoyment as a reason for owning forestland continue to increase and will ownership for timber production continue to decrease?"

45. The stewardship program can be followed on the State and Private Forestry section of the U.S. Forest Service Web site. However, this "official" record does not give a significant picture of how it worked out in the various states. One can get a bit closer to the degree to which the individual states gave expression to objectives other than wood production by following the subject in the Web sites of the various state forest agencies. In Pennsylvania, for example, there was considerable dispute over the availability to stewardship applicants of professionals other than consulting foresters. The agency was criticized for providing this professional advice by giving consulting foresters weekend "short courses" in various specialized forest-related biological and hydrological subjects, rather than identifying specialists in those fields on which applicants could rely for advice. A detailed account of the Pennsylvania program can be obtained from Stewardship Program folders, Pennsylvania section, Forest List 2, EA.

46. The work of the Forest Stewards Guild can be followed in the folder under that name in Forest List 2, EA, and especially on the guild's Web site: http://www.foreststewardsguild.org/. See especially its publication "Distant Thunder."

47. For an informative account of the Menominee Forest see Thomas Davis, *Sustaining the Forest, the People, and the Spirit* (Albany: State University of New York Press, 2000).

48. The Menominee "continuous forest inventory" is followed in Davis, *Sustaining the Forest*, 150–52 passim.

49. Davis, *Sustaining the Forest*, 129.

50. See Opinion Research Corporation, *The Public's Participation in Outdoor Activities and Attitudes toward Wilderness Areas* (1977); Deborah J. Shields et al., *Survey Results of the American Public's Values, Objectives, Beliefs and Attitudes* (see preface, n. 4).

51. The many cases cited in chapter 2 reflect a wide range of public involvement in national forest planning.

52. The diaries of John Ward Thomas, the first chief forester during the Clinton administration, reflect this distrust. Thomas consistently expresses vitriolic criticism of the citizen reform movement, finds little positive in it, and even considers it responsible for morale problems within the agency. Among the several sources of those morale problems, for example, he cites "the continual appeasement of confrontational environmentalists." These hostile attitudes are expressed throughout his diaries. For the quote see Harold K. Steen, ed., *Jack Ward Thomas: The Journals of a Forest Service Chief* (Durham, N.C., and Seattle, Wash.: Forest History Society and the University of Washington Press, 2004), 391. At the same time the diary contains almost no mention of ecological forestry as an evolving sector of scientific work in forestry.

53. A rather sharp statement of this practice came from the ecologists who

engaged the Forest Service in the management of the Nicolet and Chequamegon National Forests in Wisconsin. To them the new language of ecology was clear and precise and they were affronted with the way in which the agency was adept at using the same language and infusing it with traditional commodity forest meaning. Their confrontation over such language is elaborated in William S. Alverson, Walter Kuhlmann, and Donald M. Waller, *Wild Forests: Conservation Biology and Public Policy* (Washington, D.C.: Island Press, 1994). See especially chapter 13, "Case History: The Wisconsin National Forests," 209–34. ·

54. For the internal sociology of the Forest Service and its implications see references in note 25, above. In the late 1980s these erupted into considerable and well-publicized criticism of the dominant commodity policies of the agency by personnel especially in the mountain states of the West. Agency leaders avowed a major change in its policies toward greater recognition of other forest uses, but considerable skepticism remained as to how much this was a change in rhetoric rather than a serious change in management practice. A brief, but excellent account of these events is in Hirt, *A Conspiracy of Optimism*, 281–92.

55. The DeMeo letter was signed by over two hundred Forest Service employees, almost all of whom were from non-traditional specializations such as wildlife and fisheries biologists, ecologists, landscape architects, and none of whom were from the more traditional categories of "forester" or "forest technician." E-mail communications between Samuel P. Hays and Tom DeMeo.

56. For a lucid account of the relationship between the agency line and staff personnel and the impact of environmental and ecological factors in that relationship, see Jack Ward Thomas, "Appropriate Roles of Line Officers and Technical Staff" in "Northwest Forest Plan Review," which Thomas conducted at the request of Jack Blackwell, regional forester in the Pacific Southwest (California) region, dated June 26, 2003, in Northwest Forest Plan Review folder, Forest List 2, EA.

57. See file, Forest Service Employees for Environmental Ethics (FSEEE) in EA, and the publication, the *Forest*, a quarterly issued by FSEEE beginning in 1998.

Chapter 4: Ecological Forestry in the States

1. For a brief account of Matthew Kirchoff's role in the Alaska Department of Fish and Game, see "Wildlife Biologist Recognized for Outstanding Professional Contributions," *Raven Call* (newsletter of the Southeast Alaska Conservation Council), Fall 2003, 13.

2. For the opposition of developers to decisions by the habitat conservation division of the Alaskan Department of Fish and Game, see Paula Dobbyn, "Controversy Dogs Habitat Biologists 'Just Doing Their Job,'" *Anchorage Daily News*, March 2, 2003, copy in Alaska folder, Forest List 2, EA.

3. Events in the progress of Executive Order 107 issued by Governor Murkowski, which authorized the change, can be followed week by week in "Alaska Conservation Watch" for 2003, issued regularly by the Alaska Center for the Environment

and available on its Web site. The events can also be followed on the Web site of the Southeast Alaska Conservation Council, for example an item titled, "Hang on to Your Habitat: Legislative Hearings on Governor's Plans to Gut Fish and Wildlife Habitat Protections." For details of the administrative reorganization see "Minutes of Board of Forestry Meeting, Juneau, April 29–May 1, 2003."

4. "Senate approves bill to change primary purpose of state forests," in the *Fairbanks Daily News-Miner*, May 21, 2003, copy in Alaska, Forest List 2, EA. In another twist of Alaska forest politics, the state legislature passed a law at the request of Governor Murkowski requiring plaintiffs to pay legal fees in unsuccessful court challenges against the state, a measure assumed to be aimed at environmental organizations. A Juneau Superior Court judge struck down the law. See Mike Chambers, AP, "Judge Strikes Down Law Making Challengers Pay," in *Anchorage Daily News*, April 9, 2004. See also news release, "Judge Rules Alaska State Law Illegal," *Earthjustice Newsroom*, April 7, 2004.

5. See Washington Forest Law Center folder, Forest List 2, EA.

6. The role of the Forest Practice Act in Washington can be followed in documents in Timber, Fish and Wildlife folder and Forests and Fish folder, Washington section, Forest List 2, EA.

7. Controversy over the position of state lands commissioner with a focus on the more ecology-minded commissioner, Jennifer Belcher, elected in 1992, and the more commodity-minded commissioner, Doug Sutherland, elected in 2002, with a special emphasis on the role of the timber industry in these contrasting administrations, can be followed in documents in the Washington DNR folder, Washington section, Forest List 2, EA. See especially, Kimberley L. Crawford, "Timber Lobbyists Seek to Axe Legislative Reforms," *WFP Special Report on the Environment* 9 (April/May 1994); Susan Gordon, "DNR Under Pressure to Limit Logging," *News Tribune*, April 15, 2002; Solveig Torvik, "Our Laws Are Failing Us, Says Jennifer Belcher," *Seattle Post-Intelligencer*, January 21, 2001; Ed Hunt, "Washington's Five Million Acres," *Tidepool*, January 26, 2001, http://www.tidepool.org/. More detail about the events involving these issues can be followed in the newsletter of the Washington Environmental Council. See folder in Washington file of Forest List 2, EA.

8. For a comprehensive picture of Washington forest issues from the viewpoint of the state Department of Natural Resources see http://www.dnr.wa.gov.

9. For Timber, Fish, and Wildlife, see folder in Washington file of Forest List 2, EA.

10. The buffer issue led to an extensive analysis of the relationship between watersheds and aquatic habitat sponsored by environmental organizations. See "The Salmon Recovery Proposal: A Low-Risk Strategy for Protecting and Restoring Salmon Habitat in Washington's Forested Watersheds; A Proposal Submitted to the Washington State Forest Practices Board by the Washington Environmental Council and the Washington State Field Office of the National Audubon Society, December 1998."

11. For the circumstances and negotiations involved in producing the "Forests and Fish" program see material in "Forests and Fish" folder in Washington file of Forest List 2, EA. Especially useful are Kelly Stewart, "The Origins of Forest and Fish," *Tidepool*, September 3, 2003, http://www.tidepool.org/; James R. Karr, David Montgomery, and Reed F. Noss, "New State Timber, Fish Rules Are Weak and Will Be Ineffective," *Seattle Post-Intelligencer*, May 16, 1999; Chris McGann, "Salmon Report Critical of New Logging Rules," *Seattle Post-Intelligencer*, February 3, 2000; Robert Mc-Clure, "Forest-fish Plan: Was It Too Political? Scientists Raised Doubts about the Justification for the 1999 Agreement," *Seattle Post-Intelligencer*, January 29, 2001.

12. The Teanaway project is especially useful in pinpointing the details of controversy over owl habitat, involving circles of 1.8 miles around nests, and the program of listing and de-listing owl circles. These details are laid out with especial clarity in the sixty-day notice of intent to sue issued by the "Washington Law Center, November 3, 2003: "60-day notice of intent to sue for violation of section 9 of the Endangered Species Act, Teanaway region of central Eastern Washington—U.S. Timberlands to conduct forest practices in the Teanaway region that have taken and will continue to take the owl." Documents from which this reconstruction is drawn are in the Washington Forest Law Center folder, Washington section, Forest List 2, EA.

13. For the certification proposal see "Washington State DNR Certification Proposal" in Washington file, Forest List 2, EA. The certification report is "Public Summary, Certification Report for the West-Side Trust Forestlands Managed by the Washington Department of Natural Resources," prepared by Scientific Certification Systems, Oakland, Washington, May 2001. See also the account of the public meeting held on the certification proposal, June 8, 2001, prepared by a representative of the Washington Environmental Council, June 12, 2001, under title of "Washington State DNR Certification Pilot Project," and a variety of newspaper accounts and statements concerning the project in the Washington file, Forest List 2, EA. The proposal to certify the state trust lands took the form of legislation sponsored by the Northwest Ecosystem Alliance and the Washington Environmental Council to require it. See Becky Kelley, "Legislature Considers Certification, Old Growth Protection for State Forests," *Voices* (publication of the Washington Environmental Council), Winter 2004: 5. The legislature reduced the bill to certification study only. An earlier study by DNR decided that certification was too expensive and "it is unlikely that a new study by the same agency will yield a different result." See *Northwest Ecosystem News* 57 (Spring 2004): 8.

14. Citizen opposition to the DNR proposal to expand timber production on state lands by 35 percent tended to focus on old growth, and it led to legislation that the DNR define, inventory, and map state forest old growth and publish public notice before logging old growth. Commissioner Sutherland issued his own old-growth measure in January that left out the Olympic Experimental State Forest, the location of much of the old growth, allowed "thinning" in old growth, and applied only to stands larger than twenty acres. Despite publicly declaring sup-

port for old-growth protection, Sutherland wrote to the senate budget committee chair urging him not to support the old-growth study. See *Voices* (publication of the Washington Environmental Council) Spring 2004: 1, 6; Summer 2004: 1, 12–13.

15. A considerable number of documents from which this account of the salmon issue in Oregon is drawn are in the Oregon Forest Practice Program folder in Forest List 2, EA. Some of the more helpful documents are an essay on the evolution and contemporary context for the Oregon salmon issue, Roy Hemmingway, "Salmon and the Northwest," in *Open Spaces Quarterly*, February 28, 2004; an account of the evolution of the Oregon Forest Practices Act by John J. Garland of Oregon State University, "The Oregon Forest Practice Act, 1972 to 1994," which not only describes the development of the act itself, but conveys the skeptical, even negative, reaction to those changes by a professional forester; and two state documents, "The Oregon Plan for Salmon and Watersheds," and the "Statewide Riparian Management Policy," May 2002. Various Web sites provide access to many relevant documents, especially those accessed under the Oregon Department of Forestry and the "Oregon Plan" at www.oregon-plan.org.

16. An introduction to the history of and current issues on the Tillamook is Gail Wells, *The Tillamook: A Created Forest Comes of Age* (Corvallis, Ore.: Oregon State University Press, 1999); see also Larry Fick and George Martin, *The Tillamook Burn: Rehabilitation and Reforestation* (Forest Grove, Ore.: Department of Forestry, 1993). For more elaborate information about the Tillamook forest issue see items in the Tillamook Forest folder, Oregon section, Forest List 2, EA. A rather lengthy five-part article on the issue by reporter Benjamin Romano is in the *Daily Astorian*, July 11, July 14–17, 2003.

17. The Web site of the Oregon Department of Forestry, on which there is a copy of the Tillamook Forest Plan issued in 2003, is http://www.odf.state.or.us.

18. The Web site of the Tillamook Rainforest Coalition is: http://www.tilla mookrainforest.org/. The standards for the "permanent restoration of a native old growth forest structure" identified in the referendum provide a comprehensive list of such management objectives: (a) protection of areas that contain current or potential drinking water sources; (b) protection of critical fish and wildlife habitat; (c) protection of areas of important native biodiversity; (d) protection of current or potential forest recreational opportunities that are consistent with restoring or protecting Oregon forest structure; (e) protection or creation of corridors for wildlife movement; (f) protection of groups of trees seventy years and older; (g) protection of current and future hunting and fishing opportunities; (h) protection of threatened and endangered species habitat; (h) protection of cultural heritage; (i) protection of natural wetlands; (j) protection for areas with high landslide risks, especially where they occur upstream of productive spawning and rearing habitat for anadromous fish; (k) protection of areas with the lowest existing and abandoned road densities. See copy of the referendum in Oregon file, Forest List 2, EA. When this list of forest management objectives was included in a proposed bill in the Oregon legislature, the analysis by the ODF was that it "would essentially in-

validate nearly nine years of forest management planning." See Benjamin Romano, "Environmentalists criticize plan to balance habitat, logging," *Daily Astorian*, July 16, 2003.

19. The relevant Web sites are: Ecotrust, http://www.ecotrust.org; Oregon Trout, http://www.ortrout.org; the Wild Salmon Center, http://www.wildsalmoncenter.org.

20. *A Salmon Conservation Strategy for the Tillamook and Clatsop State Forests* (Ecotrust, Oregon Trout and the Wild Salmon Center, October 2000, updated March 2001).

21. Coast Range Association, *Forestry and Salmon: A Report on Oregon's Coastal Watersheds and the Need for Forestry Reform* (Coast Range Association, 2001); Charles W. Huntington and Christopher Frissel, of Clearwater BioStudies, Inc., and the University of Montana's Flathead Lake Biological Research Station, respectively, *Aquatic Conservation and Salmon Recovery in the North Coast Basin of Oregon: A Crucial Role for the Tillamook and Clatsop State Forests* (prepared for Oregon Trout, June 1997).

22. Reed F. Noss and Allen Y. Cooperrider, *Saving Nature's Legacy* (Washington, D.C.: Island Press, 1994); Reed Noss, *A Preliminary Biodiversity Plan for the Oregon Coast Range* (Coast Range Association, 1992).

23. National Wildlife Federation Scientific Panel on Ecosystem Based Forestry Management, *Simplified Forest Management to Achieve Watershed and Forest Health: A Critique* (National Wildlife Federation, 2000), http://www.coastrange.org/documents/forestreport.pdf.

24. Thomas M. Power and Philip J. Ruder, "Economic Realities in the Tillamook and Clatsop State Forests: Possibilities for Economic Expansion and Diversification" (Tillamook Rainforest Coalition, January 2003), http://www.salmonandeconomy.org/pdf/TillamookSF.pdf.

25. Folders under "California" (EA) contain considerable information about forest public affairs in the late twentieth century, including the role of the California Department of Forestry (CDF) and the State Board of Forestry.

26. The Planning and Conservation League of California produced a comprehensive report on Sierra Pacific Industries to "illuminate the timber giant so that environmentalists can decide how best to approach the task of limiting SPI's power to transform our forests." The study includes considerable insight and detail about the workings of the California Board of Forestry. A copy of the report is in the California folder, Forest List 2, EA.

27. The relevant legislation and its significance is covered in "Calif. Water Boards to Have Veto Power over Logging in Watersheds," *Land Letter*, October 16, 2003, 20–21.

28. For a comprehensive statement of the role and importance of cumulative watershed impacts, see letter from Dr. Leslie M. Reid to Fred Keeley, Speaker Pro Tem of the California State Legislature, May 24, 1999, copy on the Web site of the Environmental Protection Information Center, http://www.wildcalifornia.org?THP/Pacific Lumber/reid-fpr.html; copy also in California folder, Forest List 2, EA.

29. For events in this history of the relationship between the State Water Board

and the California Department of Forestry, see the publications of the Environmental Protection Information Center, Garberville, Calif., and especially its newsletter *Wild California*, archived for 2001–2004 at http://www.wildcalifornia.org/publications/publication-1; see also California folder, Forest List 1, EA. In 2003 the California Forest Practices Board granted California's logging industry a broad exemption from California's Clean Water Act, applying to industrial logging operations on public and private land throughout the Sierra Nevada and affecting the municipal water sources for approximately two-thirds of the state's population. Several environmental groups—EPIC, Deltakeeper, Sierra Club—represented by Earthjustice, filed suit challenging this decision. See news release from Earthjustice, March 18, 2004.

30. One account of water issues in the Southern Appalachians from the viewpoint of citizen forest reform organizations is Marshall, *"Lord, We're Just Trying to Save Your Water"* (see chap 1, n. 46).

31. See Virginia folder, Forest List 2, EA. See several documents in this collection, e.g., Press Release, Virginia Forest Watch, September 12, 2000; "Virginia Forest Watch Calls for Resignation of Forestry Officials," *Richmond Times Dispatch*, December 17, 2000; Shireen Parsons, "The Timber Industry Prevailed: State Chip-Mill Study Was a Fruitless Exercise," *Roanoke Times*, January 11, 2001; "The Forestry Department Must Know Where the Sites Are to Inspect Them: Forest Watch Reports Logging Jobs Because, Too Often, Loggers Don't," *Roanoke Times*, April 6, 2001; Press Release from Virginia Forest Watch, "Foresters Urge to Support Stricter Regulation of Logging in Virginia," statement from Rupert Cutler and Steve Brooks; text of speech by Rupert Cutler before the Virginia Division of the Society of American Foresters, Norton, Virginia, June 14, 2001; Jana Brickett, "Foresters Don't Think More Regulations Is the Answer," *Coalfield Progress*, June 21, 2001; Press Release from Virginia Forest Watch, "Virginia's Forests and Streams Being Devastated to Make Paper: Logging in South 13 Times Greater than Logging Nationwide," November 26, 2001; Press Release, The Virginia Organizing Project: "VAFW Calls for Stronger Logging Laws on Private Lands."

32. For an evaluation of BMP effectiveness in Virginia see Dogwood Alliance to John Greis, co-chair, Southern Forest Resource Assessment, January 28, 1002, copy in Southern Appalachians folder, Forest List 2, EA.

33. On West Virginia, see Sandy Fisher and Kaey Russell, *The Timber Reform Research Project, Introductory Report*, published by the West Virginia Highlands Conservancy, 2000, revised in July 2001, copy available from the Conservancy and in the West Virginia folder, Forest List 2, EA. The folder also contains a number of related documents that provide more extensive details. For an extensive analysis of the chip mill industry in West Virginia see articles by Ken Ward, reporter for the *Charleston Gazette*, located in Box 32, Forest List 1, EA. For Tennessee, see Tennessee folder, Forest List 2, EA. On Missouri, see Missouri folder, Forest List 2, EA.

34. The Southern Forest Resource Assessment was led by the U.S. Forest Service in cooperation with three federal agencies—the U.S. Fish and Wildlife Service,

the Environmental Protection Agency, and the Tennessee Valley Authority—and southern states represented by their forestry and fish and wildlife agencies.

35. The compliance report for North Carolina sponsored by the Assessment maintained that there was compliance on 95 percent of the sites inspected, but this conclusion was faulty because there was no information about either the number of total harvest sites and the percentage of these that were inspected; hence there was no information as to whether or not the agency was inspecting a statistically significant number of harvest sites. A similar optimistic statement about the Tennessee program led to the conclusion in the Dogwood report that "Ninety two percent of Tennessee's logging operations are not inspected for BMP compliance and water quality protection." See Dogwood Alliance to John Greis, co-chair of Southern Forest Resource Assessment, January 28, 2002, pp. 53–55, copy in Southern Appalachians folder, Forest List 2, EA.

36. For a relevant overview of the region see The Tulane Institute for Environmental Law and Policy, *State Water Quality Laws Relating to Silviculture: A Status Update for the South*, Research Agreement No. SRS 00-CR-113301133-126, January 5, 2001.

37. The conclusions of the Southern Forest Resource Assessment were shaped heavily by the limited perspectives of the state agencies and their commitment to plantation pine forest production as the region's future. See its report, "Southern Forest Resource Assessment, USDA Forest Service Southern Research Station and Southern Region," http://www.srs.fs.fed.us/sustain/report/.

38. Material describing the application of ecological objectives to southern private forests is scattered in the various regional and state folders in the Southern Appalachian section, Forest List 2, EA. The most thorough statement of those objectives is in the extensive comments by the Dogwood Alliance on the Southern Forest Resource Assessment, in Danna Smith, director of programs, Dogwood Alliance, to John Greis, co-chair, Southern Forest Resource Assessment, February 28, 2002, Southern Forest Resource Assessment folder, Forest List 2, EA.

39. This brief description of forest issues in Maine is based upon a number of news items and other documents in the Maine folder, Forest List 2, EA. Especially useful are the in-depth articles by investigative reporter, Phyllis Austin, who wrote earlier for the *Maine Times*, and after its demise for *Maine Environmental News* issued by the Maine Environmental Policy Institute at the University of Maine. The documents include a detailed description of the 1989 Forest Practices Act and the various proposed referenda. A useful capsule summary of Maine forest issues is Emily Hoffhine, "An Overview of Forest Harvesting Practices, Forestry Referenda, and Related Issues in Maine," Maine folder, Forest List 2, EA.

40. For a description of the Nature Conservancy strategy of cores and buffers see Colin Woodard, "Protecting the Heartwood: By Saving the Core of the Forest Scientists Hope to Safeguard the Whole," *Nature Conservancy* 54, no. 1 (Spring 2004): 42–50.

41. One of the more comprehensive statements of an ecological forestry program for the Great Lakes States is Anne M. Woiwode, *A New Way of Thinking: Biological*

236 NOTES TO PAGE 105

Diversity and Forestry Policy in the Northwoods of the Great Lakes States (East Lansing, Mich.: Sierra Club, 1994).

42. For the "logging quota mandate" see "Seek Renewal of Logging Mandate," *North Woods Call*, March 7, 2001, 1; "State Forest Logging Comes under More Scientific Scrutiny," *North Woods Call*, June 26, 2002.

In early 2004 the Michigan House of Representatives approved three bills which would have increased the dominance of wood production on the state's forests and, at the same time, have given the industry significant, if not controlling, influence in their management. The forests would be managed primarily for fiscal and income-producing purposes, the managing authority would supersede that of the Department of Natural Resources, in which the chief forester would have only one of seven votes, and the forest industry would have four votes, in a procedure in which four votes would be sufficient to approve action by the board. The financial authority would be independent of the legislature in its actions and responsible to the legislature only by submitting an annual report. See copies of the bills and their history in the Michigan folder, Forest List 2, EA. The proposals were strongly supported by the timber industry. See "Michigan Forest Products Council Applauds Bi-Partisan Forest Management and Jobs Package," PRNewswire, March 8, 2004, describing the support of the three bills by the Michigan forest industry. They were opposed by the environmental/ecological forestry community. See "State Forests Seen as under New Attack by Timber Industry," *North Woods Call*, August 20, 2003, 1–2; "Resist Industry Bid to Take More Control of State Lands," *North Woods Call*, December 10, 2003, 1; "Conservationists United in Opposition to Forest Bills," *North Woods Call*, March 17, 2004, 1–2. A strong industry statement attacking the biodiversity objectives of the Michigan Sierra Club is David B. Olson, the first president of the Michigan Forest Association, "Variety of Forest Conditions Will Meet Society's Demands," Michigan folder, Forest List 2, EA. As of this writing, the bills, approved by the House, have not been acted on by the Senate and the governor is described as threatening a veto. See *North Woods Call*, March 31, 2004, editorial, p. 4. Instead the governor called for certification of state forest lands. See "Granholm Wants Audit of Forest Overseers: Governor Pushes Independent Certification for Management of State's 4 Million Acres," AP dispatch from Traverse City in the *Detroit News*, February 13, 2004.

43. For old growth on the Michigan state forests see "Cool Reneges," *North Woods Call*, November 2, 2000, 1; "Sides Line Up over Proposed Old Growth Plan," *North Woods Call*, March 7, 2001, 1–2; "Old Growth Forests: Two Views," *North Woods Call*, January 23, 2002, 3.

44. For old growth on the Huron-Manistee National Forest see, "First Old Growth Set Aside OK'd on Huron-Manistee," *North Woods Call*, August 22, 2001, 3; "See Doomsday for Hunters Due to Old Growth Decision" and "Old Growth Appeals in Works," both in *North Woods Call*, September 5, 2001, 3.

45. For the Pittman-Robertson EIS lawsuit see "Sierra Club Legal Challenge Seen

as Anti-Hunt Measure," *North Woods Call*, November 2, 2000, 3; "Sue to Block Wild-life Habitat," *North Woods Call*, December 12, 2001, 1–2; "Woiwode Denies Aspen Attack," *North Woods Call*, January 23, 2002, 3; "Court Rejects Sierra Club 'Aspen' Suit against DNR," *North Woods Call*, March 20, 2002, 1.

46. A copy of the Minnesota Generic Environmental Impact Statement on Timber Harvesting and Forest Management in Minnesota, published in 1992, is in the Forest Affairs section, EA.

47. The Sierra Club report, *Sierra Report on Minnesota Forests*, is on the Minnesota club chapter Web site: http://www.northstar.sierraclub.org/Forestry%20Home.htm.

48. The Web site of the Minnesota Forest Resource Council contains its monitoring program. See http://www.frc.state.mn.us/monitor/monitrng.htm.

49. The Minnesota old-growth policy can be followed on the Web site of the Department of Natural Resources: http://www.dnr.state.mn.us/forests/old growth policy. See also other pertinent documents in the Minnesota folder, State Records section, Forest List 2, EA.

50. A good account of the Wisconsin County Forest system can be obtained from material on the Association's Web site: http://www.wisconsincountyforests.com.

51. For a brief history of the development of Wisconsin's Managed Forest Law see the Erin Twp, Wisconsin, Web site: http://www.erintownship.com/townhall/wiforestlaw.htm. A variety of related documents are in the Wisconsin folder, Forest List 2, EA.

52. The historical development of the "natural areas" programs throughout the United States can be followed in the publications of Natural Areas Association: *Natural Areas Journal* (1980–); and *Natural Area News* (1986–) (the location of the association executive offices as of 2003 was at Bend, Oregon). See also its Web site: http://www.naturalarea.org/.

53. The description of the Wisconsin Natural Areas program is taken from Paul Matthiae, "Persevering for Preservation," *Wisconsin Natural Resources*, April 2002, 31–36, and Camille Zanoni and Charlie Luthin, "Saving the Best of the Best: Saving the Remnants of Our Natural Heritage Starts with Committee Folks," *Wisconsin Natural Resources*, April 2004, 4–9.

54. For the Chicago wilderness program see *Chicago Wilderness* (1997–) and the organization's Web site: http://www.chicagowilderness.org.

55. The history of the nation's state parks can be followed in the annual reports of the National Association of State Park Directors; for reference see chapter 5, note 11.

56. For an account of the land trust movement see Richard Brewer, *Conservancy: The Land Trust Movement in America* (Lebanon, N.H.: University Press of New England, c. 2003).

57. An overall view of conservation trusts in the United States can be obtained from following the activities of the Land Trust Alliance. See its publication, *Exchange*

(Washington, D.C., 1981–). A more detailed account of on-the-ground conservation trust activities can be obtained from the publications of individual organizations. A list, by states, can be obtained from the Alliance Web site.

A cluster of three successful trusts in the northern section of the lower peninsula of Michigan are the Little Traverse Conservancy, located at Harbor Springs Michigan (*Little Traverse Conservancy Quarterly*); the Grand Traverse Regional Land Conservancy, located at Traverse City (*Landscript*); and the Leelanau Conservancy located at Leland (*Leelanau Conservancy Newsletter*). Newsletter publications for all three are located in separate folders in the Michigan section, EA.

58. The Web site for Project Learning Tree is http://www.plt.org; information about its sponsoring organization can be obtained from the American Forest Foundation Web site: http://www.affoundation.org.

59. See Project Wild, http://www.projectwild.org/.

60. The Leopold Education Project is an environmental education program built around the person and writings of Aldo Leopold. It is "an education program of Pheasants Forever" and "works in partnership with the Aldo Leopold Foundation (ALF) . . . assisting [the ALF] . . . to accomplish our mission of creating an ecologically literate citizenry so that each individual might develop a personal land ethic." The Web site for the Leopold Education Project is http://www.lep.org; its newsletter, *Strides toward a Land Ethic*, can be downloaded from the site.

61. The FSEEE program, "The Secret Forest Experience" can be downloaded from the FSEEE Web site: http://www.fseee.org/. A copy is in the file Environmental Education in Forest List 2, EA.

62. The Web site of the Biodiversity Project is http://www.biodiversityproject. org. For a running view of its work its quarterly newsletter is available on its Web site. One of its educational kits, *Eastern Forests and Biodiversity*, is, along with the FSEEE curricular materials, directly relevant to ecological forestry.

63. A more biodiversity-focused curriculum drawn up by Fred Powledge grew out of the International Biodiversity Observation Year, conducted in 2002. See Fred Powledge, "A Look Back at the International Biodiversity Observation Year," *BioScience* 52, no. 12 (December 2002): 1070–79; further information can be obtained on the relevant Web site, www.nrel.colostate.edu/projects/iboy/.

64. An overall view of the Forest Legacy Program of the U.S. Forest Service is http://www.fs.fed.us/spf/coop/programs/loa/flp.shtml. The annual reports of the program provide information about its progress in each state. A more detailed picture of individual parcels of land under easements, which reveal the variety of objectives and in particular the inclusion of environmental and ecological objectives, can be obtained from the relevant Web sites in each state.

65. The Web site for the national Gap Analysis Project is http://gapanalysis. nbii.gov/. Gap projects were organized by states and this Web site provides links to some of these. The national venture was organized as a project of the United States Geological Survey.

66. The Web site for the Oregon Biodiversity Project is http://www.biodiversity partners.org/state/or/obp/001.shtml.

67. The Web site for the Pennsylvania Important Bird Areas project, the first in the nation, is http://pa.audubon.org/iba/. This project gave rise to a similar project for mammals, organized by the Pennsylvania Wildlife Federation with funds from the Pennsylvania Game Commission.

68. In a number of cases state ecological forest proposals reflect the belief that existing forest agencies do not have available the technical skills needed for ecological forest management, and identify what skills are required. For example, in the ecological forest program for the Tillamook Forest in Oregon the referendum requires that management recommendations presented to the Oregon Board of Forestry, the Oregon Department of Forestry, and the State Forester be developed by an external Independent Restoration Science Team that is to be selected by the Biology Department chairpersons from Portland State University, Oregon State University, and the University of Oregon. They also stipulate that the science team be composed of thirteen members with expertise in one of the following: restorative forestry, wildlife biology, silvicultural science, soil science, geology, limnology, forest ecology, salmon biology, forest planning, forest management, and any other appropriate scientific field.

Chapter 5: The Pennsylvania Story

1. During this forty-year experience in Pennsylvania, I accumulated a considerable number of documents relevant to Pennsylvania forest affairs which are deposited in the Environmental Archives of the Archives of Industrial Society at the University of Pittsburgh, EA. Fifty selected documents have been reproduced in Hays, *Forest Papers*.

2. The Administrative Code of 1929 identified the primary purpose of the state forest management, in terms similar to past statements, as "lessening soil erosion [and] the silting up of reservoirs" and "to control stream flow"; it relegated wood production to a subordinate role under the provision that "whenever it shall appear that the welfare of the Commonwealth . . . will be advanced by selling or disposing of any of the timber on the State forests," then it could be disposed of. However, by 1952, the Administrative Code rearranged the "purposes" of forest management to put wood production first by requiring that rules and regulations should be compatible with the "purposes for which the State forests are created, namely to provide a continuous supply of timber, lumber, wood, and other forest products, to protect the watersheds, conserve the waters, and regulate the flow of rivers and streams of the State, and to furnish opportunities for healthful recreation to the public."

3. The quotation is from the cover letter to the new State Forest Resource Management Plan released by the Bureau of Forestry in 2003, letter signed by James R.

Grace, State Forester. See Bureau of Forestry, *State Forest Resource Management Plan* (Harrisburg, Pa., 2003).

An episode which reflects the limited interest of the Bureau of Forestry in forest watershed issues was reported in December 2002 when it was announced that the Pennsylvania Department of Environmental Protection (DEP) had ordered the timber company, Seneca Resources, to halt timber harvesting activities in Cameron, Elk, and McKean counties because of significant water quality violations. The company had "acted with disregard to erosion controls, stream and wetland impacts, and our Special Protection Waters program," said a spokesman for DEP, Regional Director Robert Yowell. The most significant aspect of this order was that it came from joint inspections by the DEP and the Pennsylvania Boat and Fish Commission, and there was no indication that the Bureau of Forestry was involved in the inspection or the enforcement. In other words, much like the case of California, enforcement of water quality standards in forested operations came not from the forest agency but from entirely independent agencies, in this case both the Fish Commission and the Bureau of Water Quality in the Department of Environmental Protection. See news item from the organization, Citizens for Pennsylvania's Future, as reported on the Sierra Club Forest list serve, January 2, 2004.

4. The standard history of the Bureau of Forestry is Lester A. DeCoster, *The Legacy of Penn's Woods, 1895–1995: A History of the Pennsylvania Bureau of Forestry* (Harrisburg, Pa.: The Pennsylvania Historical and Museum Commission and the Pennsylvania Department of Conservation and Natural Resources, 1995). DeCoster describes accurately the watershed events in the early history of the state forests. An important source of information about the early Pennsylvania state forests is a biography of the first state forester by Eleanor Maass, *Forestry Pioneer: The Life of Joseph Trimble Rothrock* (Mechanicsburg: Pennsylvania Forestry Association, 2003).

5. Such questions were also far from the minds of district rangers on the Allegheny National Forest, as revealed in my correspondence with several in response to their invitations to comment on proposed plans. The relevant letters are in Hays, *Forest Papers*, 189–207. The exchanges confirmed my belief that the Forest Service had only very skimpy ecological information on which to base plans or policies, and that as a result of this weakness the agency was not prepared to think constructively about ecological forest objectives.

6. DeCoster, *The Legacy of Penn's Woods*.

7. Joan M. Hocking, ed, *Centennial Voices—the Spring of Mont Alto, A Continuing Story 1903–2003* (privately printed, 2003).

8. Wildlife was hardly mentioned in Bureau of Forestry publicity in the years after World War I and assumed little visibility in later forest planning. In advisory meetings leading up to the new Forest Plan in 2003, the bureau was roundly criticized by wildlife specialists for this lack of attention, but it seemed to bring about little interest in the subject in its plans, except for the deer problem which it quietly "resolved" by fencing regenerating areas until they were above the reach of the deer.

9. The subject is briefly mentioned by DeCoster in *The Legacy of Penn's Woods*, but there seems to have been a management problem (little explored by historians) with lands that were formerly farmed and then purchased by both the U.S. Forest Service and state forest agencies throughout the East in the first half of the twentieth century for growing trees. The problem also surfaced in the many state laws which reduced property taxes for woodlands placed under a special classification for growing trees and replaced them with a severance tax at the time of timber harvest; these invariably required that such lands be fenced and that grazing animals be excluded. The conflict between grazing and growing trees was well understood.

10. See Ernest Morrison, *A Walk on the Downhill Side of the Log: The Life of Maurice K. Goddard* (Mechanicsburg: Pennsylvania Forestry Association, 2003).

11. See Samuel P. Hays, *Pennsylvania State Parks Plan*, report prepared for the Sierra Club, Pennsylvania Chapter, 1998. The comparative statistics about state parks were drawn from annual reports, the first one, *State Park Statistics, 1970* (Washington, D.C.: National Conference on State Parks, 1971), then followed beginning in 1990 with an annual publication, *Annual Information Exchange*, issued by the National Association of State Park Directors, and distributed by park agencies in various states, most recently by the Parks and Recreation program of Indiana University at Bloomington, Indiana. The materials cited in this note are included in the first mentioned document which is included in Samuel P. Hays, *Forest Papers*, 1:219–34. The Web site of the NASPD is: http://naspd.indstate.edu.

12. My electronic newsletter, *Forest Papers*, which was issued over a period of several years on the Pennsylvania chapter's Forest Issues List Serve, received more response from out of state than from Pennsylvania.

13. These conclusions about the Pennsylvania Environmental Council came from periodic conversations with its staff director, Curt Winsor, over the course of the 1970s and participation in many of its annual conferences. I also was involved in negotiations between the state environmental community and the council over the council's unwillingness to support returnable container legislation in Pennsylvania. Because of its divorce from the general public as a constituency for its activities, I declined on several occasions to be a member of its board of directors.

14. See Samuel P. Hays, "The Presidential Oil Tract: A Modest Proposal," paper presented to the Western Pennsylvania Conservancy, Pittsburgh, Pa., 1998. The Conservancy was primarily a land-brokering organization that acquired land and then sold it to the state primarily for state parks; it did not retain ownership of forest land and as a result did not develop its own forest management capabilities. After the turn of the century it became associated with the use of conservation easements to assure the permanence of land for wood production and gave no evidence of action to incorporate ecological objectives into the easements. See its publication, *Conserve*, Spring and Summer issues, 2003.

15. The work of the Forest Issues Working Group can be followed in my files on the group and its meetings, under the file heading by that name in EA.

16. For a more complete assessment of the role of the Pennsylvania Forestry Association see Samuel P. Hays, "The Pennsylvania Forestry Association, a Lost Opportunity" (1979). The publication of the association, *Pennsylvania Forests*, provides a running account of its activities. A substantial run of the issues are in Forest List 1 and Forest List 2, EA.

17. Activities of the School of Forest Resources can be followed in its publication *Biennial Report* (1973–).

18. Activities of the stewardship program in Pennsylvania can be followed in my file under that heading in EA.

19. See "Forest Terminology" in the newsletter *Pennsylvania Woodlands* (Cooperative Extension Service, Pennsylvania State University), Spring 1989.

20. See Samuel P. Hays, "A Challenge to the Profession of Forestry," in James C. Finley and Stephen B. Jones, *Practicing Stewardship and Living a Land Ethic*, Proceedings of the 1991 Penn State Forest Resources Issues Conference (Pennsylvania State University, 1992), reprinted in Samuel P. Hays, *Explorations in Environmental History* (Pittsburgh: University of Pittsburgh Press, 1998), 172–84.

21. The work of the Ecosystem Management Advisory Committee during my attendance is documented in the file under that title in Forest List 2, EA.

22. See my report, "The Penn State 1995 Forest Conference, March 15–16, 1995," copy in Hays, *Forest Papers*, EA.

23. See my report, "Northwest Pennsylvania Field Trip, Sept. 27–28, 1993," in which a group of about fifteen visited research sites at the Moshannan State Forest and the Allegheny National Forest, a trip organized under the leadership of Steven Thorne of the School of Forestry, Department of Natural Resources, Pennsylvania State University, copy in Hays, *Forest Papers*, EA.

24. "Pennsylvania Biodiversity Issues," minutes of the joint meeting of the Forest Issues Working Group and the Forestry Task Force of the Pennsylvania Legislature, October 15, 1996, copy in Hays, *Forest Papers*, EA.

25. See the report to John Oliver, secretary, Department of Conservation and Natural Resources, Commonwealth of Pennsylvania, by Bob Hill, biodiversity coordinator and chief of ecological services of the department, "An Open Assessment of DCNR's Role in Pennsylvania's Biodiversity Conservation Efforts" (n.p., n.d.). Copy in Hays, *Forest Papers*, EA.

26. In 1974 I was invited to give a talk about the Pennsylvania Wilderness proposal at the annual meeting of the Pennsylvania Forestry Association in Pittsburgh. As soon as I had finished, Bob LaBar of the Hammermill Paper Company rose to submit a resolution in opposition to the proposal. It was tabled on the grounds that such precipitous action was inappropriate and that it should be taken up later.

27. Citizens Advisory Council, Department of Environmental Resources, "Clear Fragments of a Whole" (Harrisburg, Pa., 1976).

28. School of Forest Resources, *Clearcutting in Pennsylvania* (State College: Pennsylvania State University, 1975).

29. My letter to *Econotes*, publication of the Department of Environmental Resources, is in Hays, *Forest Papers*, EA.

30. Samuel P. Hays, "Clearcutting for Kids," a review of a booklet, "Let's Talk about Clearcutting" (published and distributed in 1998), issued jointly by the Pennsylvania State Bureau of Forestry and the Pennsylvania Forestry Association. Copy of the initial publication is in the Pennsylvania section, Forest List 1, EA, and copy of the review in Hays, *Forest Papers*, EA.

31. See Samuel P. Hays, "An Off-Road Vehicle Management Plan for the Allegheny National Forest" (1972).

32. A convenient time-line history of both natural areas and wild areas is included in the section, "Natural Areas and Wild Areas," in the Pennsylvania Bureau of Forestry, *Resource Management Plan* (2003) under the section "Ecological Considerations." The bureau's views on old growth are contained in the section "Old Growth" and also under the section "Ecological Considerations." Old-growth proposals from the Sierra Club are described in "The Beautiful Woods of Pennsylvania: Our Heritage and Our Future," insert in the *Sylvanian*, newsletter of the Pennsylvania Chapter of the Sierra Club, Spring 2003.

33. See the report by S. G. Thorne et al., the Pennsylvania Biodiversity Technical Committee, *A Heritage for the 21st Century: Preserving Pennsylvania's Native Biological Diversity* (Harrisburg: Pennsylvania Fish Commission, 1994). Also the section, "Natural Diversity Conservation" of the 21st Century Environmental Commission Report (1998). Five years after the state forest certification approval, in which a biodiversity program was to be instituted as one of the conditions of certification, the certification review team reported that "EMAC has designated a bioreserve subcommittee that is currently developing guidelines for a bioreserve system in Pennsylvania on state forest lands." By the time of the 2003 State Forest Plan (see note 35), a bioreserve system was still in the planning stage, the victim of continued internal bureau and interagency disageement. At the same time, the plan reported that the bureau had in 1995 instituted the Wild Plant Sanctuary Program, authorized in 1982; however no specific sites were mentioned as having been designated for protection.

34. Robert B. McKinstry Jr., Coreen M. Ripp, and Emily Lisy, eds., *Biodiversity Conservation Handbook: State, Local, and Private Protection of Biological Diversity* (Washington, D.C.: Environmental Law Institute, 2006).

35. See the report to John Oliver, secretary, Department of Conservation and Natural Resources, Commonwealth of Pa., by Bob Hill, biodiversity coordinator and chief of ecological services of the department, "An Open Assessment of DCNR's Role in Pennsylvania's Biodiversity Conservation Efforts" (n.d., n.p.).

36. The Pennsylvania Natural Diversity Index was a part of the Pennsylvania Natural Heritage Program; see http://www.dcnr.state.pa.us/forestry/pndi.

37. Bob Hill, in his report to Secretary John Oliver on the biodiversity program of the Department of Conservation and Natural Resources, elaborated on

this problem and recommended that "DCNR should no longer be party to the 'east-west divide.'" "It [the department] has collaborated in maintaining a divided state through the agency's funding behaviors. The department should require full cooperation on projects that it supports so that the initiatives are joint endeavors between the TNC in the east and WPC in the west. To put it bluntly, 'separate and equal' allocation of money for natural diversity conservation should be abandoned. Pennsylvania is one state, DCNR is a statewide agency—those who would guard their provincial, special interests—and thus fracture this unity—should be challenged, not financially supported." See Hill, "An Open Assessment," 10.

38. Report of the Forestry Task Force Pursuant to House Resolution of the PA General Assembly Joint Legislative Air and Water Pollution Control and Conservation Committee, March 1997.

39. For the work of the Ecosystem Management Advisory Committee see my personal files under that heading in Forest List 2, EA. The assessment in quotations is from the Hill report, "An Open Assessment."

40. Discussion of the inventory proposal is in two sets of notes covering the EMAC meeting on December 12, 1996, one, official notes distributed after the meeting and another of my own. According to the first, "It was generally agreed that the past inventory was basically timber-oriented and that it needed to be revised or expanded." My own notes read that after an initial presentation by Bureau of Forestry representatives, "a discussion started by a question from Kim Steiner, who asked why all this wood inventory needed to be refined so much (isn't there enough known now?) and especially why more of the inventory was not devoted to identifying other parts of the ecosystem. I gave support to his concern, as did Ann Rhoads and others." "There was a general view in the discussion that an ecosystem approach at least required that much besides wood production was needed to be known." See my notes of the December 12, 1996, meeting of the EMAC, EMAC box, Forest List 2, EA.

41. "Special Roles for Pennsylvania's State Forests and the Pennsylvania Bureau of Forestry: A Position Paper of the Ecosystem Management Advisory Committee to the Pennsylvania Bureau of Forestry," adopted February 10, 1999, State College, Pennsylvania.

42. The outcome of the bioreserve proposal in the new forest plan can be found in the State Forest Resource Management Plan, "Bioreserve System," under "Ecological Considerations," http://www.dcnr.state.pa.us/forestry/sfrmp/eco.htm.

43. My review of the certification report is "Forest Certification in Pennsylvania: An Evaluation of the Report Concerning Pennsylvania State Forests by Scientific Certification Systems," March 20, 1998. Copy in Hays, Forest Papers, 407–38.

44. The Department of Conservation and Natural Resources seemed to be more interested in the publicity which came with certification and which was the subject of several departmental news releases, than it was in saying anything at all about the conditions and recommendations. To my knowledge it never mentioned these publicly or in the private groups in which I participated.

45. See my papers on certification, "Forest Certification in Pennsylvania: An Evaluation of the Report Concerning Pennsylvania State Forests by Scientific Certification Systems, March 20, 1998," copy in Forest Papers, 407–38, and "Certification Reviewed—1998," a paper concerning the wider certification movement, in Forest Papers, 489–502.

46. For the eastern old-growth movement see Mary Byrd Davis, Eastern Old Growth Forests: Prospects for Rediscovery and Recovery (Washington, D.C.: Island Press, 1966).

47. See my report of the conference, "Northeastern Old Growth Conference, Report, Williamstown, Mass., Oct. 28–30, 1994," in Hays, Forest Papers, 343–62.

48. See Samuel P. Hays, "Eastern Old Growth," in Forest Papers, 337–42.

49. See Samuel P. Hays, "Evolving Eastern Old Growth Forest Policies," paper presented at the Third Eastern Old Growth Conference at Fayetteville, Arkansas, in conjunction with the annual meeting of the Natural Areas Association, Spring 1996, copy in Hays, Forest Papers, 363–68. The survey materials on which the analysis is based is in Box 29, "Environmental and Ecological Standards," Forest List 1, EA.

50. The Pennsylvania "old-growth" program was elaborated extensively in Dylan H. Jenkins, Daniel A. Devlin, Nels C. Johnson, and Stephanie P. Orndorff, "System Design and Management for Restoring Penn's Woods," Journal of Forestry 102, no. 3 (April/May 2004): 30–36.

51. Jim Nelson presented a written version of Pennsylvania forest history quite similar to his slide show under the title of "Forest Background Reports" to the Conservation and Natural Resources Advisory Council on July 23, 2003. It was confined to the history of the wood products industry and was not extended to the history of the forest. It is in the Pennsylvania file, Forest List 2, EA. The questions raised by the council members following the presentation were equally limited in perspective. This almost exclusive focus on wood production in Jim Nelson's account is typical of state-based forest histories. See, for example, "100 Years of Wisconsin Forestry," Wisconsin Woodland Owners Association, P. O. Box 285, Stevens Point, WI, 54481, which is reviewed briefly by Randall E. Rohe in Wisconsin Natural Resources, February 2004, 17–21. A similar history for Michigan is William B. Botti, Green Gold: Michigan Forest History (Ann Arbor: Michigan Forest Association, n.d.), video.

52. A copy of the Pennsylvania curriculum, both in draft and final form, is in the files in EA. See my review, "Comments on the proposed curriculum on forestry for the Pennsylvania public schools," preceded by other documents pertaining to the circumstances under which the comments were prepared, in Hays, Forest Papers.

53. The Petersham field trip is described in Hays, Northeastern Old-Growth Conference, included in Hays, Forest Papers.

54. The newsletter "Monitoring Matters" published by the Pennsylvania Department of Environmental Protection Citizens' Volunteer Monitoring Program devoted much of its January 2004 issue (vol. 7, no. 1) to riparian monitoring. However, crucial policy issues such as the width of the riparian zone, its extension

from the main stream to headwaters, or zone management such as allowable tree harvest or biodiversity protection and restoration, received little or no attention. See also "Riparian Forest Buffers: A Practical Guide on Restoring and Protecting Riparian Buffers," published by the Canaan Valley Institute.

The Susquehanna River watershed constitutes 40 percent of the Chesapeake Bay's total watershed. While the interagency Chesapeake Bay Program has developed plans for the "Tributary Program" it has made no steps toward implementation. For the three states as a whole, Virginia, Maryland, and Pennsylvania, the "Tributary Strategies" were declared by the Chesapeake Bay Foundation as "Tributary Tragedies"; four years after the states agreed to reduce tributary contributions to the Bay's water quality there are statements on paper but no action toward implementation. See CBF news release by Melinda Downey, April 5, 2004, of the organization Save the Bay.

55. These issues were covered in a paper I wrote on behalf of the Pennsylvania Chapter of the Sierra Club, "Pennsylvania's Water Quality Special Protection Program: An Analysis of Recent Policy Developments" (1992), copy in Hays, Forest Papers, 209–17. While the bureau in its 2003 plan included a riparian protection program as part of the Pennsylvania role in seeking to reduce Susquehanna River pollution flows into the Chesapeake Bay, the strategy seemed to remain limited to riparian strip protection and not to involve a wider watershed inventory and protection program. See State Forest Resource Management Plan, "Water Resources," http://www.dcnr.state.pa.us/forestry/sfrmp/water.htm.

56. My brief involvement in small group meetings on research programs to deal with the state's forest problems led to some exchange with one of the group's main participants, Susan Stout of the Northeastern Forest Experiment Station branch at Warren, Pennsylvania, pertaining to her interest in fostering research on the deer problem. I was skeptical about the research design that she was proposing, which seemed to me to be devoted primarily to a rationale for moving deer around, and I emphasized especially the focus of similar research in Wisconsin on the effect of deer on plants other than wood fiber seedlings. See my comments on this under "Research Proposals for the Warren Station, ANF, March 1993," in Forest Papers, 165–78.

57. Two publications came from the Pennsylvania State University Conference on Acid Rain: William E. Sharpe and Joy R. Drohan, eds., The Effects of Acidic Deposition on Pennsylvania's Forests, volume 1 of Proceedings of the 1998 Pennsylvania Acidic Deposition Conference, September 14–16, 1998; and a collection of the conference papers, The Effects of Acidic Deposition on Aquatic Ecosystems in Pennsylvania (University Park, Pa.: Environmental Resources Research Institute, the Pennsylvania State University, 1999).

58. James A. Lynch and Robert S. Corbett, "Atmospheric Deposition: Spatial and Temporal Variation in Pennsylvania" (University Park, Pa.: Institute for Land and Water Resources, the Pennsylvania State University, 1982–1994), annual reports in Box 11, Pennsylvania section, EA.

59. The two contrasting views were presented as part of a larger set of talks on

acidification at the Forest Issues Working Group, April 30, 1996. See manuscript box labeled "Forest Issues Working Group," Pennsylvania section, EA.

60. See references in preface, note 3, to the two surveys of attitudes of Pennsylvanians about the importance of forests in the state. While the results of these surveys, which indicated the very high public ranking of clean air, clean water, soil protection, and wildlife in forest management objectives, were well known to the state's forest leaders and were widely publicized by the Sierra Club, they were ignored in the public statements of the state's forest establishment leaders and not mentioned in the meetings conducted by the Bureau of Forestry on the 2003 State Forest Plan.

61. During the twenty-seven meetings throughout the state on the State Forest Plan held in the summer of 2000, neither the certification report nor its attached conditions or recommendations were mentioned by Dan Devlin, the bureau's chief forest planner, who opened each meeting with extensive general remarks about forest planning. The limitations in state forest management that were identified by the certification team were introduced into the meetings only by citizen participants and were dismissed as irrelevant.

62. Bob Hill, in his review of his work as biodiversity coordinator, remarked about the response of the bureau to the certification report: "Other examples of DCNR's resistance to foster an unbridled ecological approach can be seen in the way that the agency has responded to the recommendations of the third party 'Green Certification' sustainable forestry report. Numerous examples, such as increasing the skills mix of staff, could illustrate the point. Rather than seriously addressing most recommendations, they have been met with rhetoric or silence."

63. See Allegheny Defense Project, *Allegheny Wild! A Citizen's Vision for the Allegheny National Forest* (Clarion, Pa.: Allegheny Defense Project, 2003).

64. For its report see Pennsylvania Wildlands Recovery Project, *The Pennsylvania State Forest Resource Management Plan: A Wildlands Perspective*, submitted to the Bureau of Forestry by the Pennsylvania Wildlands Recovery Project, September 28, 2003.

65. A description of the Sierra Club program is in "The Beautiful Woods of Pennsylvania: Our Heritage and Our Future," insert in the *Sylvanian*, newsletter of the Pennsylvania Chapter of the Sierra Club, Spring 2003, Pennsylvania section, EA. For the awards in the sixth annual Huplits grant competition see the *Sylvanian*, Winter 2003.

66. See *Pennsylvania's Wildlife and Wild Places: Our Outdoor Heritage in Peril*, authored by Ben Moyer and funded by the Pennsylvania Wild Resource Conservation Fund, the Pennsylvania Fish and Boat Commission, the Pennsylvania Department of Conservation and Natural Resources, and the Pennsylvania Game Commission (2003). It grew out of a previous report by Laurie J. Goodrich of the Hawk Mountain Sanctuary; Dr. Margaret Britingham, wildlife specialist at the School of Forest Resources at Penn State University; Joseph A. Bishop at the Cooperative Wetlands Center, Penn State University; and Patricia Barber of Hawk Mountain Sanctuary, *Wildlife Habitat in Pennsylvania: Past, Present, and Future*.

67. See the Pennsylvania Biodiversity Partnership (PBP), a loose combination of varied individuals which grew out of the biodiversity recommendations of the *Report of the Governor's 21st Century Environment Commission*. This was the first of an anticipated sequence of reports on the state's biodiversity resources and circumstances, *Biodiversity in Pennsylvania: Snapshot 2002* (Pittsburgh: Pennsylvania Biodiversity Partnership, 2002).

68. See Bureau of Forestry, *Final Draft, State Forest Resource Management Plan* (Harrisburg, Pa., 2003), available on disk and on the Bureau of Forestry Web site.

69. See Pennsylvania Biodiversity Program folder, Pennsylvania section, Forest List 2, EA, and especially news releases from the DCNR.

70. Correspondence from the Conservation and Natural Resources Advisory Council and the secretary's office is in the Pennsylvania Biodiversity Program folder, Pennsylvania section, Forest List 2, EA, and is available on the council's Web site: http://www.dcnr.state.pa.us/cnrac/biodiversityprogramcomments.

Chapter 6: The Skirmishes Become a Full-Scale War

1. See items in Box 20 and Box 21, Forest List 1, EA.

2. A remarkable and unique insight into the operation of the U.S. Forest Service within the larger context of national administrative affairs is revealed by the diaries of Jack Ward Thomas, spanning the years from 1992 to 1996, published in May 2004: Jack Ward Thomas and Harold K. Steen, *The Journals of a Forest Service Chief* (Durham, N.C., and Seattle, Wash.: Forest History Society and the University of Washington Press, 2004). A retrospective view of national forest issues by Thomas is his testimony "Regarding the Future of the Forest Service" presented to the U.S. House of Representatives Committee on Resources Subcommittee on Forests and Forest Health, September 21, 2000, a copy included in Statements of Forest Service Officials folder, Forest List 2, EA. For a view of Thomas's career as chief by a citizen environmental leader see Andy Stahl, "Notes from the Other Side," *Forest Magazine* (Spring 2004): 48–49.

3. The Dombeck National Resource Agenda is outlined in Dombeck, Wood, and Williams, *From Conquest to Conservation*, much of which is an outline of Dombeck's ideas about how the agency could establish a leadership that would restore public confidence in the agency. Copies of some of his speeches are in the Forest Service Leader Statements folder, Forest List 2, EA. See also copies of several of his speeches while chief of the Forest Service, in Statements of Forest Service Officials folder, Forest List 2, EA.

4. Material on the 1982 regulations is in National Forest Regulations 1982 folder, National Forest Issues section, Forest List 2, EA.

5. Documents pertaining to the work of the Clinton Committee of Scientists are on its Web site titled Committee of Scientists, http://www.cof.orst.edu/org/scicomm, and are included in the folder Committee of Scientists, Year 2000, National Forest Issues section, Forest List 1, EA.

6. A straightforward and understandable account of this thorny issue is Barry R. Noon et al., "Conservation Planning for US National Forests: Conducting Comprehensive Biodiversity Assessments," *BioScience* 53, no. 12 (December 2003): 1217–20. See also Species Viability Issue folder, Forest Plan Regulations section, Forest List 2, EA.

7. See Survey and Manage folder, Pacific Northwest Forest Plan section, Forest List 2, EA. The ecological forestry community often objected that the Forest Service scheduled timber harvests without prior surveys and thus had not determined the presence or absence of "at risk" species. For a case in Florida, see Craig Pittman, "The Forest Service Concedes That It Needs to More Thoroughly Account for Rare Animals," *St. Petersburg (Fla.) Times*, May 17, 2001. In this case the agency agreed to postpone plans to cut pine trees on about 1,000 acres of the Osceola National Forest in North Florida. This was a result of a suit brought by the Southern Appalachian Diversity Project in North Carolina; as the suit pointed out, the agency's own biologists had written that "no surveys have been done"; they were never done. WildLaw and the Southern Appalachian Diversity project sued the agency in 2000 over the lack of such surveys on fifty-six other timber sales throughout the Southeast. Still another case in the form of a preliminary injunction involving a timber sale in the San Juan National Forest in Colorado involved a fire salvage sale in which the judge ruled on January 30, 2004, that the forest had not done the required species surveys. See news item, "Colorado Wild Lawsuit Blocks Missionary Ridge Postfire Logging," in *Colorado Wild*, Spring/Summer 2004, http://www.coloradowild.org/CWNews letterSpring2004.pdf; and in Colorado Wild folder, Mountain States section, Forest List 2, EA. Still another "survey and manage" case was the Dutton timber sale on the San Juan National Forest in Colorado; this litigation involved the failure to inventory for management indicator species. See "Residents and Conservation Groups Sue to Stop Colorado Timber Sale," *Earthjustice Newsroom*, August 28, 2003. See the court case complaint under the file title, *Forest Guardians, et al. v. Mark Stiles, et al*. While the Missionary Ridge case involved a post-fire salvage logging project, the Dutton sale involved a green timber proposal; however both alleged a failure on the part of the Forest Service to inventory selected management indicator species.

8. For documents on the work of the Committee of Scientists, including those pertaining to the actions by committee members Norm Johnson and Roger Sedjo, see note 5, above.

9. Several compilations of the Bush administration actions concerning environmental issues that include forestry issues are: Robert Perks and Gregory Wetstone, "Rewriting the Rules: The Bush Administration's Assault on the Environment," Annual Year-End Reports, 2001, 2002, and 2003 (Washington, D.C.: Natural Resources Defense Council, January 2003); "The Bush Administration's Anti-environmental Actions, as Commented on by America's Editorial Pages, March 2001–May 2003" (Washington, D.C.: National Environmental Trust, 2003).

10. The agenda of the Society of American Foresters for the fourth year of the Bush administration was presented in a document, "National Forest Reform in

the Second Session of the 107th Congress: Viewpoints of the Society of American Foresters," a copy of which is on the SAF Web site, http://www.safnet.org/policy andpress/psst/FSreform_62102.cfm.

11. Arguments used by the administration in environmental litigation cases are an example. See the positions of the administration in the proceedings in environmental cases as detailed in William Snape III and John M. Carter II, "Weakening the National Environmental Policy Act: How the Bush Administration Uses the Judicial System to Weaken Environmental Protections: A Report of the Judicial Accountability Project" (Washington, D.C.: Defenders of Wildlife, 2003); William Snape III, Michael T. Leahy, and John M. Carter II, "Undercutting National Forest Protection: How the Bush Administration Uses the Judicial System to Weaken Environmental Laws," a report of the Judicial Accountability Project, Defenders of Wildlife (Washington D.C.: Defenders of Wildlife, Summer 2003).

12. Several items pertaining to Rey and his role in forest affairs are in Statements by Forest Service Officials folder, Forests: Nationwide section, Forest List 2, EA. See, for example, Craig Welch, "Issues Evolving in Forest Debate: Federal Official, UW Professor Sound Off," *Seattle Times*, October 14, 2003; Joe Scott, "Forest Official Spins Bush Policy," *Seattle Post-Intelligencer*, October 30, 2003. See also "Rey Nominated Under Secretary for USDA," *Forestry Source* (publication of the Society of American Foresters), August 2001.

13. For Dombeck's National Resource Agenda, see note 3, above.

14. The new agency views expressed by Dale Bosworth appeared in speeches which he made especially throughout the West. For an account of one given in Denver, Colorado, see editorial, "Forests Face Fresh Threats," *Denver Post*, September 28, 2003; for another see Michel Milstein, "Forest Service Chief Suggests Way to Cut through Logging Appeals," *Oregonian*, December 7, 2001; a public statement of his objectives by Bosworth is "Statement," Dale Bosworth, Chief, USDA Forest Service, Subcommittee on Forest Health, Committee on Resources, U.S. House of Representatives, Washington, D.C., December 4, 2001; all items in Statements by Forest Service Officials folder, Forests: Nationwide section, Forest List 2, EA. See also "The Source Interview: A Talk with the New Forest Service Chief," *Forestry Source* (publication of the Society of American Foresters), September 2001. A perceptive recognition of the differences in agenda on the part of Dombeck and Bosworth appeared in editorials in the *Idaho Falls Post Register* after a visit by Bosworth to the paper's editorial board. See J. Robb Brady, "Bosworth's Agenda" and "Gaps in Bosworth's Goals," *Idaho Falls Post Register*, January 25 and January 26, 2004.

15. The wider implications of the Bosworth "four threats" agenda appeared gradually over the years. One of these became known in March 2004 when Bosworth announced that reviews of Forest Service actions by outside agencies for compliance with laws under their primary responsibilities would no longer be required for subjects other than the "four threats." Consultations or any other "process" the Forest Service deemed unrelated to the "four threats" would be dropped. This included all endangered species consultation on inland aquatic species and

"all land management activities." See PEER news release, "Forest Service Dropping Endangered Species, Riparian and Archaeological Reviews; Forest Service Will Self-Certify Compliance under New 'Streamline' Plan," March 18, 2004. Also *Environmental News Service*, March 19, 2004. See Statements by Forest Service Officials folder, Forest List 2, EA.

16. Under a rule proposed in September 2003, "public land management agencies will begin determining on their own whether wildfire prevention projects, like forest thinning, will impact species protected under the Endangered Species Act." See *Greenwire*, September 11, 2003, as reported by the Red Lodge Clearinghouse under caption, "Administration to Hasten Forest Thinning by Minimizing FWS Oversight." Later, at the same time as President Bush signed the "Healthy Forests" bill in December 2003, his administration removed from the regulations the requirement that the Forest Service seek an "advisory opinion" from the Fish and Wildlife Service as to whether a particular species was threatened or endangered and therefore subject to action under the Endangered Species Act. Steve Williams, director of the Fish and Wildlife Service, argued that the Forest Service had a great number of expert biologists who could make that determination themselves. See the *Los Angeles Times*, December 4, 2003.

17. The population studies for the northern spotted owl are a case study. As a result of the 1993 Pacific Northwest Forest Plan, an interagency committee was established to monitor the owl numbers; it was led by Eric Forsburg, who was considered to be the most authoritative specialist on the owl. The timber industry's own owl researchers, however, disputed the work of established owl experts and challenged the findings of the interagency committee. As a result, the industry petitioned the administration to seek the views of still another source, and for this purpose drew upon an ecological consulting group that the industry helped to finance and on which it often drew for its own scientific arguments about endangered species. Materials pertaining to the owl issue are in the Spotted Owl folder, Forest List 2, EA.

18. Documents on the survey and manage issue in the Southern Appalachians are in the Survey and Manage folder, Forest List 2, EA.

19. A brief but accurate account of changes in the diversity regulation by the Forest Service is Jamey Fidel, "The End of Counting Critters? Biodiversity Management on the National Forests," in *Wild Earth*, Spring/Summer 2004, 41–43. For more extended coverage see the earlier citation to "survey and manage" documents in EA. In particular explore a comprehensive account of the development of the issue in "Bush Administration to Eliminate Rare Wildlife Surveys," issued by the Western Environmental Law Center, January 23, 2004. An extensive analysis of the issue as it evolved in the early George W. Bush administration is Keith Easthouse, "The Wrong Side of the Law: Logging at the Expense of Northwest Old-Growth Creatures Once Again Lands the Government in Court," *Forest Magazine*, November/December 1999, 14–20. The administration removed the "survey and manage" requirements for the Northwest Forest Plan with a Federal Register notice, January

23, 2004. It prompted several news articles in Pacific Northwest media, some of which are in the Survey and Manage folder, Forest List 2, EA.

Several examples of "survey" scientists illustrate the situation more precisely. Joel E. Pagel, specialist in wildlife biology and in particular research on the peregrine falcon in the Pacific Northwest, was Forest Wildlife Biology Program manager and threatened and endangered species biologist for the Rogue River National Forest in Oregon. In a memo to his supervisors during his work on that forest, in the Ashland and Applegate Ranger Districts, in January 2004, he said that he was "unwilling to allow his reputation to rest on the poor work of his predecessors" with respect to surveys on "survey and manage" issues. He stated that much of the information collected and collated over the past eighteen years was, for the most part, invalid. His report was obtained by the Klamath-Siskiyou Wildlands Center in Ashland and made public. See Sean Wolfe, "Whistleblower Lobs Volley at Forest Service Wildlife Surveys," *Ashland Daily Tidings*, April 6, 2004.

Another case is that of Charles Crisafulli, who specialized in the Larch Mountain salamander in the Gifford Pinchot National Forest. His "Survey Protocol for Larch Mountain Salamander" describes in detail the work of population surveys for a relatively immobile species, the focal point of much of the debate over "survey and manage" in the Northwest Forest Plan. This type of work, with a focus on Crisafulli, is described by Kathie Durbin, "Northwest Forest Plan: Federal Lands Reveal 'Hidden Diversity,'" *Columbian* (Clark Co., Wash.), April 13, 2004. Durbin reports that Crisafulli "is the only Forest Service research biologist working almost exclusively in Southwest Washington, an example of the limited resources which the agency devoted to its survey and manage responsibilities." These documents are available in the Survey and Manage folder, Northwest Forest Plan section, Forest List 2, EA.

20. For an account of the document disclosure by Earthjustice, dated April 22, 2003, "Documents Expose Timber Industry Control of Northwest Forest Plan Rollbacks: Freedom of Information Act Release Spells Out Timber Industry Plan to Weaken Old-Growth, Salmon and Ecosystem Protections on Northwest Federal Forests"; see http://www.earthjustice.org.

21. Documents pertaining to the forest industry initiative in the Bush administration are on the Earthjustice Web site, including "A Global Framework for Settlement of Litigation Challenging Federal Agency Actions Relating to the Northwest Forest Plan"; "Administrative Tools to Fix the Northwest Forest Plan"; letter from Wells Burgess, assistant section chief, Environmental and Natural Resource Division, U.S. Department of Justice, to Mark Rutzick, attorney for the forest industry, August 1, 2002; and "Response to the Federal Settlement Offer of August 1, 2002" by the three plaintiffs in the four legal cases, the American Forest Resource Council, the Western Council of Industrial Workers, and the Association of O&C Counties, dated August 13, 2002.

22. These observations are based on a wide range of materials in the Biodiversity and Survey and Manage folders in Forest List 2, EA.

23. In 2001 scientists wrote the panel of federal agency leaders who implemented the Northwest Forest Plan that since 1994 studies had shown that some species had a harder time migrating from one spot to another than previously believed. They urged a ban on cutting old growth. Statement by David Montgomery, professor at the University of Washington. See Kristian Foden-Vencil, Oregon Public Broadcasting, "Scientists Want to Amend Northwest Forest Plan," September 6, 2001.

24. The Bush administration announcement of changes in the Aquatic Conservation Strategy stated that the nine ACS objectives "would be attained at the fifth-field watershed scale and not at the project or site level." The change was described as a "clarification" with the statement that "Without clarifying the intent of the ACS, the agencies will continue to be constrained in their ability to achieve the sustainable and predictable level of timber sales envisaged under the Northwest Forest Plan." See joint news release of the USDA and the BLM dated October 31, 2003, Portland, Oregon. Documents pertaining to the Pacific Northwest salmon issue are in Aquatic Conservation Plan folder, Pacific Northwest Forest section, Forest List 2, EA. See especially several items: "Review of Scientific Information," by Gordon Reeves, Ph.D., March 20, 2003; Doug Heiken, on behalf of six Pacific Northwest regional organizations, to Joyce Casey, SEIS for Aquatic Conservation Strategy, December 26, 2002, including a copy of "A Common Sense Alternative to Bush's Rollback of the Northwest Forest Plan," and later attachment, "Restoration Principles," February 4, 2002. See also, developed under the Interagency Monitoring program for the Pacific Northwest Forest Plan, Gordon H. Reeves, David B. Hohler, David P. Larsen, David E. Busch, Kim Kratz, Keith Reynolds, Karl F. Stein, Thomas Atzet, Polly Hays, and Michael Tehan, "Aquatic and Riparian Effectiveness Monitoring Plan for the Northwest Forest Plan."

25. The attacks on the Pacific Northwest Plan led, in response, to the development of a "Citizen's Alternative for the Northwest Forest Plan," submitted to the Forest Service and the Bureau of Land Management in a new Draft Environmental Impact Statement for Amending the Northwest Forest Plan, and signed by ninety-eight national and regional organizations. For a copy see Northwest Forest Plan folder, Forest section, EA. A review of the course of the Northwest Forest Plan was carried out in a one-day conference at the Oregon Convention Center, Portland, Oregon, April 13, 2004, on the tenth anniversary of the adoption of the plan. The program was sponsored by twenty-one environmental/ecology organizations and was titled "The Northwest Forest Plan: Ten Years Later: A Community Forum to Examine the History, Current Situation, and Future under the Northwest's Landmark Forest Management Plan." Fifteen speakers participated. These included Jim Lyons, Jack Ward Thomas, Norm Johnson, Jim Furnish, Lyn Jungwirth, Julie Norman, Tom Spies, Eric Forsman, Kim Erion, Andy Kerr, Bot Guenther, Patti Goldman, and Brock Evans. For a series of articles about the Northwest Forest Plan ten years after its adoption, see the folder Northwest Forest Plan—A Ten-Year Retrospective. All these items are in Northwest Forest Plan, Forest List 2, EA.

26. Issues on Alaskan national forests can be followed in the *Raven Call*, newsletter of the Southeast Alaska Conservation Council, and its miscellaneous publications; under the heading "Alaska" in the organizational list in Forest List 2, EA; and under the heading "Alaska" in the topical section in Forest List 2, EA. See especially, for the scientific component of Tongass National Forest issues, Kent R. Julin and Charles G. Shaw III, "Science Matters: Information for Managing the Tongass National Forest," Alaska section, in the topical section in Forest List 2. For Bush administration action to resume extensive timber cutting on the Tongass National Forest see news release, "Lawsuit Challenges Forest Service Plans to Clearcut Premier Alaska National Forest," *Common Dreams Progressive Newswire*, December 10, 2003; this is a lawsuit challenging the Tongass Land Management Plan and especially six roadless area timber sales under that plan. See Tongass folder in Forest List 2, EA. For a laudatory statement about the role of the Native Corporations in Alaskan resource development see Carl Marrs, president of the ANCSA CEO Association, "Native Corporations: An Epic Story Benefiting Alaska," March 21, 2002, Alaska section, Forest List 2, EA. The issues can be followed on Web sites of the Southeast Alaska Conservation Council and the Alaska Forest Association (the forest industry organization).

27. See Sam Bishop, "Alaska Rider Passes," *Fairbanks Daily News-Miner*, February 15, 2003, in Alaska folder, Forest List 2, EA. The rider, sponsored by Senator Ted Stevens, "prevents environmental groups from suing over a pending U.S. Forest Service decision that likely will recommend against establishing any more official wilderness areas in the Tongass."

28. For the karst issue on the Tongass see the Alaska folder, Forest List 2, EA, especially, "Ice Age Paleontology of Southeast Alaska," which follows the Tongass Cave Project and its development into a research program under the direction of Professor Timothy H. Heaton of the University of South Dakota; and a description of the resulting cave protection issues in Paula Dobbyn, "Cave Experts Oppose Plans for Timber Sale: Forested Limestone Covers Cave Networks That Some Scientists Consider Priceless," *Anchorage Daily News*, November 2, 2002, in Alaska folder, Forest List 2, EA. See Stephen W. Lewis, Pete Smith, and Kevin Allred, all of the Tongass Cave Project, to Forest Service Planners, USDA Tongass National Forest, August 14, 2002, concerning the karst formations and the Tongass National Forest Roadless and Wilderness Reevaluation SEIS. The folder contains a number of documents, obtained from the Web site of Timothy H. Heaton, one of the two principal investigators of the "Ice Age" project, of which research on the karst formations is a part. A brief account of the Tongass Cave Project, its significance, and its leading figure Steve Lewis, is Sarah Lemagie, "An Obsession with Caves," *Raven Call* (The Southeast Alaska Conservation Council), Spring 2004, 16.

29. The Bitterroot issue can be followed in news reports contained in the Bitterroot National Forest folder, Montana section, Forest List 2, EA. For the 2004 phase of the Bitterroot National Forest issue see Sherry Devlin, *Missoulian* (Missoula, Mont), February 7, 2004, "Group Simmers over Wildfire Funds: Environmental-

ists, Forest Service at Odds over Recover Plan for 2000 Blazes." "Logging has proceeded while restoration has slowed down; the Forest Service blamed the lack of
funds and withdrawal of funds from the national forest level back to Washington
to fund fire fighting." A more detailed analysis of the restoration program two
years after it was agreed to is "Bitterroot Wildfire Restoration Money Gone," *Environment News Service,* February 9, 2004, stating that funds which were used for restoration were withdrawn by the Washington office to pay for fighting fires. Copy in
Bitterroot file cited above.

30. The Sierra Nevada issue can be followed in various documents and news
reports in Revised Sierra Nevada Forest Plan folder, and Sierra Nevada Forest Protection Campaign folder, California section, Forest List 2, EA.

31. The revised Sierra Nevada Plan emphasized measures intended to reduce
fuel loads and thereby reduce the threat of forest fires in which the Forest Service
proposed to use the sale of larger trees to finance the removal of smaller trees and
downed wood. However, this strategy continued to founder on the problem of
limited response on the part of the logging industry to bids solicited by the Forest Service. An in-depth analysis of a proposed sale on the Tahoe National Forest
illustrates the problem. Bids submitted by the industry offered two cents a board
foot instead of the eleven and a half cents on which the agency had relied, and
proposed to cut trees at least sixteen inches in diameter, whereas the agency had
proposed limiting the cutting the trees up to eleven inches in diameter. For this
case see Bettina Roxall, "Dead Trees Fail to Bring Life to Forest," *Los Angeles Times,*
December 10, 2003.

32. The proposed revisions to the Sierra Nevada Framework prompted the same
differences of opinion as for the original proposal, with the timber industry favoring the changes and the environmental community opposing. In a September
12 report, an interdisciplinary team of fish and wildlife experts within the Forest
Service emphasized the nature of the policy shift: "While the document alludes to
ecosystem restoration," it said, "the only action being proposed is fuels treatment."
And James Quinn, director of the University of California, Davis, Information
Center for the Environment, emphasized that the changes were driven not by science, but rather by a policy shift that came with President George W. Bush. Quinn
said: "The emphasis changed from a cautious approach to wildlife to managing
the forests for fire prevention. The preferences driving the framework have been
reversed. The old plan was put together by scientists. This was put together by land
managers." See David Whitney, "Forest Care Shift Sparks Controversy," *Sacramento
Bee,* December 7, 2003.

33. An extensive critique of the revision to the framework was produced by the
office of the California Department of Justice. See Bill Lockyear, attorney general
of California, to Sierra Nevada Forest Plan Amendment DSEIS, September 9, 2003,
in Revised Sierra Nevada Plan 2003 folder, Forest List 2, EA. See also in the same
folder the proposal of the California Resources Agency for state-federal collaboration in place of the plan revision in agency release, "State Proposes Plan for Sierra

Forests to Protect Communities and Habitat from Wildfire and Gridlock," March 17, 2003. The release, signed by Mary Nichols, head of the agency, states that the revision recommendations "essentially abandon the Sierra Framework plan adopted in 2001" and that "We invite the Forest Service to join us in collaborative on-the-ground projects now that will reduce fire risks, and protect communities and the environment."

34. For the "viability" issue in the three Colorado national forests and the actions of various parties, including the Bush administration, see Theo Stein, "Colorado Forest Rulings Scrutinized," *Denver Post*, March 14, 2001.

35. For the limited acceptance of the "Southern Appalachian Forest Vision" in the proposed management plan for this area, see the article by Jackie Dobrinksa, "Forest Service's Proposed Management Plans a Blow to Conservation," in Southern Appalachian Forest Coalition folder, EA.

36. The Bass reports, their implications and some associated relevant articles are on the Web site of the Southern Appalachian Forest Coalition, http://www.safc.org. See especially the "Statement of Quentin R. Bass II Regarding a Violation of Rule, Law and/or Regulation," a "disclosure" by Bass presented to the U.S. Forest Service, June 16, 2003, and a summary of the issue, "USFS Stifled Ecological Documents."

37. See press release from the organization Public Employees for Environmental Responsibility, "Forest Service Secretly Targeting Southern Mountains for Major Logging," in Southern Appalachian Forest Plan folder, Southern Appalachians section, EA.

38. See documents in Roadless Area Review folder, George W. Bush Administration Forest Policies section, EA, including a report by Taxpayers for Common Sense, "Road Wreck: Why the $10 Billion Forest Service Road Maintenance Backlog Is Bad for Taxpayers" (Washington, D.C., March 2004).

39. Documents describing events in the roadless area issue are in the Roadless Areas folder, Forests: Nationwide section, Forest List 2, EA. Forest Service chief Michael Dombeck's statement of the Forest Service road problem is in Dombeck, Wood, and Williams, *From Conquest to Conservation*, 93–116.

40. For progress in implementing the road closure strategy, see the Web site of the Wildland Center for Preventing Roads.

41. For the running debate over the forest health legislation see Forest Health Issue folder, National Forest Issues section, Forest List 2, EA.

42. In 2002 the environmental community released a "Community Fire Protection Plan" that emphasized clearing fuels for 500 feet around homes. See American Lands Alliance Web site. In 2004 several citizen environmental groups produced a small pamphlet that urged communities to take protective action. See "Putting Wildfires in Perspective," "Wildfire Protection Begins at Home," in Forest Fires folder, EA. The two most emphasized issues in the public debate over how to cope with western fires were illustrated by proposals in the Arizona legislature, one to provide funds for fire protection measures for homes in the "red zone" and the

other to help finance a program to jump-start mills that could process the small tree thinnings harvested to reduce ladder fuels. See "Legislating Forests: Hard Political Decisions Need to Be Made," *Arizona Republic*, April 6, 2004.

43. For a succinct statement as to the ecological forestry view of "forest health" see the *Highlands Voice*, West Virginia Highlands Conservancy, April 2004, 18: "For the Forest Service and the timber industry the focus in 'forest health' is on 'tree health' and especially trees that have commercial value as timber. However, a more ecologically sound definition of forest health implies much more than just trees. A forest includes many interacting plants, animals, insects, and micro-organisms that live and reproduce there. For example, the soil alone contains thousands of types of fungi, bacteria, earthworms, and insects, all of which are essential to growing future generations of healthy trees (as well as other organisms). What's more, dead trees, insects and disease are a part of the natural forest cycles of growth and death and are not necessarily cause for human intervention (logging)."

44. For the letter from the scientists see "Scientists Say National Forests Need Protection, Not Logging," dated April 16, 2002, in Scientists National Forest Letter folder, National Forests, EA.

45. For the letter from the forest organizations, "Joint Letter to President Bush Regarding the Management of National Forests," dated April 30, 2002, in Scientists National Forest Letter folder, National Forests, EA. See, in same folder, an elaboration of the letter from the commodity forest organizations, "SAF Urges President Bush to Support Scientific Forest Management."

46. See the Bitterroot folder as cited in note 29, this chapter.

47. The collaborative effort at restoration on the Gifford Pinchot National Forest is described in *Northwest Ecosystem News* 57, Spring 2004, 9. One project is the Cat Creek Restoration Thin which will use new "stewardship contracting" legislation to retain the money from wood by-products to do more restoration work in the project area. This "has received funding," but the source is not indicated. "We are also working with the University of Washington to make sure that our treatment implements the best available science while incorporating a detailed monitoring plan so we can continue adaptive management." The project is summarized as follows: "The efforts of NWES staff, working with the Gifford Pinchot Collaborative Working Group, have given the Forest Service a new vision: conduct business that avoids controversial old-growth and roadless logging, while restoring forests simplified by past clearcuts."

48. For the Wildlands Project see folder with that title in the New Mexico section, Forest List 2, EA.

49. See Executive Summary of the Biscuit Fire Recovery Project issued by the Forest Service. Jessica MacMurray Blaine, "Logging by Any Other Name," *Forest Magazine*, Spring 2004, 14–19; Scott Maben, "Plan to Log Biscuit Fire Draws Flood of Comments," *Register Guard*; "Biscuit Fire Salvage Deemed Too Costly," *Seattle Post-Intelligencer*, October 21, 2003; "Biscuit Fire Timber Sale Public Hearing, Comments Still Needed," January 6, 2004; Conservation Biology Institute, "Ecological Issues

Underlying Proposals to Conduct Salvage Logging in Areas Burned by the Biscuit Fire"; Siskiyou Regional Education Project, "Unprecedented Logging Proposed for the Siskiyou: Biscuit Fire Logging Plans Push a Billion Board Feet"; Jerry F. Franklin, "Comments on Draft Environmental Impact Statement for Biscuit Recovery Project," January 20, 2004; "Old Growth Forest Expert Questions Biscuit Fire Salvage Logging," *Daily News* (*Longview, Washington*), January 27, 2004; Lindenmayer et al., "Salvage Harvesting Policies after Natural Disturbances," *Science Magazine* 303 (2004): 1303; Paul Fattig, "Study Kindles Anger: Forestry Subcommittee Hearing Gets Contentious over OSU Research Paper," *Mail Tribune*, February 25, 2006; Michael Milstein, "Reform Needed after OSU Controversy, Students, Dean Say," *Oregonian*, April 8, 2006.

The Biscuit salvage proposal elicited severe criticism from both the federal Environmental Protection Agency and the U.S. Fish and Wildlife Service, as well as giving rise to 23,000 comments from the public, most of them critical. These reactions as well as a considerable amount of information about the proposal are available on the Web site of the Siskiyou Project, http://www.siskiyou.org. A number of news articles about the issue are printed from the Internet and are available in the Biscuit Fire folder, Forest List 2, EA. An excellent coverage of the post-fire salvage controversy is Kathie Durbin, "Unsalvageable: With Environmentalists Fuming, Logging Companies Grousing, and Timber Rotting, the Bush Administration Tries to Save Face—and a Sliver of Its Giant Plans to Log the Northwest's Forest Sanctuaries," *High Country News*, May 16, 2005.

Controversy over the Baird-Walden bill is covered in Kathie Durbin, "Baird Logging Bill Passes House Committee," *Columbian*, March 30, 2006. The science used by the commodity groups is reflected in the release from the House Committee on Resources that approved the bill, titled "The Science behind FERRA." The science supporting those with an ecological approach is expressed in "Scientists Warn against Fast-Track Logging in Forests Recovering from Fire," a news release from the Unified Forest Defense Campaign, with accompanying letter, March 14, 2006, to "members of Congress," with the 169 signatories identified.

Litigation arising from the Missionary Ridge fire and the subsequent proposed salvage cut gave rise to similar different viewpoints as to its implications for "forest health." See letters from Rep. Scott McGinnis to Secretary of Agriculture Ann Venneman, February 12, 2004, and from Jeff Berman, executive director of Colorado Wild, also to Venneman in reply, signed by eighty-eight conservation groups, April 1, 2004, illustrating the controversy over salvage logging. See Missionary Ridge Fire folder, Colorado section, Forest List 2, EA.

50. "Citizens' Call for Ecological Forest Restoration: Forest Restoration Principles and Criteria," copy in Box 33, Forest List 2, EA.

51. See ibid. for the list of organizations joining in support of the ecological forest restoration paper.

52. See Community Forest Act file in Forest List 2, EA.

53. One secrecy issue involved formation of the new forest-wide regulations.

Defenders of Wildlife and other plaintiffs sought documents involved in revision of the NFMA regulations, including documents from the office of Undersecretary Mark Rey. Rey responded that not a single document pertaining to the rule-making process could be found in the office of the undersecretary. The court said this response was "inadequate." The Forest Service was also reprimanded that it was so vague in its reasons for withholding nearly three-quarters of the documents requested that neither plaintiffs nor the court could assess whether the withholdings were proper. News item from Environmental Media Services, March 31, 2004, heading "USDA Stonewalling Effort to Shed Light on Bush Rewrite of Nation's Forest Rules."

54. The larger context of the Bush administration assault on the EIS is included in William Snape III and John M. Carter II, "Weakening the National Environmental Policy Act: How the Bush Administration Uses the Judicial System to Weaken Environmental Protections: A Report of the Judicial Accountability Project" (Washington, D.C.: Defenders of Wildlife, 2003).

55. See an extensive analysis of outsourcing of the content analysis team, by Greg Hanscom, "Outsourced: As the Bush Administration Rushes to Put the Public Lands into the Hands of Private Industry, a Model Group of Forest Service Employees Gets Canned," *High Country News*, April 26, 2004, 7–12.

56. For the use of "informed responses" in the 2003 FS Survey, see Deborah J. Shields et al., *Survey Results of the American Public's Values, Objectives, Beliefs, and Attitudes* (see preface, note 4).

57. For a concise summary of the Bush administration litigation strategy see Tom Turner, "Unsettling Development," *Environmental Forum*, January–February 2004, 32–41.

58. An extensive review of the Bush administration attempt to reinterpret forest-related statutes in an anti-environmental direction is William Snape III, Michael T. Leahy, and John M. Carter II, "Weakening the National Environmental Policy Act: Undercutting National Forest Protection," a report of the Judicial Accountability Project (Washington, D.C.: Defenders of Wildlife, Summer 2003).

59. See Gloria Flora folder, in file on Forest Service administration, Forest List 2, EA. A rather general and only partially informative article is Jim Robbins, "Town in Montana Wilderness Is Divided over Drilling Plan," *New York Times*, March 21, 2004. Considerable documentation about this issue is on Web sites under the titles of "Friends of the Rocky Mountain Front" and "Sustainable Obtainable Solutions." They detail the activities of Gloria Flora since her departure from the Forest Service.

60. Two of a number of cases in which FSEEE took up the case of scientific personnel involve Mary Dalton, an ecologist, and Rick Golden, an aquatic biologist. Mary Dalton was a researcher on the Tongass National Forest, counting eagle nests and bear dens on Baranof Island; when her work was not included in the formal environmental impact statement and she complained to her superiors without response from them, she filed a formal administrative appeal challenging the 2,000-

acre timber sale, whereupon she received a thirty-day suspension, followed by a 2,000-mile transfer to the Coronado National Forest in southern Arizona, where she was assigned to fighting fires. See FSEEE news report citing Fox News and Associated Press, April 21, 1997, under headline, "Forest Service Worker's Challenge to Logging Prompts Suspension." Rick Golden, aquatic biologist, was hired by the Ozark–St. Francis National Forest and asked to create a fish conservation program for the forest. He discovered that the forest rangers were relying on an incorrect and misleading sediment model to determine whether road construction and logging were appropriate. He met resistance from FS management and was told that if he didn't like the model he should come up with a new one that would allow the timber sales to continue unimpeded. FSEEE stepped in to help Golden achieve an ecologically appropriate solution, to have the flawed sediment model invalidated and develop a new one that involved collecting data on stream conditions and analyzing whether the impacts from a timber sale would be appropriate for that specific area. See http://www.fseee.org/.

61. Dombeck repeated this proposal before the conference of the National Center of Environmental Law Societies at Lewis and Clark College. See Erik Robinson, "Ex-Forest Service Chief: Spare Old Growth Trees," *Columbian* (Clark Co., Washington), March 27, 2004.

62. Dombeck, Wood, and Williams, *From Conquest to Conservation*.

63. See Jim Furnish, "Logging Change Is Shortsighted," http://www.ecoisp.com/perspectives24.asp.

64. Rob Mrowka, "Thoughts upon Leaving the Agency I Love."

65. For news stories about these activities see Sportsmen and Bush Environmental Policies folder, Forests Nationwide section, Forest List 2, EA.

66. Herbert Kaufmann, *The Forest Ranger* (Baltimore: Johns Hopkins University Press, 1960), is the classic statement of this sociological characteristic of the Forest Service.

Chapter 7: In Search of the Future Forest

1. The Web site of the Biodiversity Conservation Alliance is http://www.biodiversityassociates.org/mbnt.

2. The most important relevant documents are "Keep the Medicine Bow WILD—Citizen's Plan for the MBNF," and the Biodiversity Conservation Alliance, "The 2004 Medicine Bow Forest Plan: An Overview." See also *Land Letter*, January 22, 2004, item 9, "Forests: Enviros Concerned Medicine Bow Plan Neglects Important Wilderness Areas."

3. A brief review of the revised Comprehensive Management Plan for the Hells Canyon National Recreation Area, as well as the Hells Canyon–Chief Joseph National Preserve Project is in *Hells Canyon Falcon* (journal of the Hells Canyon Preservation Council) 12, no. 1 (September 2003): 1–9.

4. See *Lingua Botanica*, http://www.fs.fed.us/biology/resources/pubs/plants/index .html, initial issue in 2000.

5. A striking example of the role of the Republican Party in support of commodity forest objectives was the joint action of Republican Party leaders in twenty-five counties in Oregon calling for the regional forester in the Pacific Northwest to "remove the 21-inch DBH rule [which restricts the harvest of trees over twenty-one inches in diameter] for each national Forest on the east side of the Cascade Mountains in Oregon and Washington." See copy of resolution and the counties supporting it in the Oregon folder of Forest List 2, EA. Another example of the Republican role in advancing commodity forest objectives was the request by twenty-five Republican lawmakers in Wisconsin to the Bush administration that the Chequamegon and Nicolet national forests in Wisconsin be transferred to the state Department of Natural Resources for management, on the grounds that the new plan for those forests placed too much emphasis on recreation and "passive management" while limiting timber harvests and threatening jobs and corporate profits. The proposal was strongly supported by the Wisconsin Professional Loggers Association and opposed by the environmental community. Relevant documents are in the Wisconsin folder in EA.

6. One can follow the activities of Republicans for Environmental Protection and its associated organization, the REP Educational Foundation, on its Web site. In 2003 the foundation became ConservAmerica, a non-membership organization, to establish more clearly its party independence, but it still worked closely with REP. They jointly sponsored a "Land Conservation Conference" in Albuquerque, New Mexico, the location of both organizations, May 21–23, 2004. For details about ConservAmerica see http://www.conservamerica.org. For the conference details see "Land Conservation for Conservatives: Protecting America's Great Places," Environmental Media Services, April 15, 2004.

INDEX